LEGENDS OF THE KONKAN

LEGENDS OF THE KONKAN

ARTHUR CRAWFORD C.M.G.

GYAN

Published by

Gyan Publishing House
5, Ansari Road
Daryaganj, New Delhi-110002
Phone: 011-47034999, 9811692060
E-mail: books@gyanbooks.com

Distribution Network
gyanbooks.com
India, USA, Canada, UK, Australia, France

ISBN : 978-81-212-9462-1 (PB)
First Published, 1909

2nd Impression 2023

Printed at: Gyan Press, Delhi.

LEGENDS OF THE KONKAN
Author: ARTHUR CRAWFORD

LEGENDS OF THE KONKAN

BY

ARTHUR CRAWFORD C.M.G.

(AUTHOR OF "REMINISCENCES OF AN INDIAN POLICE OFFICIAL," "OUR TROUBLES IN POONA AND THE DEKKHAN," &c.)

PRINTED AT THE PIONEER PRESS

ALLAHABAD

1909

DEDICATION

(By Special Permission)

TO

HIS HIGHNESS THE MAHARAJAH
SIR SAYAJI RAO III, G.C.S.I.,
Gaekwar of Baroda.

PREFACE.

In these legends I have endeavoured to make each tale complete in itself; generally giving the English translations of vernacular words and phrases.

The old Bhutt of Chiploon is not an imaginary personage, introduced for mere literary convenience; nor are the *seances* fictitious. During my twenty years' employment in the Southern Konkan as Assistant Collector and Magistrate, District Collector and Magistrate, and (finally) as Commissioner of the Southern Division of the Bombay Presidency, my duties necessitated my camping for weeks at a time at Chiploon, one of the most important towns in the Ratnagiri District. When young in the service (1859 to 1862) I made the acquaintance there of one Râghoba Mahâdewrão, a famous Bhutt, there residing, with the object of continuing my study of Sânscrit and perfecting myself in the Marâtha language as spoken by Chitpâwan Brâhmins. He was nearly sixty years of age: he possessed such a collection of ancient Sânscrit *slöks* (ballads) and tattered manuscripts as would be worth their weight in gold to the Royal Asiatic or any Public Library; but he would never part with one of them: for example, I offered him as many rupees as would thrice cover a manuscript entitled *The True*

Chitpawan Legend. It was printed by a Poona Deshast Brâhmin in (or about) the year 1812 A.D. but, inasmuch as it related the origin of Chitpâwans to be their miraculous creation by Pursharâm (Máhá-Indra) from the corpses of Arab sailors stranded by the tide or *Samudra**, whereas they claim that the deity created them from the spume of the ocean; the Peishwah Bâji Rao (himself a Chitpâwan) was so enraged that he ordered all the copies to be called in and burnt by *Mhângs* †, decreeing that any person thereafter found to possess a copy should be hanged; a sentence which was actually suffered subsequently by one Deshast Brâhmin.

My friendship for the Bard ripened to intimacy ‡. Many a weary hour did the amiable old gentleman beguile by reciting from his store of *folk-lore.* He was wonderfully versed in the tenets of Christianity and our Bible; having attended lectures, and heard sermons by Dr. Wilson, Mr. Bowen, the American Harbour Missionary at Bombay, Padré Ballantine (Satàra American Mission), and other Missionaries (Protestant, Roman Catholic and Lutheran) at Kolhapur. The old fellow, in fact, was as near being a Christian as a bigotted Brâhmin can be: and he deeply deplored the atheistical tendency of young Brâhmins

* The Indian Neptune.

† Usually employed as public executioners.

‡ We corresponded for more than 18 years.

of his later years, and abhorred Theosophism and all *isms*. He was poor, and possessed no land: late in life he adopted a young Chitpâwan of Sungumeshwur, becoming a Sunyássi in 1887 (I think): he died two years later in the odour of sanctity, and was buried on the sacred hill of Parèshram (also called Máháindra or Mâindra) near Chiploon. I was never able to discover what became of his manuscripts, but I am instituting searching enquiries, and do not despair of tracing them during my approaching visit to that part of the Konkan.

CONTENTS.

Legends of the Konkan.

CHAPTER I.

PROLOGUE.

INTRODUCES THE OLD BHUTT.

The old Bhutt mentioned in the Preface, on the evening he first visited my camp at Chiploon at my special request, brought with him, carefully wrapped up in linen, quite a load of manuscript Sânscrit " pothis " (poems), which he displayed with pride.

By far the rarest " Pothi " (Sânscrit manuscript) in my old friend the Chiploon Bhutt's possession, was a tattered document, most beautifully emblazoned in coloured inks, with marginal pictures of birds, beasts and fishes. The ancient bard himself could scarce decipher it—he had pieced the fragments together with the viscid gum of the milk bush (*euphorbium*), which had, of course, attracted all sorts of ants, from whose ravages the horn case in which he carried them was no protection whatever. The old cover, thick as our ordinary mill-board (being made of rice straw), was eaten round the edges, drilled through and through by these voracious insects. In a word, the manuscript was as illegible as the papyrus manuscripts in the British Museum, and perhaps nearly as old as some. Like all "Pothis" it measured about 12 inches by 4½ inches and had originally been bound in crimson tinted and highly glazed kid skin, of which little remained.

I offered the venerable seer as many rupees as would cover it three times over (say Rs. 150) for the original. He gravely shook his head "Naheen Saheb, your slave would do almost anything at my lord's command but this must not be done". "Well," said I, "then let me have a copy of it for Rs. 50, for the Bombay Branch of the Asiatic Society". "Arè Khâwand, be merciful to your poor slave and tempt him not! This sacred 'Pothi' was written by your humble servant's ancestor five hundred years ago and more at Máhá-Indra, which we now call Parèshrâm. It was dictated to him by Brâm Âchârya Vishnâcharya, the famous blind head priest at the sacred shrine, who was then 103 years old and died a few days later. He was the most learned of all the pundits south of Benâres, and great Ishwar had blessed him with the gift of prophecy. When the dread spirit moved him, he could not help bursting forth into a flood of fell prophecy, no matter where or in whose presence he was. Thus, it befell him at his last visit to Benâres when he was in the Golden Temple (the Saheb has seen it I know) in the heart of the Sacred City, when he was called upon to divine the omens in the 'holy of holies where no layman may put foot; he cast ashes on his bare head, prostrated himself before the deity, and in a voice of thunder foretold the coming of white men in thousands and thousands who would wage war upon each other, incite Moguls to attack the people of Bengal, the Maráthas to attack the Moguls, and that the 'Frangistánis' (the French) should at first prevail in Southern India, but that ultimately the Feringhis (called Angreezis now) should drive them out of India, and overrun Hindostan from the Himalayas to Ceylon, from the Indian Ocean to the confines of China. The assembled people arose as one man to resent this daring sacrilege, the other priest seized and bound him, he was stoned, his poor eyes knocked out! He was about to be sacrificed to Kâli, the dread goddess, when the whole city being in an uproar, a band of at least a thousand pilgrims who had accompanied him from Maharashtra, fought their way to Kâli's shrine and rescued him from a cruel death; for his bleeding heart would, in another moment, have been torn from his bosom and offered to the goddess! It was two years after the marvellous escape by Shri Parèshrâm's evident intervention, Oh! Saheb! that the pious Brâm Âchârya's intellect recovered, quite suddenly; Khâwand! these be true words! and then he remembered nothing of what had happened.

True talk this, Saheb. Shall I sell my holy ancestor's pious sayings for silver? Náheen! Oh Protector of the poor! I cannot! must not! and (raising his voice to a shrill scream) I will not!" Thereupon the venerable old fellow tottered out of my tent in great dudgeon, and refused to come near me, though I repeatedly sent him kindly messages by my clerks. It was not till the following year that he could be, with much difficulty, prevailed upon to renew our readings. Of course, I flattered the old fellow to the top of his bent, and at last one evening he brought and unrolled his "Pothis", selected this one and began to recite the *slöks* (verses) in nasal sing-song with many gestures of hands, and much wagging of his pious poll. I made such notes as I could, the while, and cast them into shape before I slept that night.

"The village gossip is," began the old Bhutt, "that Khâwand has been up the Hârt-lot Ghaut. "I have often" I replied, "and I have been up that ricketty hundred foot ladder too, very often." "Hán Saheb!" interposed the bard, "but that was in broad daylight, of course, so your honour did not see the demons that guard the place. First and most formidable is an enormous dragon which spits venom, then there is near it a huge cobra uncoiled, ready to strike an intruder. A python, of many folds, more than 200 feet long, lies curled up near: tigers, wolves, jackals, hyænas howl round. On the summit of the rock the Saheb speaks of, a monstrous bull bison, fifty feet high, with flaming eyes snorts defiance. Wild dogs bark around him. No

Hindu, not even those reckless *Rámoshis* and *Mhángs* from Satára, durst approach the ladder in broad moon-light. No Konkani would venture near the foot of the rock by night, for ten lakhs of rupees!"

"Well, hurry up! Bhuttji," said I. "Let's hear the legend." "Bulla! Saheb! Bulla," quoth he, and began to read the "Pothi" to the following effect:—

CHAPTER II.

LEGEND OF THE HÂRT-LOT GHAUT.—PART I.

GOD'S VIGIL.

Many hundreds of thousands of years ago, as my lord knows, the gods were in the habit of visiting this puny little planet of their creation, to work good or evil to mankind, as they desired. Our sacred Parèshrâm with his *Chèla* (or disciple) brother Luxmon often, or at least three times, came down from the "Dèsh" (Deccan) to Chiploon, to see how we twice-born Chitpâwan Brâhmins were behaving, as we shall read later. This "Pothi" relates to the first visit they ever made.

The gods had been wandering somewhat aimlessly on what Saheb *lok* call "the roof of the world," (Central Asia, North of the Himalayas) till Buddha taught all that vast region his new and pure religion. Peace and good will was thereby soon established. Their divine presence seemed to be no longer needed. They heard so much in Thibet of a vast torrid and arid region to the south, encompassed by almost interminable salt water, wherein Shri Sâmudra (the Indian Neptune) reigned. Tired of ice-bound mountains, Shri Parèshrâm told his disciple brother Luxmon to accompany him to Sâmudra's shores.

It was at the beginning of the Mrig-sal (the Indian spring at the end of May), the black clouds, rain charged, of the south-west monsoon rolled up every night from the sea, only to be dispersed by the fierce red morning sun. The heat was so suffocating during the day that all nature seemed to wither away : only the cicados chirrup, and the kawil's* maddening reiterated cry was heard, or the hoopoo's metallic tapping. All nature was asleep at noon. Shri Parèshrâm and his disciple brother slept also heavily. They had just made one march from Nasik (250 miles) and only twice slaked their thirst from the Naera (at Wai), and from the Krishna (at Helwak).

"To you Khodâwand! who know so much, it can be no news that when the gods assume human form they are subject to human ills. Your own great God whom you call Messiah, when he visited the 'Ajuda log's' (Jews) sacred city, suffered unspeakable tortures, so the Missionary Padrè Sahebs preach. Bulla!" Our god Parèshrâm and his brother Luxmon also suffered that broiling day from the pangs of thirst. They discussed, while resting at Helwak, by what route they should descend the Syadris. They had travelled twice down the Kumbharli Ghaut and their recollection of the last journey were not pleasant. "Your Honour," interrupted

* We call the Kâwil "the fever bird" because of its monotonous prolonged note which almost brings on fever. It is a species of cuckoo or magpie and always calls "Káwil! Káwil Káwil"! (crescendo) just before the rains.

the bard, "remembers about the black soil and red soil.". I nodded. "Bulla Saheb, then I'll read on." Luxmon pleaded hard that his great brother should try another route, for he dreaded, he hated Helwak. A troop of *langurs* (large black faced monkeys) perched overhead, had heard the discussion, and chattered among themselves, and then the father of apes (from his grey hair and stature) descended to the ground, prostrated himself humbly before the gods, saying "we, the ever faithful servants of Shri Máhá-Indra,* will gladly guide our lords to Chiploon by a short cut; but it must be in the day time because of the demon guardian of the passes." "Arè baprè! Arè! golam (slave) what sayest thou? Do *we* fear the demons"? "Naheen! Khodâwands! but"—"But me no buts" thundered Parèshrâm. "We'll fight the demon guardians! Arè, Lukkoo Bai, see my bow has a new string and don't let that cursed carpenter bee come near me this time! You *langur* log take us to the spot, we'll sleep on the crest of the mountain and descend at daybreak." "Khâwândâchi marzi (as my lord pleases)" said the *langur* patriarch submissively, and hopped on in front to the gigantic rock at the head of the pass which was only a few miles off. On its very verge the procession stopped. ["It is a much more extensive panorama than that from Helwak as your Honour knows," said the old man looking up, "for it is a 1,000 feet higher."

---

* Another name for Parèshrâm or Pursharâm.

"Don't pull the long bow Bhuttji" quoth I, "it is only 400". "bulla! Bulla! asò! (well, well, be it so)" humbly murmured the bard.] '"One can see 40 miles all round four points of the compass, and on very clear days can even make out, like little flies, the big *shibâds* (native craft) anchored at Dabholl, Mhaiput Ghur (which Saheb log call the 'saddle back') to the north the Bhyroo Ghur, jutting out from the Mulla Ghaut to the South,— but I'll read on."

The *langurs* collected a large heap of bracken for the gods' bed, wood-apples, "corindas" (a sort of damson) graceful fragrant orchids, wild "anand" blooms, abundance of "maiden hair" and other ferns. A she-bison came near hesitatingly, and submitted to be milked into a gourd by the partriarch *langur*. The two god brothers ate and drank to repletion, then stretched their wearied limbs on the fragrant, springy, bed prepared for them and sank to sleep; the *langur* troop fanning them the while, with broad leaves of the jungle toddy palm.

All nature slumbered as did these great deities. The very cicadas ceased to chirrup, fearful of disturbing the divine repose. A couple of imprudent carpenter bees came buzzing from the forest, bent on mischief, but the *langurs* promptly knocked them down, and a greedy Kâwil gobbled them up.

(Our gods did not actually view the Indian Ocean, Saheb, till sunrise of the day after their arrival in its vicinity. Tired out, for even divine beings tire Khawand,—they slept at Karád about fifteen *coss* from the Syadri Mountain range as we now call it.)

All nature slept; the gods slept; the sun sank fiery red in "Sâmudra's" (Neptune's) bosom, "Shri Chând" (moon) arose in the east, cross shadows from sun and moon deepened gradually. A soft breeze stole up the mountains from the Indian Ocean.

All nature would have slept gladly, gratefully but that the forest resounded with the lowing of bison herds, with the sharp yapping barking of wild dogs, and the bell-like challenge of sambhar stags to each other. The Kâwils uttering their melodious cry, flew up to roost on the lofty tops of teak trees. The shadows cast by "Shri Chând" spread ever further westward. "Shri Surya" (the sun) sank suddenly with inflamed visage, his last rays gilded "sâmudra's" broad bosom, illuminating the heavens with crimson, fading into orange on the horizon. Darker and yet more darkly purple grew the west, where huge storm clouds began together rolling landward. "Sri Chând" anon coyly veiled her face with fleecy clouds. Anon she burst forth into glistening silver, light as noon-day. Her shadows deepened, ever darkened, lengthened ever. Three "singh-ooloos" (large horned owls) special watchmen of the gods on earth by night [as three "guruds" (hornbills) are by day] perched themselves on trees half a mile from each other and began their vigil. "Hán" growled out one inquiringly, "Ha-àn" loud hooted the furthest, "ooloo," "Hán Hán, Hori Hori" groaned out the third in the centre, as if they cried "Are you there," "I am here"! "Yes, yes, we're all here"! Night fell, all nature slept; the great gods slept on their fragrant couch the solemn sleep of gods. Gentle zephyrs rustled among the evergreens and undergrowth. Clumps of graceful bumboos bent to it gratefully, shedding splendid showers of tears on the black rock of the defile gate.

"They have come our Lords, 'Ah, dear'!
"They have come! our Lives our Fate!
"The Asokha blooms cry 'They are near, they
are near';
"And the Anandi weeps 'They are late';
"The cactus listens, 'I hear, I hear';
"The cobra lily whispers 'I wait'."

All nature slept, except the three horned owls. The god brothers slumbered also till Shri Chând passing southward smiled a loving smile upon her favourite Parèshrâm her hero, her cherished lover. 'Twas the first "prahar" (three hours) of the highest, when beasts of prey do roam about to seek their food; when serpents, large and small, do glide undulatingly, in grass, in reeds, in undergrowth, seeking the nimble frog, the beetle, and "do-tonda" (blind worm, of which it is difficult to tell the head from the tail), when the huge python uncoils from under the rock and slowly, slimily, noiselessly, works his sinuous way to the foot of some giant forest there, ascends it spirally, and glares round for prey. Lo! a pair of "háril" (green pigeons) roosting on that branch—the fell monster stretches his huge head over them, the birds (favourite fowls of the Mogul Prophet Mahomet) awakened by falling twigs, perceive their relentless foe, his emerald eyes fascinate them, they strive to flutter away; the cock bird escapes screaming shrilly, his poor mate flutters also feebly, but into the gaping jaws of her enemy, which close upon her with vicious snap. All nature awakes, the god brothers awaken also. The three horned owls wheel around the divine heads with emphatic discordant notes of warning "Danger is near, Oh! Holy Ones"—they cry "Hán! Hân,! Hori! arise".

Parèshrâm, our unconquered, unconquerable deity, ever alert, seizes his 15 cubic bow, kicks up his always slothful brother "Arè Lukkoo! Lukkoo Bhai! the demons are upon us, arm thyself speedily with spear and shield! and thou lovest me!"

"Bulla Bulla! Mera Bhai," grunts Luxman "Kahi zhalè?" "Ishwarás máhit" ejaculates Máhá-Indra, "Zarur paha, thou son of a burnt father!" (God knows! look quickly!)

Shri Luxman sought in vain for a reason for the outcry! was it a false alarm? But the sky, till then so bright, was overcast with clouds drifting from the west, a mighty tempest followed, and, in it the two god brothers reached the defile of the Hârt-lot Ghaut where, for the first time, they beheld Sâmudra (the Ocean). Sâmudra in his wrath! mighty waves dashed against the iron-bound cliffs, their spray drenched the brothers as they stood spellbound for, there below them, arose the puissant Sea God, blowing a huge conch shell defiantly—leviathans, whales, dolphins and hideous sea-monsters gambolled, as it were, around him, rising and falling on the foam. "What do ye here, tresspassing on my domain! Shri Parèshrâm and Luxman, are ye? I know ye not. Puny terrestrial deities! begone, I say, lest I overwhelm ye and cast ye to these my outraged subjects of the Deep."

Shri Parèshrâm replied never a word, but lifting a huge boulder, cast it with such unerring aim, that it struck the conch shell from Sâmudra's very lips. Down dived the sea monsters all in fear, but the great Sea God roared "War! War! to the bitter end; so let it be! Tomorrow's morn shall decide whether thou or I control these waters." Then Shri Parèshrâm retorted with the one word "Agreed" and shook his mighty bow at Sâmudra in defiance—The Sea God quailed (yes Khodawand he quailed), and raising his slimy sea-weed covered arms spread them aloft and around, and behold a terrific dazzling flash of lightning, followed instantly by a fearful thunderclap, split the very summit of the mountain as the huge mass tumbled into the waves casting up sprays to the highest heavens. The Sea God sank, crying once again "Tomorrow!" Immediately there was a great calm! Shri Surya (the Sun God), who in fear had hidden behind a bank of clouds, again shone over the weird scene. Shri Luxman, always weak and irresolute, lay prone on the verge of the fathomless abyss; but Parèshrâm stood firm and defiant, knowing his power, trusting in the mighty bow he brandished, confident of victory on the morn.

"Well, Bhuttji! Jey Parèshrâm ki jey!" I said. "But what about that coward Luxman? Was he dead? I devoutly hope so." "Nay Khodâwand! thou must not say such words! No deity that ever visited this sinful world, in human form, besides Shri Parèshrâm, but would have succumbed at such a time! But with my lord's permission I will read the few *slöks* (verses) that remain," and the bard continued.

Having restored his poor weak brother to consciousness Shri Parèshrâm led him affectionately on (by the hand). The twain returned to Karâd to rest, to prepare for the great duel of the morrow. The mighty bow had to be minutely examined, oiled, polished. Shri Parèshrâm fitted a new bowstring to it, made of fibres which the *languars* (monkeys) cut from forest creepers and twisted carefully. Shri Parèshrâm caused the *langurs* to test it, to tug at either end, a hundred at each end. At last Parèshrâm was satisfied, and directed his still quaking brother to hang his favourite weapon to the limb of a giant teak tree. The day passed dreamily away, the god brothers twain conversed in under tones; countless song birds of the forest soothed them melodiously, the while; myriads of forest insects buzzing around as the sun sank in the west, lulled them to rest, and the *langurs* and great horned *ooloos* (owls) kept watch and ward till morn.

CHAPTER III.

LEGEND OF THE HÂRT-LOT GHAUT.—PART II.

SHRI SAMUDRA'S PRECAUTIONS.

At dawn of the morrow, the *bul-buls* (Indian nightingales) awoke the divine brothers (read on the old Bhutt). After ablutions and quaffing great draughts of milk, they prepared to return to the trysting place to encounter Sâmudra in battle. The *langurs* and horned owls assured the brothers that no evil spirit or beast had approached Shri Parèshrâm's mighty bow suspended on the teak tree, but the deity was not satisfied till his brother had examined the weapon and the arrows and pronounced them in good order.

But as Luxman was still very drowsy and at no time was very observant, he did not notice a tiny blemish in the centre of the bow's curve, nor did he see a little pile of dust on the earth under the branch to which it had been suspended. But the *langurs* saw both, and chattering among themselves fled with loud whooping into the densest forest. The god brothers wended their way westward to Hârt-lot; Luxman, as usual, carrying both bow and quiver. Once or twice his heart failed him for fear, for he seemed to find the great bow much lighter than it usually was; but in his dread said never a word to Parèshrâm.

Now, Sâmudra had not been idle, and fortune had greatly favoured him before the sun set on the preceding evening. This was the way of it! Sâmudra was floating on his back in smooth water below the Hârt-lot cliffs, when a big carpenter bee blundering in his flight, as these insects are apt to do in waning light, blundered against the cliff and fell half stunned within reach of Sâmudra. A fish on the alert for such prey was about to swallow the insect, when Sâmudra rescued it, and let it recover and dry its wings in the palm of his holy hand. While the insect was doing this and buzzing forth its gratitude, a brilliant idea flashed o'er Sâmudra's mind. (Quoth the old bard "All the world knows how crafty is the great Sea God. Hán? Saheb!)

[Quoth Sámudra "Thou art grateful for thy life sayest thou? then prove thy words, go to Parèshrâm's camp. 'Tis a short flight hence. My sea-gulls will bear thee to the spot, will show thee where the braggart's bow is placed. Myriads of other insects will be buzzing about in the gloaming. All thou hast to do is to settle on the inner side of the bow—the inner side mark me—then bore thy way along as ye so well know how. I shall know in the morning what thy gratitude is worth! Fail, and my gulls will relentlessly put thee and thy kindred to the death!"

The carpenter bee buzzed consent. Sâmudra whistling to a flock of gulls floating on the water near, gave them their orders, placed the half bewildered insect on the soft back of the king gull, and, in less than a *ghutka* (24 minutes), the bee was buzzing round the mighty bow as it hung aloft, in company with thousands of others of the insect tribe! Carefully selecting the spot at which he could commence work, the carpenter settled on the branch and waited till it was dark and all the other clouds of insects had flown away, attracted to the adjacent camp fire; then he noiselessly settled on Shri Parèsbrâm's bow and set to work, labouring diligently till dawn, till his task was quite achieved, then he backed out by the channel he had bored, and plugged the tiny aperture with the ichorous sweat from his own body, and a little of the dust thereto adhering. "Of the insect's fate thou shalt hear anon, Khấwand!" said the old Bhutt as he wiped his horn-rimmed spectacles. "Now will thy slave read the marvellous end of this miraculous tale!" He read on.

THE DUEL.

It was a heavenly morn, not a cloud in the azure sky. Surya (the Sun God) was rising in the east, his rays lit up the distant ocean horizon, which was scarcely ruffled by a light land breeze. The Sun God would fain have risen rapidly, so eager was he to behold the encounter, but he was constrained to hold his appointed course. ["Yea Khấwand, his appointed course, appointed by that Omniscient Being who controls us all. Who yet in his wisdom, permits poor mortals such as I am to calculate that very course and Shri Chând's (the moon's) course also, multitudes of years beforehand !'" observed the old seer solemnly.]

Shri Parèshrâm and Luxman, his bow-bearer, appeared on the edge of the cliff and the gilded tops of the bow and arrows glistened in the sun's rays. Sâmudra still lay below the surface of the pellucid deep, scanning the great demi-god narrowly, to divine if he had any suspicion of the treachery that had been wrought. His gulls had hours before apprised the sea God that the carpenter bee had admirably executed his behest. He saw no symptom of faltering in Parèshrâm's noble mien, as he turned to take the mighty bow from his trembling brother's hands and to string it slowly. As Shri Parèshrâm bent to select a steel-topped shaft from the quiver on Luxman's shoulder, Sâmudra suddenly rose to the surface of the waters and blew his conch-shell in derisive challenge. "Art come then stripling ! to court defeat ?" he thundered—"Knowest thou that shouldst thou fail, I even I, will o'erwhelm thee and thy craven brother where ye stand—will burst through the iron-bound cliffs at thy feet—will sweep away thy temples—thy temples, forsooth ! like chaff—will flood Máhárásh-tra and all South Ind down to Lunka (Ceylon) and gather half this Continent into my broad bosom ?"

"I know it well," simply rejoined Shri Parèshrâm. "If 'tis a big word 'if'."

With these few confident words, our beloved patron deity drew his arrow to the very steel tip, aiming–Ah! a crashing sound followed the bow string's twang—the mighty bow broke in half, but so great was its strength, so superhuman was the power of the demi-god who bent it, that the arrow went forth into space and, quivering, pierced the bosom of the Ocean—18 *coss* (36 miles) from where the brothers stood!

Then ensued a scene only to be compared to that chaos when the Supreme World Creator separated the waters from the waters!! No mortal can adequately portray it!

Samudra, as in honour bound, retreated, defeated to a line, 18 *coss* from the Syadri range of mountains, leaving a long basin, as it were, thousands of cubits deep, wherein in the mud wallowed whales and sea monsters innumerable, only the two leviathans escaped destruction floundering out beyond the now sacred border line of the Konkan.

The chasms below opened and shut again convulsively, volcanoes innumerable burst out beneath, and all around vomitted forth fire, molten lava, ashes, and red hot rocks. 'Twas as if the end of the world had come. A dense black pall of smoke and noxious vapours began to rise from the newly created Konkan which had but a *ghatka* before been covered fathoms deep by the briny ocean. Sated with his victory Shri Parèshrâm murmured exultingly to his brother "If, indeed! Oh Lukkoo bhai! What thinkest thou now of Sâmudra's 'if'?" Luxman fell at his brother's feet and kissed them a thousand times in admiration. Then Shri Parèshrâm said "Well Lukkoo bhai, 'twill take many cons ere the land we have won is fit for human habitation! Meantime, we will betake ourself to Lunka and see what mischief those Titans are doing in that beautiful land, but first we'll fathom this treachery, for treachery there must have been!" At this moment Luxman picked up the broken bow and eagerly exclaimed, "See here, brother mine, it is quite evident some insect has been sent to bore its way through the arc of your noble bow, but it was not large enough to do the work thoroughly!" The brothers then returned to Karad, by which time it was dusk. The *langurs* were summoned at once and questioned, but they, of course, could afford no clue, beyond declaring the fracture might have been the work of a carpenter bee. At last as the brothers were about to close the enquiry, one of the large horned owls who had been on guard flew down and exhibited in its claws the wretched carpenter bee, aforesaid, half dead, with broken wing. The bird explained that during the previous night he had heard a sort of grating, grinding, noise proceeding from Shri Parèshrâm's suspended bow, and had noticed dust, fine dust, dropping from it. He had called his two mate owls, they had watched, and at daybreak had seen the carpenter bee emerge backwards from the arc of the bow and fly away; they pursued the insect and would have caught and produced him before, but the rising sun's rays dazzled them. However, they had watched all day and had at last caught the insect. "Should he be destroyed?" they asked.

Shri Parèshrâm took the wretched creature, stroked it kindly and persuaded it to tell the whole story. Then he said "Náhin, (no) thou shalt live. What thou didst was done from gratitude to the Sea God for sparing thy life. Gratitude is a divine virtue. Mercy is another. Therefore, we restore not only thy life, but thy strength. Begone in peace." Laxmon, who was not so tender-hearted could only ejaculate "Wáh, Wáh," but all the birds and beasts heartily applauded.

CHAPTER IV

THE CHITPAWĀN LEGEND.

This is the second of three "Pothis" or Sânscrit poems, which no doubt were fragments of a work entitled "The Syadri Khind" clandestinely printed about the middle of the eighteenth century. The first related to the conquest of the Konkan from the sea by Parèshrâm as described in my last Legend. The second (which is related here), dealt with the origin of the twice-born or Chitpâwan Brâhmins during the period when they were, as Parèshrâm had promised, immortal for a long series of years. The third poem relates how these immortals sacrilegiously demanded from the God a guarantee that they should never die, how they tried to hoax the deity and how Parèshrâm punished the sect by summarily cancelling their privilege. I have here for convenience sake connected the two last together.

It is not very well known why this particular work "The Syadri Khind" was detestedby the Brâhmins—unless, indeed, it included the Shenwi version of the Chitpâwan origin.

Chitpâwans denied (and, I believe, still deny) that the Sáraswati (Shenoys, or Shenwis) have any sort of claim to Brahminism alleging slanderously that the latter were descended from a low-caste girl who was ravished by a Brâhmin while engaged in making fu e cakes from "Shen"* (cow dung). The Shenwis from the Saráswati river region in Kathiawár retaliated by alleging that Chitpâwans were not miraculously created by Parèshrâm from the spume of the ocean as they claimed to be, pointing to the fact that Chitpâwan has at least two meanings—"pure hearted or sinners pardoned" and "a dead body raised"—they insisted that the latter was the true description of Chitpâwan origin. Shenwis, admitting that Chitpâwans were in a sense miraculously "twice-born," created by Parèshrâm, insisted that, as a matter of fact, when the deity visited the Konkan first after it had become habitable, he was somewhat at a loss from whence to people the country, till Sâmudra (the Indian Neptune) in revenge for his defeat by Parèshrâm, derisively cast upon the beach of the river Wáshisti, the corpses of certain Arab sailors, which Parèshrâm then proceeded to resuscitate! Small wonder that the Chitpâwan Peishwas loathed the Shenwi version of their origin, and made the possession of a copy of the "Syadri Khind" an offence punishable by death. Certain it is that so late as 1814 A.D., Bájee Rao, Peshwah, disgraced and ruined a respectable Deshast Brâhmin of Wai, who had incautiously shown a copy of the obnoxious pamhplet to some friends who betrayed him.

My aged friend, a Chitpâwan of Chitpâwans, produced these two Sânscrit manscripts with a triumphant grin as if to say "See what a holy caste is ours," adding

* This is Dr. Wilson's version in "Indian Caste."

"My lord must not credit the Shenwi slanders, of course, they are all lies." "There is not much to be said, Bhutjee, I fear, for either version; they seem much of a muchness to my mind. However read on, said I". So he began in his usual nasal sing song.

Several eons rolled by before the Konkan or lowlands won by Parèshrâm were explored by the "*dhangurs*" (herdsmen) of the Ghatmâla (mountain plateaux) with their buffaloes. They, every year, penetrated further till they overran the Payeen Ghauts (*i.e.*, the foot hills) whence they brought back to the uplands, marvellous accounts of mighty rivers navigable to the very foot of the Syadri Mountains, of magnificent forests of every kind of valuable timber, of trees laden with delicious fruits, of a coast line fringed with cocoanut palms, of lush forage on every hillside and wild rice growing in all the valleys. Next, attracted by these tales, the hardy Mhârs of the Dekkhan ventured to explore, ran up their huts, roofed with "*cadjans*" (cocoa palm leaves interlaced) and walled with split bamboos and red clay. ("The outcaste Mhârs, my lord knows, were the aborigines who first owned and peopled the Konkan," observed the old bard. I nodded assent.)

These Mhârs hired bands of ryot cultivators from above the Ghauts, Sudras, by caste—who began to till the land lying at their feet, after the best modes of cultivation then known in Ind. Good rice seed yielded enormous harvests in that rich alluvial soil composed of decomposed lava, laterite, and trap. Waishya (trading) castes followed, bought up and conveyed the produce into the interior on bullocks driven by Brinjáris (Indian gypsies) from the far east Dekkhan. The Kshatrya caste (warriors and true Maráthas) made incursions and built strongholds, here and there, and warred against each other as is ever their custom. But, with the exception of a few Brâhmins occasionally summoned by the ryots to officiate at religious ceremonies, none of the Deshast Brâhmins ventured to make their permanent residence in the Konkan.

The whole of the hard won Konkan was still but sparsely populated when Shri Parèshrâm, then in distant Burmah, received constant reports from the birds of the air, ever his messengers, that it were well that his godship should visit the region he had won from Sâmudra (the Indian Neptune) which sadly lacked governing and guiding, especially a guiding priesthood. Thereupon, Shri Parèshrâm and his brother wended their way back rapidly by way of Bellary and Karár to Helwak, whence they gazed astonished at the beautiful country lying at their feet. At the north, to their right, rose a lofty hill, beneath it flowed a grand tidal river (afterwards the sacred Wáshisti) on which they could descry numbers of small sailing craft and fishing boats. At the head of the tidal basin, nestled in palms and mango groves, was a straggling town of mud huts, from and to which droves of pack bullocks were being urged along by Brinjáris. Descending the Koombharli Ghaut easily, they came to a large expanse of fertile land but half cultivated, though there were seven adjacent *talaos* (small lakes) from which a large area could be easily irrigated with small labour. A crowd of the aborigines came out to meet the god brothers, worshipping them. Half-naked, with matted locks, nearly black were they, and their women and children following them at a distance, were as abject in look as they were.

Shri Parèshrâm accosted them "Where are your gods? Where are your temples? Where your priests?" The trembling creatures cried "We have neither gods, nor temples, nor priests! We beseech thee to be our God henceforth and protect us. Oh Shri Parèshram we know thee now! Thou didst win this Konkan from Sâmudra! Thou art he who should come, whom the Deshast Brâhmins, when they come sometimes to perform ceremonies for heavy fees, declare hast deserted thy kingdom! Leave us not, thy people, we beseech thee! Give us priests of our own! Teach us to pray, Deoba!".

Parèshrâm was deeply moved by this appeal. He despatched Luxman forthwith with guides to the sea-shore, telling him to gather and bring back with him in earthen jars some of the spume or dried foam of the ocean. This was soon done. Parèshrâm poured it out and shook it over the ground around him, when, behold, a goodly band of handsome young men, fair in complexion, with green grey eyes, clad in saffron coloured robes, arose miraculously from the ground and prostrated themselves before him crying "Jey! Shri Parèshrâm—Parèshrâm Deo ki Jey!"

Anon Shri Parèshrâm addressed these holy ones, and blessing them said "Be ye for ever my *chelas* (disciples). Ye are, with the aid of these poor people, to build a shrine to me on yonder hill. Ye are to be the spritual guides of the Konkani people, to teach them and to protect them from other gods. To you I give these "*sath malas* and *sath tulaws* (seven meadows of rich soil and seven lakes) from which to irrigate them. Obey my behests religiously, honestly, and ye shall never die, like those Deshast Brâhmins who have neglected and oppressed these my poor people. My spirit will always be at my shrine to appeal to. We hall often visit it unknown to you and all men". And immediately the god brothers faded from view : but lo! a meteor descended from heaven on the summit of the hill Parèshrâm had pointed to, indicating the precise spot on which his shrine was to be built. That hill has been called "Parèshrâm" or "Mâhâ-Indra" ever since.

For centuries the Chitpâwans did increase and multiply, for, sure enough, they never died. Becoming prosperous, they waxed bumptious, as Brâhmins are apt to do, and became a nuisance to mankind. The birds brought Indra intelligence of their oppressions and licentiousness. He saw that he had made a great mistake ; and, to rectify it, he bethought himself of instilling some of the "*goon*" or spirit of the red soil into the Chitpâwan mind. Accordingly, at the next meeting of the Brâhmin elders under a certain wide-spreading Banyan tree, when the conversation turned on their wondrous prosperity and immunity from death, he put it into the heart or stomach (which with them is synonymous) of an old gentleman to observe.—" 'Tis all very well, my brethren ! True that none of us have yet died like these Deshast Brâhmins above Ghauts; or these impure Shudras (working men) round about us," (here he spat vigorously on the ground). " But what security have we after all that we never shall die, eh ? " Animated discussion followed, in the course of which it was determined to test the god's faith in this way :—One of the party should sham death, they would carry him to the temple on the hill, and there extort some guarantee from the deity. No sooner said than done : the counterfeit corpse, decently laid out on a bier, his face besmeared with ochre and red pigment, was carried toilsomely up to the shrine, escorted by a *posse* of caste mourners, naked to the waist, " ugada bodka" (bareheaded), swinging pots of burning incense, and making the welkin ring with their wail " Arè Narrayen Ból ! " Narrayen' ". Depositing the burden before the idol and ringing the bell overhead to attract the god's attention, an old grey-beard took up the parable " Arè, Deoba (look here, 'old god), you promised we should never die, but see what we have brought you" (pointing to the shammer). "What security will you give us that death shall not again visit us?" A solemn silence followed, broken only by the muttered "muntrees" (imprecations) of the Poojárree (priest) as he walked round and round the altar, ever and anon dropping flowers on the idol and sprinkling it with holy water. Lo! the blossoms drop withered, will not rest on the idol! The water evaporates into steam. Horror of horrors! The priest faints, and pitchy darkness fills the shrine-room! Suddenly a terrific flash of lightning reveals the deity to the terror-stricken conspirators, and a voice thunders "Treacherous and accursed race! the cup of your iniquities is filled to overflowing (apale páp bharile gèle)! Ye ask a sign! Take it from the bier! So shall ye all die in future!" Behold, the shammer was as dead as any Deshast!

"The story is quite true, Saheb," said the old bard. "There is the Banyan tree out there by the tank; *there* are the seven 'Mullas' and 'Tullas' still so registered in the Revenue Register of the Town, and Chitâwan Brâhmins die, Vishnoo be praised! like other people!"

CHAPTER V.

HOW PARESHRAM CURSED THE KONKAN.

"Thy servant has read Khodâwand, how Shri Parèshrâm conquered the Konkan from the Sea God; how he created the Chitpâwan Bhrâmins and promised them immortality on condition of their faithfully carrying out his behests, how they lamentably failed, and how the deity, incensed at their treachery, withdrew his promise and made them mortal, like other men"—said my old friend. "Thou hast now to learn how he and his brother cursed the Konkan with a curse so bitter that it has lasted ever since, and will ever prevent its becoming the earthly paradise that the deity had hoped to make it. My lord shall now hear from the *slöks*, thy servant will read, the full details of the calamity."

The Bhutt then began to read as follows. But before I place the legend before my readers, it is well that I enter, at some detail, into the mode of cultivation pursued in the Konkan, which, however well known to those who have dwelt in Western India, may be quite unknown to the general European public outside the official world.

Let us picture to ourselves the fair region when it first became sparsely populated by the hardy Mhars, the aborigines, owners of the soil who ventured down from the Dekkhan attracted by the verdure. All the volcanoes which had spouted after the first upheaval from the Indian Ocean were dormant or exhausted, their slopes and all the spurs and foothills were clothed with dense forest growth, holding the soil together. Countless cascades flowed from the great Syadri Range, wending their way westward till they were lost in the volume of great tidal rivers, all more or less navigable for native craft, almost to the foot of the mountains. The lower lands, gradually drying up, became covered by the detritus of trap and basalt strata of which the range is composed, and over all was spread, as it were, a blanket of disintegrated and motly friable lava, or alluvial soil capable of producing rice in abundance.

But this fair region was doomed to be the fighting ground of nations. The Kshatryas (Marátha warriors) class descending from Maharashtra, after long guerilla warfare, conquered and made slaves of the Mhar aborigines, establishing themselves on high hills whence they waged incessant internecine war upon each other: the Bâhmani dynasty had little difficulty in subjugating these "Raos" (as they are called) one by one, and, for some hundreds of years, the Konkan enjoyed peace. Trade from all parts of the West—Arabia, the Persian Gulf and far Cathay—penetrated by the tidal rivers and found its way by countless tracks into the Dekkhan.

But the fierce Mogul hordes from the north, having established themselves eastward of the Syadris, naturally sought seaports in the Konkan, and for centuries ruled as the Pharaohs did in Egypt and not less harshly

Compelled to employ the hardy sailors of the Malabár in commerce and to protect their ports, they soon experienced the fate of all who depend upon mercenaries by sea and land. Rebel leaders arose among those mercenaries, fierce mariners who became pirates, preying alike on Mogul and Marátha. Still fiercer pirates from Arabia's coasts, from Erythrœa (the Red Sea), from Socotra Island and the Eastern Coast of Africa, commenced on their own account to seize vantage positions, to build sea fortresses, even inland forts, and thus gradually to carve out small kingdoms of their own, to the gradual diminution of the Mogul Dominion which, first shattered by Siwajee's founding the Marátha Empire, and then by conflicts on sea and lands with the Portuguese, shrank to a nominal Delhi suzerainty in the East Dekkhan.

It would be tedious, and, indeed, is unnecessary to sketch the downfall of the Portuguese, the rise of the British "ráj," the collapse of the Marátha Empire, the subjugation of the great pirates, Ángria and the Habshi, obviously these were not times in which husbandry could flourish or population increase, however much commerce might expand from the Indian Ocean to the Eastern Highlands. Immense bodies of labourers, moreover, were needed to build the fortresses which stud the Konkan: these works absorbed all the Mhárs and employed thousands of able-bodied men imported from all parts of the coast, for whom food-stuffs had also to be imported. Cultivation only existed in the immediate neighbourhood of forts, and yielded barely sufficient grain for their garrisons. This was the state of affairs when the Peishwah dynasty was established. The Peishwahs, being all Konkani Brâhmins, naturally desired to develope their native country, and to this end granted large tracts on perpetual or long improvement leases, to their relatives and Court favourites. Thus sprang up a system of cultivation of a most disastrous nature, which continued up to nearly 1850. The grantees (middlemen farmers or "*Khotes*" as they are called) encouraged by the liberal terms of their "*Sanads*" (title-deeds) imported from the Dekkhan bodies of husbandmen under short agreements of one, two or three years, levying an almost nominal grain rental from them, and granting them free right to cut timber, fuel, and fodder wherever they thought fit. These "*ooprees*" or wandering husbandmen proceeded to denude the hillsides in the wasteful mode known as "*Kumri*" cultivation which consisted in firing the jungle and sowing on the plots thus cleared. Heavy crops were thus raised for, perhaps, two years at most, when the "ooprees" moved on to repeat the devastating process elsewhere. In a comparatively short time, not only were the hillsides denuded of vegetation, but the soil, which the roots of that vegetation held together, was washed down by the rain and has silted up the tidal creeks for miles along their course, utterly impeding navigation except for row boats. The demand for brushwood, foliage, anything inflammable, to burn on seed beds increased year by year: forest trees especially "*Ain*" and "*Kinjal*" are lopped as soon as the foliage has grown to a head, and this material, mixed with dry grass and "*shen*" (cow dung) is spread lightly over the surface of plots selected for the seed beds, and fired in the months of May and June whence the seedling plants are dibbled into other fields after sufficient rain has fallen. This is the system known as the "*ráb*" method, so called from the collected brushwood and leaves which are called "*ráb.*"

Volumes have been written for and against "*ráb*"—learned professors, English and German, have condemned the system not only as being wasteful, but as useless. As many more insist that the burnt compost contains certain valuable salts and manurial properties in the ashes, which enrich the peculiar soils of the Konkan, destroying larvæ which would otherwise devour both seed and seedling.

Whichever party may be correct, one thing is certain, that it is hopeless to expect even a moderate crop of rice, unless the seedlings have been raised on "*ràbbed*" plots, and the same holds good as regards the millets "*nagli*" and the like, grown on the steep hillsides which need heavy manuring, after transplantation, each bunch of seedling being dibbled in with a piece of rotten fish!*

* This description of "*ráb*" and "*kumri*" cultivation appeared in the Author's work "Our Troubles in Poona and the Dekkhan" (1897).

My old bard's verses quaintly ascribe to Parèshrâm's modified curse the absolute need for "*ráb*" in the following terms:—

Shri Parèshrâm having punished the Chitpâwans (as related in Chapter IV), hied him through the air to Helwak to join his brother Luxmon whom he had appointed to wait there for him. Luxmon had already been informed by the birds of the treachery of his brother's chosen people, and had left the black rocks of the Dekkhan, and was pacing excitedly on a red laterite plateau a little below. The moment Parèshrâm was by his side he began in the most insolent manner to revile him, accusing him of deceit and ingratitude after all his own personal devotion and obedience for so many years. Parèshrâm at once divined the cause of this change of manner; taking Luxmon kindly by the hand he said soothingly: "Be it so, brother mine, but let us ascend the great rock above, which was the trysting place I appointed, and discuss the question and our future plans in the cool breezes from the sea. We can scarce breathe in this stifling heat." The instant Luxman's foot stood again on black soil he prostrated himself at his elder brother's feet, overwhelmed with remorse. Said he "Oh my brother! my dearly beloved! I know not what has bewitched me that I should have so shamelessly accosted thee, just now below! Pardon thy *chela* (disciple), I beseech thee." Shri Parèshrâm raising and embracing him mildly observed "No need for pardon Lukkoo! thou wast in truth bewitched, and I will show thee how it happened! Let us descend again for a few moments to the red soil." They did so, but no sooner did Luxmon tread on the laterite than he became more turbulent than before! Shri Parèshrâm led him up again to the black soil, again did Luxmon wallow in the dust in remorse. Quoth Parèshrâm calmly "Brother mine! Zaminâchegoon âhè! ('Tis the fault or, literally, the virtue of the soil.) See what will now happen when I have sprinkled laterite soil on this black soil path, then follow in my footsteps." Again, as soon as Luxmon stepped on the laterite strewn portion of the road, he repeated his offence, no sooner did he pass on behind his brother to the black soil then he repented. "Behold Lukkoo! said I not truly 'Zâminachi' goon 'âhè'? 'Tis the fault of the treacherous soil!" cried Parèshrâm. Whereupon Luxmon in his wrath cursed it saying "Jalo" (or may it burn)! but Shri Pârèshrâm in the kindness of his divine heart, qualified the curse "Jalo! pun piko!" (let it burn, but let it be fruitful).

"For which reason it is," said the old bard complacently, "that all seed plants must be burnt in the Konkan if there is to be any harvest." "Shah Bash! Bhutji!" said I. "I'll tell the *savants* not to vex their learned souls more about "*ráb*," and so we parte d for that time.

CHAPTER VI.

LEGEND OF RAIGHUR.*

The so called Siwajee Revival a few years ago was a remarkable circumstance which ought to have attracted the serious notice of the Bombay Government, seeing that it was got up by the Brâhmin press, by descendants of the very caste that for their own base ends and by the basest intrigues usurped the power of Siwajee's descendants. The most casual perusal of the history of Máhárâshtra should have shown that the enthusiasm was feigned, and that pretended patriotism was spurious and without doubt displayed with some sinister object, and most certainly inspired by feelings inimical to the British "Ráj." Yet his Excellency the Governor (but, let us hope, *not* his Council) was smitten with admiration, and when a subscription was started to repair Siwajee's tomb or rather the platform on the summit of Raighur Fort, on which his body was cremated, he eagerly gave his mite and thus expressed his sympathy with "a down-trod nation," his remarkable knowledge of Brâhminical character, his abhorrence of the neglect of English officials who had so long left the sacred masonry to crumble!

The subscription list must be of such historical value that it should be published, and the original, together with the account showing how much of the amounts

---

* This Chapter is partly reproduced from Grant Duff's "History of the Maráthas," and from the Author's "Our Troubles in Poona and the Dekkhan," but has been considerably enlarged.

promised were actually paid, should be deposited in the archives of the India Office! It would also be interesting to know what caused this touching outburst, why the Peishwa's caste have forgotten for 300 years to restore the monument or even to keep it in repair! Have they taken the trouble to recover from Mhâd, the Brâhmin town at the foot of the fortress, the carved corner stones, pillars and wood-work robbed from their hero's residence and Durbar halls to be built into the walls of the better classes, or into their cow-sheds?

The writer of these pages had the good fortune to visit Raighur in the train of Sir Richard Temple during one of His Excellency's celebrated "Verification tours."

A mangy, ill-clad, highly flavoured old "*poojáree*" (worshipper) led us to what people call the tomb of Siwajee; an insignificant platform of decaying stones and mortar. We then proceeded to the "chowthara" or plinth, still in fair order, of the great Durbar hall in which it was Siwajee's wont to receive each year his various leaders, to distribute the spoils he and they had collected since the last Dussera. The plinth faces east. Sir Richard mounted it, and we all stood round while he made a heart-stirring recitation. I see the scene now vividly before my eyes, seem to hear his very words He first described the wild Mawalis, Hedkaris and Pathâns armed to the teeth, with shield, spear, sword and dagger, gathered in the Durbar hall: and on the steps bales of spoil scattered about, gold and silver, jewels, rich clothing, and cash galore. The great Chiefs gathered in a semi-circle round the Founder of the Máratha Empire, who, gorgeously arrayed, his good sword "Bhowanee" lying ready to his hand, sat on the kincob cushions of the throne, awarding praise or blàme as seemed meet. A shortish wiry man with looks of unusual intelligence, his visage generally displaying frank, rough humour, his long ape-like arms (which Grant-Duff tells us, are thought a great beauty among the Marátha race) folded on his knees and anon raised in gesticulation. The whole scene mayhap was lit by the rays of the rising sun, dispelling the masses of fleecy clouds in the valleys beneath. Or, more likely still, a nocturnal Durbar lit up by waving torches the back distance all in gloom, cross-lights glinting off the polished shields and glittering spoil, fierce faces appearing and disappearing, the tocsin resounding with enthusiastic cries of "Jey! Siwajee Máháráj Jey!" An embroidered "purdah" (curtain) stretched across the back of the hall, from which ever and anon peeped faces of the wives and female members of the family exultant in the tumult. In the rear—fittest place for them—a few white-clad Bráhmins, like snakes in the grass, subservient, humble, treacherous, as was their wont.

"Anon" declaimed Sir Richard, "the scene changes." The great Siwajee is dead and burnt on that plateau. It is the craven Sumbhajee, his son, who for the first time ascends his father's fortress, his mind filled with blood-thirsty intent, a discontented soldiery following him, presaging evil—with scant spoil to divide--the very crows and vultures seeming to scent blood in the air. The last surviving Queen-mother, Soyera Bye, has been deserted by all but Ánnaji Dutto and a few faithful adherents. The white-livered Brâhmins have long fled, and are endeavouring to make terms for themselves with the nearest party in power, by the sale of secrets, by treachery of every kind.

Soyera Bye is well-nigh alone when she is summoned to the ghastly Durbar, and foully accused by her stepson. Knowing that she has no chance of mercy, in her widow's weeds she ascends the "*chowthára*" and then with all the strength given her at the supreme moment, she holds forth; the craven Sumbhajee the while, cowering on the throne his father had so recently occupied. "Unworthy son of the great Siwajee!" she screams, raising her shrivelled arm, "if son thou art, which many doubt—I defy thee! Do thy worst! Thou comest hither, I know, for my blood and that of thy father's faithful servant: thou art now about to shed it. We die!"—raising both arms with clenched fists to heaven—"but may the wrath of the great Ishwar, may the curse of Bhowánee descend upon thee and thine!" No cries of "Jey Sumbhajee!" then, but a deadly gloom over the whole assemblage—a silence broken only by the guttural curses of the Máwalees and the clash of shields.

The Royal widow, her face now veiled, is led away to execution, and the murderer seeks to drown his conscience and allay his fears by revelry and riot."

Sir Richard's declamation was magnificent, and he never faltered for a word.

The toil of ascent is at once forgotten by the marvellous beauty of the scenery when looking eastward from the "*chowthára.*" Pertabghur in its majesty, Thorna in its audacious lofty isolation, all the peaks bristling around Arthur's Seat, Elphinstone Point, the Saddle Back and Mhyputghur in placid slumber, their summits touched by the last rays of the setting sun, their shadows dark purple, rosy edged, seem within a stone's throw—while the tiny stream of the infant Sâvitree and its numerous petty tributaries glisten like silver threads as they wind about below.

On the further or eastern side of Pertabghur, in the valley beneath the Fort and Mahableshwar, not far from where the travellers bungalow now stands, at Wárra, is the site of the celebrated encounter between Siwajee and Áfzool Khán, the Mogul General.

In September 1659 the Beejapoor Government, incensed at Siwajee's successes, despatched Áfzool Khán, one of their best commanders with 5,000 horse, 7,000 picked infantry and a strong train of artillery, rockets, and camel guns, to attack Siwajee in his stronghold.

The force, owing to the rains could not reach the Western Ghauts till October. Siwajee left Raighur and went to Pertabghur to meet it; thence he despatched emissaries to the proud Mogul, pretending to be in great dread, expressing his contrition and beseeching Áfzool Khân's mediation for forgiveness. The latter "vain as a Mogul" and despising "the mountain rat," sent a Brâhmin "wukeel" one of his staff on from Wai to receive Siwajee's submission. Siwajee, after one or two interviews, visited the Brâhmin secretly in the dead of night and made this powerful appeal to him. "You are a Brâhmin, my superior in caste, my guide in religion! I tell you that all I have done has been for the sake of Hindoos, and the Hindoo faith, The great Goddess Bhowánee herself has ordered me to protect Brâhmins and cattle, to slay these impious violaters of your temples and your Gods, to resist the enemies of your religion. I call upon you as a Brâhmin, to help me to obey the Goddess's behests! Do this and you shall hereafter live here among your own caste, and in your own country, in affluence, honoured above all Brâhmins."

Rich presents followed, and richer promises, and the Brâhmin Envoy swore by all his gods to do anything that Siwajee might ask. A consultation followed at which Siwajee's confidential adviser, also a Brâhmin, assisted, when the Mogul's Envoy suggested that a vain man like his master, might be easily persuaded to meet Siwajee in friendly conference where he could be disposed of. Áfzool Khán fell into the trap, and consented to an interview at the foot of Pertabghur. Meantime, Siwajee hurried up his trusty Máwulees by thousands and hid them in the jungles. Áfzool Khán, leaving the bulk of his army on the other side of Máhábleshwur, came on with only fifteen hundred men, to within a few hundred yards of Pertabghur, where, at his Bráhmin Envoy's suggestion, they were halted, "for fear of frightening Siwajee!" What followed is thus graphically told by Grant-Duff.

Áfzool, a giant in stature, dressed in a thin muslin garment, armed only with his sword, and attended, as had been agreed, by a single armed follower, advanced in his palanquin to an open shed erected for the occasion.

Siwajee had made preparations for his purpose, not as if conscious that he meditated a criminal and treacherous deed but as if resolved on some meritorious though desperate action. Having performed his ablutions with much earnestness, he laid his head at his mother's feet, and besought her blessing, He then arose, put on chain armour and a steel cap under his turban, concealed a crooked dagger or '*beechwa*' (literally, scorpion), in his right sleeve, and on the fingers of his left hand he fixed a '*wágnuk*,' or tiger's claws, a small steel instrument made to fit on the fore and little finger; it had three crooked blades, which are easily concealed in a half closed hand.

Thus accoutred, he slowly descended from the fort. The Khán had arrived at the place of meeting before him, and was expressing his impatience at the delay, when Siwajee was seen advancing, apparently unarmed, and, like the Khán, attended by only one armed follower, his tried friend, Thánnajee Máloosary. Siwajee in view of Áfzool, frequently stopped, which was represented as the effects of alarm, a supposition more likely to be admitted from his diminutive size. Under pretence of assuring Siwajee, the armed attendant, by the contrivance of the Brâhmin Envoy, stood at a few paces distance. Áfzool made no objection to Siwajee's follower, although he carried two swords in his waist band, a circumstance which might pass unnoticed among Maráthas: he advanced two or three paces to meet Siwajee; they were introduced, and in the midst of the customary embrace, the treacherous Marátha struck the wágnuk into the bowels of Áfzool Khán, who quickly disengaged himself, clapped his hand on his sword, exclaiming 'Treachery and murder!' but Siwajee instantly followed up the blow with his dagger. The Khán had drawn his sword and made a cut at Siwajee, but the concealed armour was proof against the blow. The whole was the work of a moment, and Siwajee was wresting the weapon from the hand of his victim before their attendants could run towards them.

Synd Bundoo, the follower of the Khán, whose name deserves to be recorded, refused his life on condition of surrender, and against two such swordsmen as Siwajee and his companion, maintained an unequal combat for some time before he fell. The bearers had lifted the Khán into his palanquin during the scuffle, but by the time it was over Khundoo Málley and some other followers of Siwajee had come up, when they cut off the head of the dying man, and carried it to Pertabghur. The signals agreed on were now made; the Máwulees rushed from their concealment and beset the nearest part of the Beejapoor troops on all sides, few of whom had time to mount their horses or stand to their arms. Nettajee Pálkur with the Máwulees gave no quarter; but orders were sent to Moro Punt to spare all who submitted; and Siwajee's humanity to his prisoners was conspicuous on this as well as on most occasions."

This graphic description is now shown on very excellent authority to be not quite accurate—not quite fair to Siwajee. Mr R. P. Karkharia, a Parsee historian of high repute, has hunted out old "bakhars" (documents) of undoubted authenticity, and proves in an able pamphlet on Pertabghur (or as he calls it Pratapghur), that Áfzool Khán was only deceived so far as to believe that Siwajee was really in dread of him, that he came to the conference prepared not only to encounter treachery, but to surprise and seize, doubtless to kill, Siwajee, if the latter had not killed him, but he foolishly despised his enemy. Whatever treachery there was on both sides was suggested by Brâhmins, prepared by Brâhmins—that much is certain!

The incident reads like one of the chapters in Fennimore Cooper's Red Indian Novels. We seem to see an encounter between the Crow Chief "Clawing Catamount" (Siwajee) and the Delaware leader "Big Bull" (Áfzool Khán), and we admire Siwajee's pluck, cunning, and superior military skill. The mode of warfare, the morals of those years gone by, are not to be jüdged by Exeter Hall standards of the present day. We have been dealing with times when armed and desperate man struggled daily to take each other's lives and snuffled not at murder. We may well cry, and let Maharattas still cry, "Jey Siwajee Máháraj"!* for he *was* a fine fellow; but when a handful of the treacherous caste that nullified his patriotism, suggested all his crimes, and compassed the downfall of the Empire he had raised, use his name for the furtherance of seditious plots against ourselves, 'tis surely the time to scotch the reptiles, not to subscribe to their schemes?

I should add, in conclusion, that the old Bhutt's Sânscrit verses describing leading incidents in Siwajae's life, contained descriptions of Torna Fort also—but none so well told as those by Grant-Duff, or here by Sir Richard Temple.

* Hurrah (or victory) for Siwajee Maharaj.

CHAPTER VII.

THE LEGEND OF WASOTA.

"*This 'Pothi,' Kháwand, will have a special interest,*" observed the old Chiploon Bhutt, "*because it really describes the condition of the Konkan before the great Deluge when the great Noe and his family were the only human beings saved (so tradition says but 'tis hard to believe!). Moreover, my lord will remember (what does my lord ever forget) that there were tragedies committed in the great Fort Wásota frowning above us so late as* 1817 *of the Christian era by Báji Rao the last Peishwa. With Kháwand's gracious permission, his slave will now read and can read easily, for (Paraméshwar be praised) the manuscript is in excellent condition! But first let my lord regard the "chamátkár" (strange and amusing) pictures drawn on the title page and around the margins.*"

They were indeed beautifully executed: not the stiff gaudy pictures of red lions, green tigers, and yellow crocodiles, with distorted limbs with which Hindus to this day love to cover the walls of their dwellings, but exquisitely tinted in appropriate colours by the hand of an artist who must have carefull studied the anatomy of the animals he depicted.

"*They are good indeed,*" said I. "*Now read away.*"

"*Bulla! Saheb! Bulla! parantoo gaye karonaka*" he said *(Well! Well! Sir! but don't be in a hurry!)* "*Thou wilt perceive, Khawand, that these pictures represent birds, beasts, and fishes of gigantic size much larger than any that now exist on earth. 'Ni saonsh'* (no doubt) *they were some of those that Parameshwar created before he made puny sinful man, whom 'Missenary' (Missionary) Padrés tell us he created last of all. Is it not so? Khodáwand!*"

I nodded impatiently, not caring to hear the 1st Chapter of the Book of Genesis discussed in detail. The old man began to sing-song the sacred '*Slöks*' (verses) in long-winded compound words plentifully bestrewed with 'anuswaras' (labial-nasal aspirates ending in 'um') which made the poetry run, like liquid, melodiously from his mouth. Some linguists there be who call Sânscrit the German of Oriental languages, a very inapt description of it, in my humble judgment—German is harsh and guttural, abounding in polysyllables that have neither beginning nor end. Sânscrit is rather a compound of Italian and Portuguese—the latter language much resembling Sânscrit in the profuse use of the terminal 'anuswara' "um-um" with the addition of Italian liquid vowels.

But I must describe Wásota. It is a fortress absolutely impregnable from the Western, Northern and Southern sides, even by modern artillery; but from the East it is open to assault from the plateau of flat rock, which, however, gradually narrows to the great gateway. Looking down from above it seems as if one might drop a pebble 2,500 feet perpendicularly without its touching anything, but looking up from the nearest projection one can reach the actual sheer drop in about 1,700 feet. The bastions are mostly cut out of solid rock, entirely so on the western face. It has plenty of spring water and a few trees inside the enclosure; otherwise it is a most desolate spot. It was Báji Rao's favorite State prison; requiring a small garrison, it was really inaccessible yet sufficiently near Poona (say 110 miles). A State prisoner cost little to feed there, or to guard. Escape was quite impossible from those frowning battlements. His funeral ceremony, or execution, was simple and impressive; as the sea was the Cemetery of the Chateau d'If, so the precipice was the Cemetery of Wásota. God alone knows how many gallant warriors and statesmen there languished till death mercifully released them! how many—some of them English officers—were tossed alive into space when the order came from Poona for their despatch*.

---

* Grant-Duff mentions several white men and natives. Two English Officers were murdered there, two others, whose names he gives, were rescued after the defeat of Bāji Rao in September 1817

On the face of the rock, up to the very foot of the bastions, marine shells are imbedded, showing, that the sea once flowed over the country round, leaving Wásota (probably) a rock only bare at low tide, for shells and petrified fish and marine fossils of several kinds may be gathered in the valleys lying eastward. Somewhere not far below the summit, where the basalt overlies the laterite foundation, the river Wáshisti rises winding a silver thread down to the small village Wasi (or Wáshi) and gradually increasing in volume till it falls by what is a roaring cataract in the monsoon into a fathomless pool, whence it rushes fed by a thousand torrents to meet the Indian Ocean tide for the first time at Chiploon. It is as if Titanic hands pressed down the trap stratum on the spongy laterite beneath.

Enthusiasts of the Forest Department used to contend that these barren boulder-strewn cliffs and spurs were once clad with forest growth, till wandering bands ("Oopri") of cultivators destroyed it, in their wasteful process of "Kumri"* cultivation, but (as Mr. Commissioner Crawford pointed out at a Forest Conference, where Sir Richard Temple presided), no shrub or undergrowth could find rootbold on such steep declivities. Here and there a stunted Bábul tree may struggle on a small plateau, elsewhere nothing but the tenacious "Sábri" (thornless Euphorbium) can exist with (of course) spear grass. Sir Richard concurred, but nevertheless included all these species in Forest second-class Reserves! The writer knows no more desolate tract than that extending on the Western face of the Syadris from Rai Ghar to the Hârt-lot Ghaut.

The old Bhutt at last began to read

THE LEGEND OF LEVIATHAN AND WÁSOTA.

It was, it must have been, soon after the Great Deluge, in which (perhaps) Noah's ark bumped on Wásota's rocks, that a huge snake-like head reared itself from the ocean waves lapping Wāsota's cliffs. It lay its flat scaly head and fifty cubic yards of its neck in a shallow inlet of the sea: its body, many cubics in diameter, and a thousand cubics in more sinuous length, floated on Sâmudra's * (the ocean's) bosom, the serrated spine fringed with coarse rope-like hair, waved in the light sea-breeze. Two three-toed paws clung lizard-like, to the scarp †. It was the monster Leviathan whom Ishwar created to sport in the depths of the ocean, with his mate, a smaller reptile. But why call it *reptile* profane wretch that I am! seeing that it was the largest and most amazing of Ishwar's creation. It will never die, nor its mate either, but Ishwar in his benevolence has decreed that it shall be childless, lest it destroy and devour all the rest of his creatures. Its ordinary food is the larger fishes, turtles all the giant weeds and grasses growing at the bottom

* Ocean, the name of the Hindu Neptune.

† Many naturalists opine that the so-called "sea-serpent" (if existent) is a kind of sea-lizard or newt.

of the ocean, but it attacks also all beasts that roam along the coast, even mammoths and mastodons, but its favourite food is or was man! Just as *muggers* (alligators) seem to smell dogs below water, and to hear their pit-pat on the bank overhead, so the Leviathans smelt mankind and heard their footfall from the depths of the ocean!

One glorious *Jesht* (June) morn, the male Leviathan was thus lying at Wásota, the female curled asleep in a swamp hard by. He watched with half closed eyes for his prey. Behold a band of *Rishis* (demi-Gods) approaching, with sound of horn and baying of huge hairless polygar dogs. They were hunting down a splendid *Sámbhur* (Indian elk) 20 cubics high; foaming at the mouth, bleeding at its expanding nostrils, panting for breath, the exhausted monarch of the forest sought sanctuary in the very morass wherein the female Leviathan was concealed. She moved not nor did her mate. The stag, knee-deep in slush and reeds, turned boldly to face his enemies, his antlered head bent low. The hounds surrounded him baying noisily, some he struck down with back-breaking stamps of his cloven fore-feet, some he gored to death; others, however, swam under his guards seizing him by nostril and by dewlap, while others clambered on his broad back and bit his flanks or dragged at his hocks. The gallant beast with one last plunge forward shook off his assailants, but it was his dying effort. Sinking on his knees the poor animal raised his glazing eyes heavenward, streaming with briny tears as if to implore the gods to save him. The gods did save him. As the foremost *Rishis*, spear in hand, rushed into the mire to despatch him—with one sweep of her horny tail the she-Leviathan struck down dogs and *Rishis* in the morass—Old Leviathan extended himself nearer, and the pair of monsters greedily devoured man and dogs one by one, glaring the while at the affrighted *Rishis* on the bank, who fled incontinently. The Leviathans touched not, however, the gallant stag—still hungry though they were—knowing that the gods desired him to live. He, poor beast, slowly revived, dragged his weary limbs to the bank—where for a whole *prahar* (3 hours) he lay prone—struggling for breath—gradually recovering, he turned his head to lick his bleeding wounds—then rolled his huge carcase on the sand, rose, shook himself, and with pathetic eyes raised gratefully to the azure canopy of heaven, slowly limped away into the forest. He did not know how his foes had perished, or he was unconscious and at the point of death when the great sea-lizards devoured them. When he came to himself, all nature was seemingly asleep, he could not discern his saviours among the rushes and the rocks. So departed that noble stag to challenge with bell-like bellowing all comers that very night—to live, protected by the gods, the monarch of the forest for many centuries to come.

THE SAMBHUR'S GRATITUDE.

The *Rishis*, demi-gods as they are, were not a little chagrined at their defeat—the loss of their prey, and the loss of all their favourite hounds. But they realised that the Leviathans were no common antagonists: they, therefore, hied them to the nearest temple to Kâli, goddess of death, to whom all mortals appeal for aid when in dire straits, especially when they desire vengeance. The most famous of all Sri Kâli's shrines is at Punderpoor, as knoweth all Mâhárâshtra. There they laid the facts before the goddess dread and besought assistance. The officiating priest told them that the entrails of the cock they had brought and he had sacrificed, were knotted and inflamed, therefore the omens were unfavourable. He averred that Shri Kâli was angry with them, the petitioners, for neglecting her worship, and for resorting in preference to the shrines of that up-start young goddess Bhowáni, who held (he said emphatically) a much lower position in heaven than Shri Kâli. If the *Rishis* sincerely sought Shri Kâli's assistance, and would swear there and then to sacrifice to her at the next Dussera, and would offer up as a Meriah sacrifice a certain beauteous maiden, named Bhágirthi, the only daughter of the Marátha *Rishis* of Juth, Shri Kâli would amply avenge them on the great sea-lizards.

The *Rishis* obtained permission to withdraw into the recesses of the sacred *bun* (grove) outside for consultation. Shri Kâli's behest must, of course, be complied with—but how? It was a very perilous undertaking to kidnap Bhágirthi, carry her 60 miles to Punderpoor, and sacrifice her, seeing that until she arrived at puberty a year later she was dedicated to the service of Shri Bhowáni at Juth, and moreover, was already betrothed to the powerful *Rishi* of Phultun. It would be surely safer to carry her off to their own country around Helwak, and induce a priest from Shri Kâli's small shrine there to accompany them, who should perform the sacrifice at a temporary altar built at the very spot above Wásota where they (the *Rishis*) had been disgraced! And surely it was appropriate that the sacrifice should take place at the spot where the offence was committed! Best of all, if they found the great sea-lizards there basking in the sun (as was probable) they might, with Shri Kâli's powerful aid, destroy them then and there.

The *Rishis* accordingly returned to the temple, but the priest waived them away saying that Shri Kâli was away hunting, next day she was said to be sleeping, the next she was declared to have gone to bathe in Mother Gunga (the Ganges) at Benáres. For two whole moons did the priest (who well knew the *Rishis* to be wealthy) put them off.

They daily increased their offers to Shri Kâli nominally, but really to the priest—a cow and a calf? not enough! 3 cows? not nearly enough! 6 cows and a bull? still insufficient! By the end of the two moons the priest had extorted twenty cows with their calves, three bulls, a herd of goats, and three camels from the reluctant *Rishis*, who were compelled to pawn their gold ornaments for wherewithal to pay the purchase money of this farm-yard full of beasts.

Then the priest announced that Shri Kâli accepted their offerings, that they should at once carry Bhâgirthi off to Wásota, where the goddess would afford them a splendid vengeance.

They (the *Rishis*) had no difficulty in kidnapping the child. She was usually playing outside the temple of Bhowáni at Juth. Gagging her they carried her off on horseback to Helwak, while they were arranging with a local priest of Shri Kâli's small shrine there to accompany them. Shri Bhowáni sent a *lungur* (large monkey) to warn the *Sámbhur*, and order him at once to race off to Phultun and Juth with the news.

The noble stag—fleetest of his kind in all that country—inspired alike with bitter hatred for his late pursuers, and an earnest desire to serve his preservers the great Leviathans, performed his journey in a few hours. The *Rishis* of Juth and Phultun were already on the war path but were being misdirected by a Mhár employed by Shri Kâli—him they slew and hanged on a tree. The *Sámbhur* guided them swiftly to the morass adjoining Wásota. They arrived not a moment too soon. Poor little Bhágirthi was already bound on a temporay altar. The wicked *Rishis* were squatted around, exulting, having left their arms and horses in charge of their servants in a neighbouring thicket. They were all naked to the waist—as is customary at all such sacrifices—the loug keen knife of the priest was the only weapon in the assemblage. He had raised it glittering in the sun's rays, when suddenly the *Rishis* of Juth and Phultun rushed upon them with fierce yell, slew them like sheep, shouting "*Jey Bhowáni!* In the midst of the turmoil the Leviathans rose from their lair in the morass; the male promptly swallowed the priest, knife and all—his mate gulped down another—and the *Sámbhur* gored half a dozen of the wounded to his heart's content. Bhágirthi's rescuers having killed all but one wounded wicked *Rishi*, bound him on the temporary altar on great faggots, whereon they slowly burnt him to death with cries of "*Jey! Bhowáni—Bhowáni Máha Dewi ki jey!*" Then the grateful father of Bhágirthi calling the *Sámbhur* to his side embraced the noble animal—so did little Bhágirthi—and gilded his antlers and feet, while the *Rishi* of Phultun fastened a splendid collar of gold round the tag's neck to which a golden bell was attached. Therefore this noble *Sámbhur* has never been attacked by Tigers or "*Dholes*" (wild dogs). Therefore has he lived so many years.

The tinkle of his bell is often heard along the Ghauts and in the Koina valley, and is welcome as a happy omen by all "*Dhungurs*" (herdsmen). The votaries of Shri Bhowáni have mightily increased in numbers. Those of Shri Kâli have proportionately decreased since that day of the triumph of her sister goddess.

Sámbhur skin has since then been generally used only for honourable purposes—with the hair on, as mats to pray on to Shri Bhowáni or when cured, for saddle cloths, for sandals, for waist belts, for shields, for all kinds of harness and decoration.

The great Leviathans, of course, crawled back into Sâmudra's bosom, but the male complained greatly of his throat. "*Methinks, Bhai Májhi,*" he gurgled in his wife's ear, "*that rascally priest's long knife has stuck in my throat! Call the big lobster that he may pull it out.*" She did so, the famed dentist of the ocean put his head fearlessly into his patient's jaws, found the knife sticking in Leviathan's gullet like a fishbone, and triumphantly drew it out but the great sea-lizard has been subject to a hacking cough ever since, which is often heard by mariners at sea, and betokens bad weather, wherefore they promptly put back for shelter.

"*There! Khodáwund!*" quoth the venerable Bhutt, "*that is all! I trust my lord has been amused? It is all true!* he added solemnly, "*By Shri Bhowáni it is!*"

"I'm sure it is by Bhowáni! Bhuttjee!" said I. "Tell me another to-morrow, by Bhowáni!"

"Bulla! Khodáwund, Bhot bulla! Majhi pèteet Májhi potat azoon pushkal rahile ahet!" quoth the venerable priest ("Very good, my lord! There are plenty more in my box, and in my stomach!").

NOTES BY THE AUTHOR.

Meriah Sacrifices.—These ghastly ceremonies, like *Sutti* (widow burning), hook-swinging, suicides under the wheels of Juggernath's car, were quite common till our beneficent British Government put a stop to them and to thuggi and self-mutilation. I am not aware what the word *Meriah* precisely means or is derived from. The sacrifices were made for several objects: the commonest being to induce the Gods (Kâli, or other ferocious deity of the Hindo Pantheon) to prosper any new enterprise—to obtain a son, to perform the annual funeral obseqnies of parents hitherto childless, to avenge the petitioner on his or her enemies, to avert or abate any public calamity (famine, drought, or disease), to obtain relief from private ailments, or domestic trouble—and, especially to gain divine favour by the immolation of female infants, for whom it was difficult for poor parents, with quivers overful of female children to find suitable husbands. It was customary also among the noble classes, especially Rajputs and small families of the highly born wherein there was no suitable male infant unbetrothed. Blood and burnt offerings to the Omnipotent Power have been (and will always be) a prominent feature in the worship of Oriental races, from the time of Abraham. But *Meriah* sacrifices (religious murders we may term them) were inspired by much the same sentiment that induces modern Roman Catholic parents to place their female children in convents for life. In the distorted Hindu imagination it seemed (no doubt still seems) that, apart from the self-abnegation thereby displayed—which must be laudable and gratifying to all the gods (whether benign or ferocious) —it was preferable for the poor little girl's soul that she should be removed from this sinful world, than that unwedded she should grow up to be a devotee (in fact, a prostitute) at some temple, or the (may be) honored and powerful concubine in some prince's or nobleman's zenána. To immolate the infant while still innocent and undefiled was to insure her salvation and must be pleasing to Shiwa. Her elimination, moreover, was a palpable relief to a poor family living from hand to mouth. To all families of whatever degree it is a matter of honour that no girl arrived at puberty shall be unwedded, or (at least) betrothed. In all families, rich or poor, the cost of a wedding is a very serious matter indeed. A wedding means (perhaps) a future generation in the usurers' claws, and a perceptible present diminution of the family income.

The desire for "an heir of their loins" prompts many childless parents among Christian peoples, to perform pilgrimages, to consult astrologers and clairvoyants, to swallow quack medicines, even (as all the world knows) to sleep on the Blarney Stone at Innisfallen island in the Lakes of Killarney. Aye! even to commit great crimes. Is it surprising that a race, comparatively uneducated, steeped for countless ages in superstition, should resort to crime to procure what means their future salvation, when some difficulty obstructs adoption. Such a *Meriah* sacrifice certainly took place in 1878 at Karwar (North Kanara) when I was Commissioner of the Southern Division of the Bombay Presidency. I was at Karwar at the time, was consulted by the Police Superintendent and the Magistrate, and perused the depositions on which the murderers were committed to the Sessions.

The facts were these. The Judge's Chitnis (Head Clerk) was childless, he sought to adopt a pretty little son of the Court's Názir (Sheriff), but the latter declined the honour. Bad feeling was thus engendered. Mrs. Chitnis, a truculent woman of the "Soopya-Lat" * type, made pilgrimages in vain to Punderpoor, Násik and Benáres, the gods would not listen to her. In despair, she consulted her Joshi (astrologer) who advised a *Meriah* sacrifice to Shri Kâli, at the

* Soopya-Lat, ex-Queen of Burmah, notorious for her ferocity.

goddess's approaching annual festival. It naturally suggested itself to a woman of Mrs. Chitnis's vindictive disposition, that she would not only propitiate Shri Kâli, but gratify her own malice if the Názir's boy were sacrificed. The Názir was away conducting some Court sale. The woman employed one of her husband's peons to bring the child to her when she told him what she intended, promised him the ornaments with which she would load the little fellow, if he would do the needful—the villain was nothing loath. He was seen at the festival with Mrs. Chitnis to be carrying the Názir's little boy, gorgeously dressed, on his shoulder, and to lift him several times ostensibly to see the idol. His poor little body was found the next morning with his throat cut in an adjacent tank. The jewels he wore were, of course, gone. Mrs. Chitnis and the peon were arraigned for murder—the Chitnis for being accessory before and after the fact, but they were acquitted for want of evidence, of course. The townspeople, however, spoke openly of the little fellow's murder as a futile *Meriah* sacrifice to Kâli.*

This case is incidentally mentioned in the author's Reminiscences," which has long been out of print.

CHAPTER VIII.

THE WHITE TIGERS.

A LEGEND OF THE KOINA VALLEY.

"*This pothi*," quoth the old Bhutt, peering at me admiringly over his horn spectacles, "*will be pleasant hearing to my lord, because it describes wondrous scenes and incidents in tiger hunting, and specially because my lord is a Roostoom Báhádur of Báhádurs among Shikaris*". I salaamed modestly. "*And, moreover, Khodáwand*," continued mine ancient friend, "*these tales are true!—All my pothis are true, my lord! I swear they are, by the great Shiwa and the fell Kâli*"!

"*Oh! Oh!*" said I. "*What a fickle old philosopher thou art! Yestere'en thou wast eloquent in praise of Shri Bhowáni! and to-day*"? "*To-day, Máháráj, thy slave will read of the exploits and transfiguration of a greater than Shri Bhowáni, of Shri Shiwa, the dread, but yet merciful Destroyer*," (hear he bared his white poll, and rubbed his old nose on the tent carpet). "*Thou knowest, Khodáwand, that these sacred slöks* (verses) *are not of my inditing.*"

"*Granted, 'Budda ji'* (old man)" said I. "*Keep thy temper though" tis a bad one! Let's hear thy true tale, by Shiwa, Kâli, and all your hundred thousand gods and goddesses".*

He proceeded to read as follows :—

When the great Siwaji was yet a callow youth fresh from Poona and Joonere, when his mighty projects for overthrowing the Moguls in Máhárâshtra were as yet known but to a few trusty adherents and to his resolute mother, just widowed, she and he resided mostly at Pertab Ghur, whence the little hero with the large heart, was accustomed to make many expeditions in the Koina Valley, big game hunting accompanied by Bábaji Phakre, Bhao Rao Mâloosre, and Khundi Rao bin Bhow Rao "*Names well known afterwards in history Khodáwand!*" (observed the old Bhutt). "*Fire arms or what the Sahebs call 'arms of precision' were then unknown thou knowest, Khodáwand?*" They carried only boar-spears pointed at both ends, a short "tulwar" (sword), and a round shield made from the breast skin of the "Nilghai" (the largest of the antelope tribe) and a dagger in their "kummerbunds"* (waist band). With these simple weapons, and on foot, they followed up large games; sat up the night through to attack tigers over the carcases of cattle, the fierce brutes had killed, withstood their charge, and followed them in densest jungle if they escaped wounded. Bisons, bears and boars were mere child's play to them!

* "These kummerbands" or sashes serve for a dagger called "Beechow" (scorpion) to be sheathed in, and it is also folded with a leathern or silver girdle and a pursé.

For several years previously a pair of large tigers, very light skinned, but with very black stripes withal, had ravaged the country from Kumbárli Ghaut to Máhábaleshwar, killing hecatombs of deer and cattle. Their favourite lair was under a huge rock in the face of the cliff facing Rai Ghur. They were oft times to be seen stretched on the top of it, basking in the sun, but no Shikaris has ever been able to surprise them there. While one slept, the other kept watch and ward. The place was consequently called "*Wághâchi Baitak*" (*tigers seat*). "*The Saheb log, thy servant hears, called it* "*Arthur's Seat*"* the old man observed "*which seems a senseless name*"! No peril that the beasts of the forest can encounter but had been undergone by these two "*Gai khuṉkaris* †" (cow slayers). They had fallen into cunningly concealed pits, but had somehow scrambled out. They had once been nearly smothered by leaves smeared with a viscid mixture of lime and the milk (gum) of the milk bush ‡. On this occasion, the tiger was actually so far enveloped that he was rolling blinded on the ground: his muffled roars attracted

* After Sir George Arthur, first Governor of Bombay, who visited Máhábaleshwar, then discovered by the Honble Mr. Malet.

† "Khun" means murder.

‡ This in former days was a common method of trapping tigers, panthers, and bears. The beast finding a leaf sticking to his paw, puts it up to his face, to which it adheres; he repeats this game; his eyes become blinded, his face plaistered all over; the rolls about becomes more enveloped, and falls an easy prey to the Shikaris.

the tigress, she had just time to lead her mate to a deep pool hard by, when the Shikaris ran up. The cold water and the bath relieved the tiger of his adhesive plaisters, and cleared his sorely smarting eyes, so they were able to swim across, and evade the hunters. One night the tigress was caught in a large wooden cage-trap baited with a calf, but her mate gnawed through the bars, and they carried off the calf after all! The tiger's tail was broken in a stone-falling trap. They had eaten of a "*kill*" in which poison had been placed, but luckily did not touch the poisoned part! They had been wounded by arrows shot from high trees by Shikaris watching for them at night. At last, as they were hunting down a fine young bull bison together, the whole herd turned upon and trampled them down; the tigress's ribs were broken, the tiger was badly gored and tossed high in the air. This was the narrowest escape they had ever had; and it had important results for the country-side.

The injured brutes just managed to crawl under the shelter of a large rock; the tigress was so maimed and in such agony, that she was unable to lick her mate's deep wound, which was high on his wither where he could not reach it himself with his rough tongue.

Blow-flies settled on and deposited their eggs in this wound, these hatched out grubs, which burrowed into the tiger's muscles under the skin They were doomed to die of hunger and thirst. and rapidly wasted away to skeletons. But when they were moribund, Shiwa sent a troop of monkeys to peer at them, their natural foes, on the ground; one of these came within reach of the tiger's huge paw, and he had just strength enough left to strike it dead. Its warm life blood refreshed, its tender succúlent flesh revived and nourished the sufferers. Other curious jungle denizens a "*Mohr*" (Peacock), a "*pisoori*"* or two (Mouse deer), and more monkeys—all sent by Shri Shiwa, were similarly caught and devoured; a flock of "seven sisters" † fearlessly settled (Shri Shiwa sent) on the moaning, writhing tiger, and picked the worms from his festering wound, so that it soon began to heal. Both the beasts rapidly recovered strength to some extent, but, alas! they found that their fangs were falling from their gums, or were decaying; they were no longer vigorous, but stiff in all their joints, comparatively feeble, and partially blind and, wonderful to relate, they had become what the Saheb log called "*Albinos*" ‡ white as a snow leopard, their stripes showing faintly a pale orange color in the sun!

* The smallest of antelopes, no bigger than a small Norfolk hare, striped and speckled green grey.

† These birds which are very foul feeders, are so called by us because they are always seven. They are a species of thrush and chatter incessantly.

‡ Albino tigers are not at all common, but snow leopards are common in the Himalayas. The finest Albino tiger skin ever seen in England was set up by Edwin Ward, the Taxidermist in Wigmore street. The beast was shot by Major Craigie-Halkett in Bengal. Ward valued it at 500 guineas.

"Shall thy slave stop now Khodáwand"? queried the old man, "*thy servant seest that his lord is impatient.*"

"*No,*" *said I,* "*pray continue. I'm all anxiety to hear the sequel, but my Chitnis is coming presently with a batch of important papers; however he can wait.*"

"*Oh! my lord's Chitnis (Secretary) must not be kept waiting, he is a great man. The Nana has a good profitable 'jaga' (berth) hán? Khodáwand,*" queried the cunning old fellow. "*Hum*" said I. "*Now fire away, I want to know why your Shri Shiwa helped the tigers in their trouble.*"

Bulla! Khodawand, Bhot bulla! 'tis worth thy hearing, thy slave assures my lord. He read on—

For many years previously all Maráthas, especially those of the Syadris, had been mostly neglectful of Shri Shiwa's worship. Shri Bhowáni, 'tis true, is the patron goddess of nearly all Maráthas, and of all "Kshatryas" (or warrior caste), but that was no reason why they should contemn their creator and destroyer. His shrines were rarely frequented—few flowers were laid on the sacred "Lingum"*. His sacred Bull

---

* An obscene emblem of the female and male pubes in the act of coition worn in miniature encased in silver boxes appended to their sacred threads by all Lingayets, as emblems of Shiwa the Creator.

was not decked with garlands, nor annointed with fragrant oils, his priests complained bitterly of poverty. Shri Kâli had even greater cause for anger. The great little Siwaji's good sword, with which he was soon to hew off Afzul Khán's head, it is true was named by his royal mother after Shri Bhowáni, but she and he had forgotten that the future founder of the Maráthа Empire was named after Shri Shiwa. Máhárashtra must be made to know that Shri Shiwa is supreme in heaven, and Shri Kâli, one of the most potent deities in hell. Shris Bhowáni, Kristna, Paréshrâm, and others, now so much honoured, were all very well in their way but were parvenus at best. Shri Shiwa accordingly took counsel with Shri Kâli, they determined to enter into the bodies of the injured tigers aforesaid—so beasts and birds were enjoined to succour the latter (as has been narrated).

When the two tigers were restored to something like their pristine form, Shri Shiwa entered into the body of the tiger, and Shri Kâli into that of the tigress. Then all the country-side, from lofty Pertab Ghur along the Koina, to the Mulla Ghaut, had a terrible time. These two fearsome white tigers no longer hunted game and killed cattle; they laid in wait for, and devoured human beings far and wide. Did a couple of wood-cutters go into the jungle with their "*koitis*" (bill-hooks) one never returned—nothing but his crushed skull was discovered. Did a party of women hie them pitcher-laden, to the village well, one or two would certainly be carried off shrieking. Did they repair to prickly pear clumps under the mud walls of the village with their children at early dawn, for natural purposes, two were surely taken, and others perhaps stricken down. Whole villages were deserted; cattle wandered far and wide, unattended—the fields were left untilled, the crops uncut. No one could predict when or where the next tragedy would occur, it might be at Warra to-night, at Khelghur to-morrow, at Helwak the third night, for these White Tiger Devils as they waxed stronger, travelled great distances after every kill, usually returning once every half moon, to bask on the lofty rock at "*Wághách i Baituk*" (or Arthur's Seat).

The Royal widowed mother of Siwaji offered large rewards in gold mohurs, and villages in "*Enám*" (hereditary gifts, free of Land Tax) to any one who would rid the land of these pests, but in vain. Siwaji, her son, was away at Singhur, having just accomplished perhaps the most daring exploit of his marvellous career, when he forced his way with a few followers in disguise into the City of Poona, joined a marriage procession, surrounded what had been his Royal Mother's "wárra" (or Palace), then occupied by a Mogul noble, and entering, with his own hand cut down the Mogul's son, retreating with all his men unhurt to Singhur, with music playing.

It was, of course, out of the question to trouble her gallant son with such a petty matter, at such a time. So the Royal Mother ordered her *mánkurs* (Chiefs) in Pertab Ghur to organize a hunting party, to bring back the White Tiger skins or never to show their faces again in Durbar. A Máloosray and a Ghorepoorary led a small band of Shikaris round to a deserted village which they intended to work from. They were assembled after the evening meal in a hut over a fire, for it was very cold, the door was (as they thought) securely fastened. Two Mhárs of the village were in the room ; outcastes though they were, whose presence was a defilement to the Marathas, humanity demanded that they should not be left outside at the tigers' mercy. The hubble-bubble was being passed round, when, suddenly, the door was burst in ; with terrific roars two huge White Tigers bounded into the room, rushed through and scattered the glowing embers, seized and carried off the two poor Mhárs who were cowering in a far corner, and carried them shrieking off. The assault was so sudden and unexpected, the Shikaris had not time to seize their weapons. But they followed at once, guided by the tigers' growling, and then, when the beasts halted to devour their prey, secreted themselves by a stream hard by and waited for dawn. The White Tigers having by that time gorged themselves, drank greedily at the stream within a few yards of the Shikaris, and then curled themselves up under a bamboo clump for their siesta. Two of the

Shikaris were sent back to bring a strong rope net with which they had prudently provided themselves. This was deftly drawn round the sleeping tigers and then, with yells of vengeance, Máloosray and Ghorepooray rushed in armed only with their "tulwars" (swords) and shields.* The conflict was soon over but it was bloody indeed. Máloosray was very badly mauled, but he had killed the tiger. Ghorepooray, not so fortunate, had wounded the tigress, but had been killed by one blow of her paw—the beast, though mortally injured, her entrails trailing on the ground, had killed another man, and mortally mauled a third. She managed to crawl into the bamboos, where she was speared at last. Máloosray flaying the carcases of the beasts, burnt their whiskers and returned in triumph to display his trophies to the Royal widow, who embraced him affectionately, and cast her own priceless necklace round his neck. The glorious news spread far and wide like a forest fire, the Ryots returned joyfully to their villages, collected their stray cattle, and resumed their field work. Bnowáni's temples were more crowded than ever. But the Royal Mother had a dream, in which Shri Shiwa appeared to her and revealed that the slain tigers had been inhabited by his own and Shri Kâli's spirit, and that all the recent loss of human life had been inflicted on her people for their impious neglect of his worsihp, and that of Shri Kâli. Shri Shiwa

* The Gonds, a wild tribe in Central India, practise this method of tiger hunting to the present day.

solemnly warned the Queen Mother that a fearful famine would follow if this shameful neglect continued.

The affrighted lady consulted her "*Joshis*" (Astrologers) who advised her to hold a great festival at Pertab Ghur in honour of Shri Shiwa, to be followed by another at Satára to Shri Kâli at each of which a thousand Brâhmins should be fed and well feed. This was accordingly done, and from that day till the fall of Báji Rao the shrines of Shri Shiwa and Shri Kâli were as much frequented and honoured as those of Shri Bhowáni.

EPILOGUE BY THE AUTHOR.

Bhowáni is the favourite deity of most Maráthas, or one of them. She is the special patroness of the superior Kshatrya (or warrior) caste, of Dacoits, *et hoc genus omne.*

None of these ever embarked on any new enterprise without having first sacrificed to Shri Bhowáni at the Dassora, which is the only really propitious time for commencing any undertaking.

The worship of Bhowáni somewhat waned during the Peishwa dynasty, having many rivals in that of Shiwa, Parèshrâm and a dozen other "Ávatars" (Incarnation) of Kristna.

An incident precisely resembling that here related of the White Tigers, occurred in the Koina Valléy in

May 1855, when Lord Elphinstone (Governor of Bombay) and his Staff were at Mahabaleshwar, only there was but one man-eater, and he was not an Albino.

The whole country-side, from Pertab Ghur to Helwak (in the Koina valley) was perturbed by the ravages of a huge man-eating tiger. Villages were deserted, etc., as above described. The Author was then Assistant Commissioner of Satára province, and in charge of two sub-districts lying in the Koina valley. The man-eater devoured some forty-five persons before he was shot (I think) by Lord Elphinstone's Aide-de-Camp, Captain Hugh Elliot, who went out with another A.D.C. (Captain Elphinstone). Just as above described, the man-eater broke into a hut in which the Shikaris and Mhárs were assembled, smoking round a blazing fire, and carried of a man. He was marked down and shot at noon next day when lying asleep gorged, but mauled several of the beaters severely.

A reward at first of Rs. 100, which rose by hundreds to Rs. 1,000, was offered for the brute.

I may mention that Captain Elliot was carried off by a wounded tiger not long afterwards—he described that he felt numbed and paralysed but no pain. The tiger fortunately dropped him without inflicting more than flesh wounds on his neck and shoulders which, however, were constantly suppurating for several years, and ultimately accelerated his death.

It is all nonsense to say (as many do) that tigers will not face fire. They fly before a forest fire as do all birds, beasts and reptiles, but they will come prowling and purring round camp fires. Major Baigrie was out in the Nerbuddha Valley once, lying asleep on his "charpoy" (camp bed), when three tigers bounded through the camp in pursuit of some animal, one of them leapt over his charpoy, and bounded through the watch fire! People are equally in error in supposing that man-eaters are always worn out, aged, or diseased and mangy beasts, that can no longer kill game or cattle. They are quite as often young, but having been wounded by a bullet that has lodged in a place inaccessible to their tongues, or having been gored by bison or boars, or severely bitten in such a place in some fight over a female, the wound gangrenes, they become feeble, emaciated, and unable to hunt for their food. Hunger drives them to kill a human being: they find that so easy that they continue. Sometimes "the change of diet" cures them and they become sleek in coat (as the Author has seen). Tigers are often driven up from their lairs in low regions by the leeches (which drop off in the dry pure mountain air), having so drained the brutes of blood that they can hardly stagger along. In this condition they often strike down the first man, woman or child they encounter, and become man-eaters from that day. But, after all, man-eaters are not very numerous.

It is absurd to suppose, as many persons contend, that tigers could be destroyed from the face of the earth if the British Sirkar would materially increase the reward. Twenty-five rupees is ample to induce native Shikaris to hunt them. It is, of course, no inducement to Sahebs. We do not shoot for money rewards but for sport, and most English sportsmen in Western India will bear the Author out in averring that (not counting other big game bagged in a "big shoot") each tiger bagged costs not less than Rs. 500. One might as well hope to rid the Konkans of "Foorsa" (snakes), or County Norfolk of hares, as to rid India of Tigers--the stupendous and difficult ground they frequent affords them thousands of square miles to breed in.

CHAPTER IX.

THE LEGEND OF MHAIPUTGHUR FORT.

Mhaiputghur is a peaked hill on a spur of the Syadri range of the Western Ghauts: it is the loftiest of all; its fortifications consist merely of the natural scarp—precipitous with huge split-off boulders, peculiar to the '*trap*' formation of the Deccan. Its altitude is about 4,500 feet; the hill-side to the west drops abruptly to Sondughur or Mhanghur (called, from its shape '*the Saddle Back*'): the two hills undulate by spurs to the foot of Mâhâbaléshwar, the principal hill station of the Bombay Presidency. The eastern precipice terminates in an almost perpendicular defile nearly 1,000 feet high, separating it from the main chain of mountains, to the east of which flows the turbulent torrent river Koina, one of the five sacred rivers whose origin I have related elsewhere. There is a narrow plateau round the topmost scarp, well-clad with primeval forest of teak, ain, and other evergreen trees and shrubs: thither the Ratnagiri officials often used to pass the hot season before a good cart-road had been constructed (17 miles) to *Bombay Point* (Mâhâbaléshwar).

Insignificant in some respects though Mhaiputghur is, it has a history as thrilling as any of the great Siwaji's fortresses, except Pertâbghur and Raighur, its neighbours ; or Prachitghur (also called Oochitghur) further south on the confines of the petty Native State of Wâri, also called ('*Soond Wâri*', Beautiful Haven). There are caves in the upper scarp formed by the masses of basaltic rock, split off, falling over each other: there are other caverns lower down in the laterite stratum, that were scooped out by Siwaji's Hedkari infantry as shelters from the torrential rains of the monsoon months, or as permanent '*cliff dwellings*': these are (as they usually are on all these old Marâtha forts) screened by low walls of large stones, resembling the '*Sánghurs*' constructed by the Afghans.

It was the day after the famous battle of Pertabghur (*vide* 'Our Troubles in Poona and the Deccan' by Arthur Crawford, C.M.G.). In the valley below, the Marâthas were still beating the hill-sides perseveringly, as if beating for big game: now and again they put up a herd of *Sâmbhur* (Indian elk); a sounder of wild pig, or a tiger: but it was not for these they searched so eagerly; it was for Moghul soldiers, wounded, unwounded, or dead, the quest was being made; for the Moghuls of Áfzul Khân's great army that little Siwaji, '*the Mountain Rat*' (as the Emperor Aurungzebe had contemptuously called him), had scattered to the winds on the previous day. As the line of skirmishers descended from the Wârra * plateau, an occasional yell of

* A small village lying in the vale between Mâhâbaléshwar and the isolated Pertâbghur, where Siwaji and Áfzul Khân had their "friendly meeting".

triumph, followed by screams for mercy, arose where a wounded Moghul had been found. But no quarter did even a wounded man get: his head was off in a moment, with the eternal "*Jey Bhowâni—Jey Siwaji—Siwaji Maharaj ki Jey!*"

But, at this juncture, the discordant blast of a brass trumpet, the monotonous '*tum-tum-tum*' of the *tom-toms* resounded through the glades, and Babaji Ghâtgâ (one of Siwaji's favourite lieutenants), with Anaji Dutto (the Queen Soyerbai's Minister), and a band of fierce Mâwulis, armed to the teeth, carrying a saffron-hued flag, appeared, and peremptorily ordered the blood-stained Hedkaris to desist from slaughtering the prisoners, on pain of severe penalties; Siwaji having already issued orders to spare their lives. So the baffled Hedkaris, some 300 in number, hurried their prisoners with blows and spear-prods, up the steep sides of Mhaiputghur, where they stripped and tortured them in unspeakable ways. "*The Maharaj did not forbid us to make the harâm-zâdèhs* * *squeal!*" exultingly cried the captors, as Moghul after Moghul was strung up, some by their thumbs, some by their big toes, some by a single wrist.

The victors deposited the immense bundles of *loot* they had collected in their largest cavern, to be afterwards honestly delivered to Siwaji's *Khajindar*

* Cowards

treasurer). It would, of course, be divided among his followers by Siwaji himself. And then the barbarians, having captured a troop of Nautch girls, and brought with them skins-full of *Pheni* (the most potent liquor distilled from the toddy-juice), abandoned themselves to a debauch till day dawned and the sun rose over the Eastern Ghauts. In their drunken sleep they scarce heard Ghátgé's trumpets summoning them to march forthwith on Satâra, in which direction the remnants of Áfzul Khân's army had retreated. But, ever alert, they plunged their throbbing temples into the ice-cold springs bubbling up outside the cavern, seized their arms, girt up their loins, stowing away in their waistbands (*kummer-bunds*) any food they could lay their hands o , twisted up their moustaches, and at once set off, leaving their tortured prisoners, the quaking nautch girls and their musicians, and the pile of prize *loot* unheeded. Miriam Bibi, the *premiere danseuse*, so soon as the *tom-tom's* beats had died away in the distance, rushed with her troupe to the miserable prisoners, cut their thongs, bathed their wounds, forced drink and food down their parched throats, and when they were somewhat restored, led them by a great path down the cliff, and guided by '*Khátkaris*' (charcoal burners) working near, took them down to Mhápral on the Savitri, where the whole party crossed into the Habsân in safety, with no small portion of the abandoned *loot*. Meantime, the Hedkaris had, of course, accompanied Siwaji's triumphant armies through Máhárâshtr everywhere was the Founder of the Marátha Empire victorious. Bijapur was sacked and burnt ! The Adil-sháhi Dynasty destroyed for ever, and this little-long-armed Napoleon of the East (Napoleon-like) carved out kingdoms for his favourite Generals. Holkar the '*Dhungar*' (shepherd) of Hol (an obscure hamlet in Khandeish) was seated on the Indore '*masnad*' (throne). The Guzrathi cattle grazier and milkman was exalted on kincob cushions as the Guicowâr of Bâroda : a cousin, also a Bhonslay, made Regent of Central India : a Deccan Bráhmin (a favourite Councillor) Scindia by name—exalted to the still more potent position of Máhárajah of Gwalior ; each by intrigue, or by menaces of rebellion, held their own. Another Bhonslay cousin became Râjah of Kolhapur ; while many petty States (such as Bhopal, Idhar, Mâlégaum) were created for Siwaji's successful Lieutenants.

At last the Conqueror turned his bead-like eyes towards his favourite mountain stronghold, Raighur ; accompanied by his faithful Mâwulis, the while his Hédkaris roamed far and wide over the Konkans, collecting the booty they had '*câched*.' The Mhaiputghur band, whose exploits are already above narrated, had not forgotten the *loot* they had abandoned after the battle of Pertâbghur—not a bit of it. Hastening thither they found that all the gold mohurs, all the priceless jewels, the yet more prized arms and armour inlaid with gold, silver and steel, had vanished there remained only a few worthless rags and gew gaws!

Naturally, they fell upon the wretched '*Khâtkaris*' (charcoal burners), tortured them till they revealed truth, and confessed (poor devils!) that they had guided the Moghul prisoners and Nautch girls to Mhâpral. Cutting the throats of all but two of the tribe, whom they kept to guide them to Mhâpral, the infuriated Hédkaris took and burnt the little Mhapral fort, massacred every living soul therein, cut the dykes of the '*Khâjans*' (reclaimed salt marshes) on each side of the Sávitri. Then, wending their way dejectedly to Raighur, they pleaded to Siwaji for pardon. The little man was in high good humour, for never before had his followers brought in more plunder. He smiled graciously upon them saying "*Bhowâni-chi marziâhè! Kâhi chinta nâhin! Santosh râha! Anchè mâf dilhe gèle!*" (*'Tis Bhowâni's will! Don't worry about the matter, my children! Be comforted!* Our pardon given will go forth).

So the Hédkaris were comforted, and shared in the distribution of the plunder.

CHAPTER X.

THE LEGEND OF RISSALGHUR, SOOMALGHUR AND MANDANGHUR.

The legends of these forts is tame in comparison to those of Raighur, Mhaiputghur and other neighbours; but they had their history of carnage, cruelty, and torture also. They are but a few miles south of Mhaipütghur, Rissâlghur being nearer, Soomâlghur about the same distance from the latter. They are flat-topped and naturally scarped, with inner and outer gateways, and steep flights of rock-cut steps (which Mhaiputghur has not); they are not more than 2,500 feet above sea-level. Their garrisons must have been small, for the water-supply is deficient, and derived only from the rainfall. They were both abandoned for nearly a century, owing to a typhoid epidemic caused by the stagnant water; but the Marâthas were forced to re-garrison them in defence of the South Konkan from the inroads of the Moghuls, who firmly established themselves at Khèd on the Jogburi (an effluent of the great Wâshisti river), at Dabhol (mouth of the Wâshisti) and at Bânkote (mouth of the Sávitri). They (the Moghuls) also built a miniature fort on a low hill at Dâsgaum, the point where the roads lead to Raighur, Torna, and Pertâbghur; thus isolating all the Marâtha fortresses from Hurnee to the Syadris, from the Sâvitri to the Wâshisti rivers, and cutting them off from Siwaji's chief stronghold, Raighur, and the important and extensive fort of Mandanghur, which lies half-way between Bânkote and Mhâpral. The Marâtha garrisons in this region were further seriously imperilled by onslaughts by the Sidi (*Habshi*) from the north side of the Sâvitri, and by Ângria from Hurnee. The ryots (peasants) lived mostly in the fortress, went to their field work armed to the teeth, and helped to man the battlements when need arose. It was a precarious existence at best; nevertheless, in their constant raids, the garrisons in the course of many years amassed an immense amount of treasure, of grain, and of salt, the two latter articles have been cleared away but the first having been buried, has never been discovered—never will be.

The garrisons of the several fortresses I have named in this chapter, commanded by the Marátha Killadâr (Fort Commandant) of Mandanghur (whose name has not come down to fame) combined together after Cocoanut Day * (on 8th August, 18) to surprise the little fort at Dâsgaum aforesaid, held by a renowned Moghul warrior (name—Futteh Khân). He had only 200 men

* Cocoanut Day—called by Hindus '*Gokul Ashtami*' is the date when the S. W. monsoon is supposed to terminate. Nuts and flowers are cast into the sea to propitiate 'Sâmudra,' (the Hindu Neptune), and then ships put to sea in confidence; and the Dussora festival follows, when, after sacrifices to Bhowâni, new enterprises are begun.

and 10 cannon of small calibre. The fortress extends barely over an acre, and the walls are low: yet the gallant fellow defended the place successfully for three months; inflicting great loss on the Marâthas, and sinking their boats on the creek below. But his provisions became exhausted; his ammunition ran short; yet he would not capitulate. The Marâthas sent up to Siwaji (then at Raighur) for orders: the big-little man, always an admirer of heroism, even in his enemies, directed that the Moghuls should be offered a free unmolested passage to Bânkote and all the honours of war; but Futtéh Khân and his men (reduced to 75) though enfeebled by starvation, refused to surrender and were slaughtered to a man, for the little fort had been a sharp thorn in Siwaji's side for years past. Of course Siwaji caused the works to be strengthened and enlarged; mounted heavier guns on the bastion; put in a strong garrison, and picketted several squadrons of cavalry outside, to patrol the roads to Pertâbghur, to the Torna passes, and to Raighur itself. This outwork also gave him the command of all the inland region between the rivers Sâvitri and Wâshisti, and between Dâsgaum and Nâgotna (opposite Bombay). He was thus able to surround Habsân by land, and to menace Janjira (the Sidi's capital) by sea. He could also besiege the Bânkote, Hurnee, and Dâbhol forts by land and sea, to the great discomfiture of the Moghuls at Dâbhol, and of Angria at Hurnee.

Thus, holding these two forts in the hollow of his hand below the Syadris, he laid siege to Janjira and Bânkote (then occupied by the Sidi); the latter fort speedily capitulated; the defences being poor, and near the water's edge; whereupon Siwaji caused a commodious fort to be built on higher ground *. In another paper I have related how Siwaji's troops vainly laid siege to Janjira for 28 years.

These successes induced Angria to give in his submission to the '*Mountain Rat*,' who subsequently gave Angria supreme command at sea, on his yielding up all his fortresses on the coast to Siwaji's Killadârs.

The Founder of the Marâtha Empire had no more serious trouble below the Syadris afterwards, despising the English as a nation of shop-keepers. Nevertheless, he took every possible precaution against the encroachments of all white men, of whatsoever nationality. He forced the Dutch to give up all their so-called Factories in Guzerâth, but let them remain at Vengorla on payment of heavy annual tribute. He besieged and captured Bassein, Cheoul (on the Nâgotna river), and Chimbhoor (The *Neat's Tongue*); he carried old Goa

* When Sir Arthur Wellesley reinstated Bâji Rao as Peishwa at Poona in 1802, he was induced by the Government of Bombay to cede 11 villages, some on the Habsân, some on the south bank of the Sâvitri to the British, and a Resident was appointed who resided in this fort, thereafter named For Victoria. The writer's great uncle, Mr. J. H. Crawford, was the first Resident (1811).

by assault and fearfully avenged the cruelties inflicted on his people by the accursed Inquisition. He fortified Pânvel, Oolwa, Elephanta and the islands of Henery and Kenery; strengthened the defences of Anjanvél, Ratnagiri, Deõghur; he personally superintended the erection of Sindghur * (hard by Mâlwan); strongly garrisoned Sudâsewghur and Kârwâr, Kumpta, and Honore. He conciliated the turbulent Moplahs and the Zamorin of Calicut; made lasting treaties with the Râjâhs of Kochin, Travancore, Tinnevelly, and Trichinopoly. Siwaji even visited Bombay several times in disguise; occupying a cavern below where Government House now stands at Malabar Point, and doing 'Pooja' at Wâlkeshwar. Bhooleshwur, and Moombadevi temples. It is recorded that he actually hung a garland of flowers on a certain '*banian*' tree (*Ficus Indicus*), and himself smeared a large knot on it (familiar to all Bombayites) with turmeric †, which has a certain obscene resemblance. The wily Marâtha well knew that the most dangerous future foe of his newly-created Nation was *Ján Kampany Bahadur*, that nothing appalled those restless, resourceful, energetic 'Angreezi log.' For the present

---

* His handprint in the mortar is there shown to this day.

† This particular 'Yodi' is conspicuous at the point where the Back Bay road runs into the Wâlkeshwar road. It is always kept painted vermilion: certain priests and women from Wâlkeshwar temple daily adorn (!) it with flowers, and sprinkle rice and ghee; pilgrims hang up garlands and stick flags on the branches. It is supposed to resemble a '*lingum*' which need not qe described.

they must be bribed with small concessions, must be cajoled with specious promises, never to be fulfilled; but must never be threatened; so he left the accursed intruders severely alone. He was not only a great warrior, but he was a most sagacious and far-seeing statesman, was Siwaji.

All these important measures being indirectly the result of the stand made by the garrisons of Rissâlghur, Soomâlghur, and Mandanghur are well worth attention.

CHAPTER XI.

"TREASURE LEGENDS."

PROLOGUE.

Treasure stories have a peculiar fascination for all classes of all nationalities; and that whether they be founded on fact or fiction. For example: how interested we all were in Charles Reade's "*Treasure Island*" and Ryder Haggard's "*Solomon's Mines*"! both masterpieces of fiction. But a few years ago certain astute swindlers, by craftily "*Salting*" unlikely spots, led ignorant people to trespass on other people's property, and to dig here, there, and everywhere! The very pavement of side-walks was raised, pits were dug in main thoroughfares, trees uprooted in orchards to find treasure that rascally "*Second-sight-seers*" and "*Clairvoyante*" women pretended was hidden. But a few months ago, a well-known British nobleman freighted a steamer to search for a sunken Spanish Galleon known to contain vast treasure. A salvage company has been engaged for (I believe) 30 years past in dredging up an enormous treasure of precious gold and silver coin, intended for the pay of the British army in the Netherlands war. The ill-gotten ingots of bullion, and precious stones, the spoil of Mexico and Pánáma—that the ruthless ruffian Morgan and his pirate band looted in South America—are still dreamt of by needy adventurers, and in years past, were sometimes found. The blood-stained booty of Captain Kydd, is certainly buried in a dozen unknown spots and desert islands in the Indian Ocean, but has never been traced, and never will be, because every soul employed in secreting it was murdered and buried with the treasure.

Nowhere in the world is more treasure in precious metals, and in still more precious stones, secreted than in India, where sometimes it has been discovered in immense quantities, but oftener in small parcels.

I propose in this unpretentious, but strictly veracious paper, to relate instances that have come officially (and otherwise) under my personal cognizance, beginning with the well-known Pirate Ângrias (Mânâji, Khânoji, Toolaji and their descendants), who for several centuries before and after the Portuguese, the Moguls, and the British contended for Naval superiority on the Málábár Coast, harried the mainland and estuaries from the Gulf of Cambay to Cape Comorin—in conjunction occasionally with each other, but generally in fierce rivalry; building strong forts inland, so as to command each tidal creek, and impregnable strongholds

* Afterwards, by the irony of fate, His Britannic Majesty's Lord High Admiral of the West Indies and "*Sir Henry Mor gan.*"

with graving docks along the coast which they took and re-took from each other, which they sometimes lost to the Marâthas and Moghuls, or wrested from the Portuguese until Clive (then a Lieutenant in the Madras Infantry) and Admiral Watson (of the Indian Navy) captured Viziadroog (also called "*Gheriah*") from Ângria. The power of these pirates soon recovered this blow,—however they continued their depredations by sea and land till 1812, when (on the 12th September) the Ângria of the day captured the good ship *Ranger* (East India Company's Merchantman) as she lay be calmed off Viziadroog! In 1811, the Government of Bombay entered into a solemn treaty with the Habshi of Jinjira. This was a severe blow to Ângria, but he stuck to his guns and to his Forts—Sadâsewghur, Málwan, Viziadroog, (especially) to Jyghur; and some twenty other smaller strongholds—as the High Admiral of the Peishwa of Poona.

After Bâji Rao Peishwa's defeat and abdication, (on the 17th September 1817)* the British Government spent four or five years in capturing all the forts in the north and south Konkans, which were dismantled. The Colonel Commanding (Protheroe by name) then issued a proclamation forbidding any one to reside in the Forts, or to seek treasure known to be buried therein.

* Bâji Rao delivered his sword that day to my uncle Captain (afterwards Sir) John Low, G.C.B.

Each Fortress has, of course, its own legend. As there are 365 of them in the Ratnagiri District alone, my readers may imagine what a wealth of "*folk-lore*" there exists to dig and delve in.

By far the most interesting of all, which I give in the following two legends.

CHAPTER XII.

THE LEGEND OF JYGHUR.

This was among the *Pothis* of my old friend the Chiploon Bhutt, but I never thoroughly appreciated the tale till thirty years later.

It happened that I was sailing down from Bânkote (at the mouth of the Sâvitri river) to Vengorla in one of Shepherd and Co.'s swift coasting steamers, which used to ply in ferry fashion between Bombay and Marmagaum terminus of the Anglo-Portuguese railway); we put in at Jyghur: as we steamed out of the creek under the battlements of that formerly formidable fortress, a voice from the crowded deck below the poop where I was smoking in my deck chair, called out "*Arè! Bâbâji Bhâtkarji! Sing us the song of the old Fort!*" Whereat an alert, comical looking fellow, clambering over the passengers, perched himself on a coil of rope amid ships, and with the accompaniment of a Marâtha "*Zither*" *delivered himself in a high nasal falsetto somewhat in these words, but in verse, which I will not attempt to re-produce.

"*Baré! Baré, Mâjhe bhai log! Aikungeeya?* (well! well! brothers! listen). At least two hundred years before the Angrez log settled at '*Moombhai*' (Bombay),

---

* A kind of Mandolin.

this beautiful Konkan of ours—now so happy and peaceful under the beneficent and invincible British Raj" (these " *improvisatore* "* are always ardently—not to say obtrusively, loyal when they see a Saheb among their audience !), " was grievously harried and distracted, no man's life was safe, no woman's honour sacred " ! (here the troubadour spat greasily !). " The Habshis of Jinjira (where we put in this morning), the Ângrias from Âlibagh, the Moguls from distant Delhi, all, aye *all !* Mâjhe bhai ! robbed our miserable forbears even of their bit of " *bhâkâr* " (unleavened bread). The " *ryots* " (peasants) carried their " *talwars* " (swords) into their ricefields, the women feared to be ravished every time they left their homes to draw water, or collect " *Shen* " (cowdung for fuel). Did foolish fisher men fail to return before day-break—lo ! a swift " *hodi* " (out-rigged boat) full of armed Negro slaves overhauled them—they were forced to serve on some black-hulled pirate "*pâttiámâr* " (lateen-rigged vessel) hovering near, or (if they resisted) had their tongues (may be) torn out—their eyes pierced, their very teeth drawn, one by one, Mâjhe bhai ! and were thrown overboard to the great " *Wâgh-Machis* " (sharks) (" *Wáh ! Wáh !* " chorussed the audience). " Ah ! Great black and bloody Fortress!!" (raising his arms and fiercely shaking his clenched

* There are many of them, of both sexes, in the Konkan, who " discourse sweet music " not un-musically, and with considerable humour. They abound also in the Deccan, but there their songs are harsh and discordant for, according to a Marâthi saying " *The Deccan is the grave of melody* ".

fists) "what fearful tragedies have been enacted within thy walls! what nameless crimes have been committed in thy dank dark dungeons! What rapes! What tortures"! ("*Wáh! Wáh! Wáh!*" crescendo from the now excited people). "*Pun! Bhai log Mâjhe?* (But! my brethren!) a day came, when the terrible Habshis sailed down with an over-powering *Armâr* (fleet), defeated Kânhoji Ângria's Admiral outside the harbour—just where we are now! Driving Ângria's crippled ships over the Bar, and entering the great river with them, the Habshis sent fireships up to the *Godi* (Graving dry-dock), burnt all Ângria's Dhows and '*Shibâds,*' * therein re-fitting all his ships' stores! Little recked those reckless Negroes that those huge guns you see still gaping in the embrasures above, rained down red, red-hot shot on their own decks! Crowding into boats, the Habshis strove who should first scale those lofty bastions on bamboo ladders taken from the dockyard. Little they cared that molten lead and boiling oil found out the crevices in their armour, that catapults hurled down huge rocks, that their scaling ladders broke here and there with the weight of their forlorn hopes, that they were thrown backward with their comrades clinging to the rungs like

* Shibads are the largest native sailing ships and range from 300 to 1,000 candies (75 to 250 tons), two-masted, lateen-rigged, drawing from 17 to 22 feet. They are now usually employed in the timber trade.

bees—one outwork fell—then another! Their ships pounded away with 64lb. iron shot, silencing Ângria's uppermost tier of even heavier cannon. But Ângria's men were also brave, and defended the place stoutly. Till—Hearken to the victorious ones from the "*árkilla*" (Inner upper fortress) '*Jey! Yákhoot Khân! Habshi ki Nawáb Báhádur ki jey!*' lo! the cunning *sidhis* * guided by a renegade, have broken in the main gate above and are pouring into the main fort, driving before them like sheep Angria's Arabs, their faces always to their foes. Foot by foot the Arabi swordsmen are forced to retreat. The defenders on the bastions, too, are overpowered by numbers, and, abandoning their nearly red-hot guns, leap pell-mell into the inner moat. Many are drowned—more stick in the viscid mud, an easy prey to the Habshi sailors".

"The upper and lower storming parties rapidly meet, spearing and cutting down Ângrias' gallant men, till the stormers and a few surviving defenders crowd together in a mob on that blackened bastion above" (pointing to it). "Then arose exultant and despairing cries commingled '*Kajina battao! soorlog! Konikade hay burra Kajina? Badshakal!*' ('show us the Treasury—ye swine! wherever is the big Treasure

* The Abyssinians, called Habshis from Habesh the vernacular for Abyssinia, are fair, of fine physique—are also called Sidhis—though of course, the latter come from nearer the equator, and are coal-black like Zooloos.

vault ? ye ugly ones '!) yelled the Sidhis to the Bhandâri* sentries over a dark flight of steps—'*Pun! Bhandâri jâtpukka hai,*' Speak true! you Mussulman Polish-walla (addressing a constable among the passengers), '*Hán! such bhát*' replied the blue coat addressed ('Yes! true words!')—and a knot of sturdy but stunted '*Bhandaris*' (Toddy-drawers), with their buxom tightly-girthed women, grin delightedly and salaâm to the constable—while the other Marâthas shout 'Right you are, the world has never seen a faithless Bhandári' and a discordant yell arises, from all parts of the deck '*Jey! Bhandari zât ki jey*'! While I, standing up, call for three cheers for the Bhandâri caste—the bard leading with a shrill '*Heep! heep! horay! ânik ek heep! like saheb log*'! After this pleasant interlude, hubble-bubbles passed round below, mangoes were munched, the merry audience hawked and spat freely over the sides—chattering like a lot of monkeys—(good fellows all!)—while I drank a deep draught of iced Pumalo sherbet brought by my faithful boy-servant, Luis"—(To be conventional I ought to have said "*I discussed*" the drink—what a silly phrase that is, by the way!

* Bhandâris are notoriously *faithful to their salt.* They are a short, thick-set race—with immense chest girth—and muscular development of limbs produced by climbing lofty cocoa-palms. They are also fearless sailors. Their women-folk are equally well-developed and well-favoured, but pass their *loogadis* so tightly between their thighs that one wonders why they don't split! They are very virtuous—addicted like their husbands—to bright raiment.

as well say "*I argued*" or "*I disputed*"!)—silence was proclaimed, and the bard resumed—"The poor Bhandâris were cruelly tortured, thorns were stuck under their nails, cords tightened round their temples, they were hung up by their thumbs; their feet, smeared with oil, were slowly roasted—but the *Roostooms** wouldn't say a word! (*Shábásh*! from the audience)—so their throats were half-cut, and they were hurled over the battlements on to the jagged rocks beneath"!

"But the Sidhis could not find a way into the treasure vault, where they well knew many crores of rupees and casks of jewelry lay. It was tantalizing to the *loochyas* (rogues)! They were crowded together in the galleries underground, and on the bastion above, trying to pierce the seeming solid rock with crow-bars and pickaxes—when, suddenly, the rock walls split with a terrific roar—lo! Bhai Mâjhe! the Bhandâris had laid and lit a slow match to the large powder magazine adjoining the treasure vault. They were (almost all) hurled into the air, or blown to pieces, or crushed by the falling rocks! Great lumps of bloody flesh; pieces of arms and legs; heads scorched to cinders; human brains fell on the decks of the Sidhi war *Shibáds* riding at anchor under the Fort; and then an appalling silence, as thick volumes of black smoke drifted slowly up the

* 'Roostoom'—a brave man, a hero.

river! The Habshi Nawâb, who had stayed aboard his flagship, then landed himself, confident that the explosion must have exposed the treasure vault. But our great goddess Bhowáni is not to be flouted with impunity. Huge masses of rock falling back and into the subterranean galleries, had so piled on each other that every trace even of the powder magazine was obliterated. The Habshi searched in vain—lost the tide—was trapped within the bar by Kânhoji Ângria in person, who had just sailed up from Anjanira with a large reinforcing squadron. The Habshi lost every ship he had there, all his men were put to the sword or sold into slavery. He himself was imprisoned for many months in Ângria's Fort Sevendroog at Hurnee; for his Sidhi Sirdars could not immediately raise enough to pay the heavy ransom Ângria demanded. In the meantime, the Moghuls fitted out a fleet at Dâbhol (at the mouth of the river Wâshisti—(where we anchored to-day for two hours, ye know, jees!)—and Kânhoji Ângria thought it prudent to restore the Habshi to liberty that he might co-operate against the Moghuls. The Moghuls have never occupied Jyghur, nor the Portuguese, but the Angrezi sirkâr did. Then Colonel Protheroe Sahib explored with gunpowder, but never a trace did he find of the treasure vault. All those crores lie buried out of human sight till that *day of judgment* comes that the Missionary Padré Sahibs are always preaching about."

"Thus does Shri Bhowáni, our Máha Dèwi, avenge herself. Blessed be her name! '*Jey Bhowáni—Shri Máha Déwi ki jey*'! *'*Bulla! Bulla!*' '*Bhote Atcha!*'—'*Bálaji ki jey!*' vociferated many voices. A brass *lotah* (water vessel) was passed round, and, most of the passengers being mill-hands returning home from Bombay mills on furlough with plenty of money to spare from their savings, the bard made a very good thing of it, so far as I could see. Our certificated *Serang* Mahommed (who, of course, styled himself *Captain* and had a glazed card!) refunded him his fare, as we glided round to the anchorage under Ratnagiri Fort—adding that he should ask his Masters of Shepherd & Co., to let the bard always travel free. Captain Mahommed was wise! The man's sing-song story kept every one in good humour, prevented quarrellings, and the use of obscene language. Báláji Bhâtkurji and bards of his type are useful members of native society—instructive withal. I can imagine that they might be potent agents for dissemination of disaffection—but (as I have above said) they are invariably effusively loyal to our Sirkâr"

* Very good! Very good! Victory to Báláji.

CHAPTER XIII.

THE LEGEND OF DABHOL.

"We now come, Kháwund, to much more recent times," said my old Chitpâwan bard, taking from his well-worn wallet a thick roll of comparatively new manuscript; "these relate to those infidel Moghuls (may they be dogs after death). Consequently, they are not written in *slöks* (verse), but in continuous prose narrative. Some of their accursed names thy servant cannot decipher, but Kháwund will, of course, be able to correct me, for their boastful appellations are recorded in Marâtha History". I said I would try to supply the names, and he read on in a monotonous voice, not so pleasing as his usual sing-song.

"It was in the year 1595 (or thereabouts) of the Christian era, that the Moghul Emperor of Delhi sent his beautiful daughter by way of Satâra and the Kumbârli Ghut to Chiploon, thère to embark on small boats with an immense retinue for Dâbhol at the mouth of our sacred river Wâshisti. The child-princess, though only eight years of age, was a prodigy of piety and learning. She craved to become a '*Háji*' by making a pilgrimage to Mecca and prostrating herself before the tomb of Mahomet in, what the infidels term, the '*Kaiba*.' It is a terrible undertaking for a strong man even in these days of steamboats and railways: what must it have been then! Bands of fierce Khurds and Arabs lay in wait to rob the pilgrim's caravans; fell cholera and small-pox decimated the fanatics when and after they landed at Jeddah: pirates of all nations lay in wait for pilgrim ships throughout their outward and homeward voyages, and hundreds of them were wrecked in cyclones! Neverthless, the stream of superstitious fanatics continued unchecked. It was notorious throughout Hindostan that this Moghul princess not only would take with her gold and precious stones of fabulous value as presents for the Khâlif, but also a gold-thread carpet embroidered with seed-pearls destined to cover the Prophet's tomb. Every pirate on the seas; every freebooter on the land-route, was keeping a keen look-out for the Moghul flotilla to put to sea. Among them there were white men too, most dread of all".

"It was some years before Siwaji (Aurungzebe's '*Mountain Rat*') had broken the power of the Delhi Empire. The Moghuls had long held the port of Dhâbol and built docks and jetties on the banks of the sacred Wâshisti, and mosques innumerable. Fleets of heavily armed ships left annually for the Red Sea and the Persian Gulf after '*Gokul Ashtami* *' laden with rich merchandise, costly silks and shawls, valuable spices and oils, richly inlaid arms and armour; in

* We call it '*cocoanut day*' (8th August), when the monsoon is supposed to be over bacause cocoanuts and flowers are then cast into the sea to propitiate Neptune.

a word, all the paraphernalia of a wealthy and luxurious race. The larger craft (Shibâds, Dhows, and Gállivâts *) being of deep draught could not get up above the junction of Jogburi river with the sacred Wâshisti, but lay at anchor in deep water in the land-locked basin at Dâbhol, where they loaded, as ballast at the bottom, salted hides, then a double layer of '*ain*', '*kinjál*,' and '*blackwood logs* †; to keep the hides down; then casks and sacks of manganese, emery and antimony ‡, talc, oyster shells (flattened to glaze windows), bags of myrobolans, plums, cocoanut kernels, kegs of molasses, '*dubbers* §' of oil; then sacks of wheat and '*dari* ||'; over these goods, bales of loose cotton, covered with bamboos in thick layers; the whole topped with teak balks and boards. Thus stowed in the hold, the cargo was roofed in with '*cadjans* ¶', on which the crew

---

* These vessels have been described in former legends.

† These hard timbers sink in water like lead.

‡ These valuable minerals were washed up on the shore, or brought down by floods and deposited at low tide. What has become of this trade during the past century? The minerals are still there; mine eyes have seen them. They are mixed with a fine black sand (like emery) largely used in iron foundries for the moulds into which the molten metal is poured.

§ Huge bottle-jars of hide.

|| Called jowari or jondla in Marâtha; '*Sorghum Indicum*' the Botanical name.

¶ Mats of plaited cocoa-palm leaves sewn on bamboos with coir cording; they are most impervious to the heaviest rain and throw off the waves easily.

could tread safely. Such a cargo in a large shibâd might be worth from 50,000 to 80,000 sicca rupees *. The ship, of course, carried brass swivel guns fore and aft, and was manned by from 30 to 50 sailors, who fought like shaitans if attacked by pirates. The young princess' fleet was to be composed of fifty of these large craft, and to carry fifteen hundred well-armed men (besides the crews), infantry, cavalry (with their horses), and '*Jezailchis*' with their brass swivel camel-guns. Constantly interrupted by pirate raids, these necessary equipments were only half collected in two years, during which time the young princess resided in a small palace built for her just within the bar (north bank), or in Anjawèl fort opposite. When pirate ships appeared in the offing, she was moved up to Gowalkote fortress (37 miles) where the tide ends. The result of all this unavoidable delay was that Her Royal Highness arrived at puberty, when (of course) pilgrimage was abandoned. Re-called to Delhi she married a nephew of the Emperor". ("Futteh Khân—something—I can't decipher the rest," said the Bhutt).

"During her long residence at Dâbhol she had endeared herself to all by her gracious demeanour, wit, and generosity; to this day the time of her sojourn is recalled as "The princess' heart-gladdening years." Her principal Moslem preceptor was a devout Moollah named Yâkub Khân *bin* Isâk Khân, who had accompanied

* A sicca rupee was worth 2*s*. 3*d*. English money.

her from Delhi. He was selected by the Emperor her father for his absolutely blameless life, his profound knowledge of the Korân (which, of course, he could repeat verbatim as many Moslems can) and other sacred books, his marvellous eloquence in expounding Holy Writ, and his power in converting infidels *.

"The Princess began, directly she settled at Dabhol to study Sanscrit and soon became proficient in the Marâtha language, for she was a born linguist. One Shankerao Máhadeorao Chiploonkar, was chosen by the elders of Chiploon to be her '*Pandit*' (teacher) on a very high salary. His duties, of course, necessitated his residing at Dabhol".

"Between him and the Moollah no love was lost. Háji Yâkub was a large-minded priest who was on the best of terms with all the Bráhmins, but he was also a consummate judge of character. He decided in his own mind the first time he met the *Pandit* that he was a dangerous man, covetous, treacherous, intriguing, and immoral. He said nothing, however, to any one but watched the *Pandit* closely and had him watched in his social life outside the palace. Proofs were soon forthcoming that the *Pandit* Shankerao was boasting of the influence he possessed over the Princess, and that he was extorting large sums from persons who sought to sell jewelry to the royal lady. This, however, was

* (Author's note) I am not certain if Yâkub Khân was the Moollah's right name, but it will do.

not a heinous or unusual offence. Next, he was traced to a noted naikeen prostitute's house where he frequently passed the night. This was highly objectionable, of course, but not worth notice, provided he did not openly parade his immorality and thus scandalize the little Royal Court. This the *Pandit* was far too astute to do. But when it came to Shankerao's making lewd proposals to one of the maids of honour, and daring to speak lightly of his royal pupil, and making vile insinuations against her virtue, it was high time for the Moollah to take action! Accordingly, he despatched a confidential servant to Delhi, and asked the Emperor's authority for dismissing the *Pandit* for reasons assigned. Always prudent, he besought His Imperial Majesty to avoid scandal, which would follow the execution or other public punishment of the peccant *Pandit*. It would be sufficient to order him up to Delhi, and then banish him to Benâres".

"As a matter of course the Naikeen's people, finding out that the *Pandit* was being watched told their mistress, who promptly warned him. He guessed at once that the Moollah had set on the spies: of course, he lost no time in using a Brâhmin's favourite weapon, anonymous letters. Several of these precious documents, accusing Yâkub Khân of visiting the Naikeen himself (!) were torn up by the Princess' secretary, who would not annoy his royal mistress with such abominations. Foiled at the palace, Shankerao succeeded in persuading a brother Chitpâwan about to make a visit on business to Delhi, to drop a similar anonymous letter at the Imperial palace addressed to the Emperor himself. But that potenate was up in the Panjab quelling an insurrection, so this scurrilous epistle and the Moollah's confidential report reached His Imperial Majesty within a few days of each other, three months later. His Majesty was, of course, furious; the *Pandit's* head would have been off without more ado, had he been accessible. As it was, the Emperor followed the faithful Moollah's advice: Shankerao was ordered to present himself at Delhi forthwith '*to receive a dress of honour*', which would have been at the least a terrible bastinadoing on the soles of his pious feet"

"But before His Majesty's orders reached Dâbhol, the *Pandit* had tried his next weapon. Yâkub Khân was waylaid by the Naikeen's pimps, and but that he wore a shirt-of-mail would have been mortally stabbed in the back. Old man though he was, the courageous Moollah, single-handed, killed one of his assailants, and severely wounded another: two others fled at the approach of the night patrol. The wounded man, being at the point of death, confessed his guilt, alleging, as he was propped up to hold a cow's tail*, that the *Pandit* had instigated the crime. The Naikeen escaped to Seroda in a

* In old days this was the usual mode of swearing a Hindu; who, holding the sacred beast's tail, feared to lie.

Goanese pattiamar that (fortunately for her) was on the point of sailing for Goa, and her pimps went with her. The Moollah always patient and prudent, contented himself with inducing the princess to banish the *Pandit* from the palace till her royal father's orders should arrive. Meantime, the local *Kâzi** confiscated all the Naikeen's property, and razed her house to the ground. Shankerao *Pandit* was left unmolested, but not permitted to pass beyond the walls of Dâbhol".

"It is scarcely necessary to say that the *Pandit* was not idle. He bribed the Moollah's cook, a low-born *Sunni*, Yâkub being a *Shiah*,† to put poison in his master's pillao, but Yâkub detected a pungent flavour in the first mouthful, and gave his plate of food to a dog, which immediately expired in horrible agony. The cook trying to escape, was arrested and condemned by the *Kâzi* to be bastinadoed and afterwards strangled". Yâkub Khân, ever humane, begged the *Kâzi* to remit the death penalty on the criminal's confessing that he was employed by the *Pandit*".

"The cup of Shankerao's iniquities, most people would think, was at last filled to overflowing".

("But Kháwand!" here said the reader, "no human heart can fathom the treachery of a bad Bráhmin.

* Magistrate.

† The two sects are bitterly hostile to each other.

that I, alas! should be compelled to confess the hideous truth! who am a Bráhmin. Thoba! Thoba!"* "You are right, old friend!" I assented, "but we've some pretty bad specimens of traitors too in Merrie England! *Experto crede*!" The Bhutt interrupted, "Ah! but Saheb! even thou, who hast oft tracked them in their treacheries as in the case of Vinayek Deo of Narryengaum,† dost not know them! A vindictive Bráhmin is as wily as a cobra, or the serpent that bit the Christian Apostle Paul Saheb! Shri Kâli herself" (he prostrated his bald head on the tent carpet) "is not so cruel and resourceful, or a *dotonda* ‡ more dangerous: he bites like that serpent fatally by head and tail!" "You are right and wrong", "by Shri Kâli!" said I, emphatically, "but read away." Sighing deeply at his brethrens' wickedness, the good old fellow said solemnly— "Where'r Kháwand finds a passionate Bráhmin, cherish him in thine heart! He is a pearl of great price, my lord!" "I will, old friend, be sure! but resume thy tale; I want to hear how the *Pandit* got it hot!" He resumed).

---

* Fie! for shame! or alas!

† *Vide* my true tale of "The would-be Parricide" in my *Reminiscences of an Indian Police Official* (published in the 1st edition 1894; 2nd edition, 1897).

‡ "Two-headed"; a large blind worm. The Bhutt (like most Hindus) believe that this beast bites at both ends and is poisonous, which is a foolish superstition, for the worm is harmless.

"But a vindictive Bráhmin never relents, is never at the end of his resources. Shankerao *Pandit* bribed a half-crazy Gosaen to accost the Moollah at the '*bunder*'* as he was '*eating*' the fresh evening breeze after his prayers in the adjacent '*Muzjid*'†. Presenting a petition to Yâkub Khân, the Gosaen threw the contents of a flask of sulphuric acid over his person. Before the by-standers could seize him, the maniac plunged into the deep water at the '*bunder*' head and swam for the opposite shore. But Shri Kâli was not to be baulked of her prey! When the wretch rose a hundred yards off, he was seen to throw up his emaciated arms; he sank with a blood-curdling yell, that pierced the ears of the horror-stricken spectators. Next morning his mangled corpse was found washed up on the strand. Lo! the half-witted miscreant had been bitten in half by a huge '*Wâgh Muchi*,'‡ known and feared by all the fisherfolk who prayed to him as '*Râjáh Saheb*'. In the poor wretch's *dhoti* § letters of the *Pandit* were found, wrapped in wax cloth, which revealed the plot. So certainly, so remorselessly, so inevitably does Shri Kâli execute her vengeance on those who flout her majesty! *Jey Shri Kâli! Máha Dèwi ki jey!*"

"Allah and His Prophet had preserved the Moollah from serious injury; his chain-armour vest threw off

---

* Jetty.

† Mosque s with '*dharmsala*' (travellers' rest-hall) attached.

‡ Hammer-headed shark.

§ Under-garment.

the corrosive acid, but his coat was burnt in holes; his turban saved his bent head and face, but was riddled like a sieve; he had only suffered to the extent of a few small burns on his hands and feet, to which his attendants applied cooling "nimb" leaves,* oil and vinegar. Shankerao *Pandit* tried to escape in a 'hodi' † to Chiploon, but was arrested at Gowalkote".

"The young princess and the Moollah both pleaded hard for the miscreant to his captors, and to the very last to the Emperor, but in vain; Shankerao's crimes were past pardon. He was carried, fettered and manacled, in a bamboo cage slung between two camels to Delhi; the population of all road-side villages turning out to revile and spit upon him. The Emperor sentenced him to be bastinaded (100 blows) on his soles, and then to be tied to the foot of an elephant; trampled slowly to death before the eyes of the Imperial Court, who gloated on his agonies; Shankerao's bowels gushed out in the midst, ('*Like the Jew Judas who betrayed thy Messiah, Khodáwund!*' observed the Bhutt) and the city dogs licked up his blood ('*as they did the blood of Rájâh Ahab's queen, the harlot Jezabel*' observed the old fellow." "Verily, Bhuttjee! thy knowledge of our Old Testament is marvellous. Read on," said I.)

* A tree of the plane genus, with fragrant leaves which make an excellent poultice, and destroy moths and insects better than Keatinge's Powder; the blossom resembles lilac.

† An out-rigged canoe.

The old man complied, with a deep sigh :—

"When the news reached the Chitpâwan elders at Chiploon, after many months, they decreed that *Pandit* Shankerao's house should be razed to the ground, and that his entire family should be put out of caste for a year, and then only re-admitted on payment of a fine of five thousand rupees, sicca, leviable on his Khoti lands".

("*Which was unjust! seest thou! Kháwand! for they were not guilty!*" observed the old fellow.)

"The Emperor sent Moollah Yâkub Khân a handsome *Killat** and a bag of 101 gold mohurs† as reward for his watchful care of his daughter, who rewarded him likewise richly, while the Committee of the *Joomma Muzjid* at Delhi, sent him the '*Sanud*' ‡ of a *Syud* § for his piety. Syud Yâkub Khân *bin* Isâk Khân distributed the gold in alms to the poor with characteristic charity. The princess, his royal mistress, besought him vainly to accompany her to Delhi. "*No! my beloved Khânum! thy servant will remain at Dâbhol, where, by the Holy Prophet's favour (for ever blessed be his name!) thy servant has sown much good seed, and would fain, by Allah's Grace, reap a plenteous harvest. Allah Akbar! there is no God but*

* A '*Killat*' is a dress of honor accompanied by rich gifts.

† A gold mohur equals 16 rupees.

‡ *Sanud* is a formal deed or credential or patent.

§ A Syud (or Saayad) is at the head of the priesthood, and regarded as a living Saint.

our God and Mâhomet is His Prophet!" said the old gentleman. So he dwelt on at Dâbhol, beloved by all, celebate to the last, celebrated for his learning and piety, by his powerful preaching proselytizing many to Islamism. At the end of his life, he caused a small mosque and hermitage to be built on the summit of a high hill commanding extensive views of the sacred Wâshisti and his beloved Dâbhol where he resided when become too feeble to descend to his favourite muzjid when the '*Muezzin*' summoned true believers to prayers. Syud Yâkub Khân lived to the truly miraculous age of 128 years, preserving his sight and senses to the very last. His body was buried on the hill amid the lamentations and breast-beatings of countless mourners of all creeds and castes, so much was the holy man venerated. The Emperor caused a mausoleum (still visible) to be erected over his grave, and sent a richly embroidered shawl to cover it: the Delhi Syuds decreed him to be a '*Pir*' ("*Canonised him, as Sahebs say*" observed the Bhutt). A large subscription was collected among Moslems throughout Hindostan to keep the sacred building in repair, and well white-washed by a resident Moollah (whose salary has been amply provided) who shall daily and nightly pray for his pious soul. On each anniversary of the holy Syud's death, pilgrims of all nationalities Jews and infidels, Cretes and Arabians, Parsis and Persians, Thibetans and Burmese, Chinese and Christians, Hindus of all castes and sects flock to his tomb, which has worked many miracles, and will, by the grace of the One we all worship, continue so to work them among the sick, especially those paralysed. At these anniversaries noble but barren women offer gifts at his tomb, and their prayers for children are usually speedily granted. Then doth the attendant Moollah dream and prophesy coming events. Never have his predictions remained unfulfilled.

EPILOGUE.

"That concludes," said the good old man, "a most wonderful and true tale, as my lord well knows".

"From Syud Yâkub Khân's tomb the attendant Moollah did predict the great Sepoy Mutiny, the outbreak of Wáhábiism, the murder of the righteous Chief Justice Norman Saheb at Calcutta Town Hall, the assassination of '*Lord*' Mayo, that heaven-born '*Hutti*'* among Viceroys (may Máhá Indra rest his noble soul)."

"Yes!" I assented, "I know all this—and much more. May be the Moollahs at the Syud's or Pir's (I beg his pious pardon!) do cure many sick, for they are '*Hákims* †' as well as priests Anyhow, the sick believe that the Moollahs possess that power, and that is half the battle won! I know officially that

* Elephant.

† Physicians.

when Wábábi emissaries came to the '*Pirsthán*' * to affix the '*Jehád*' † Proclamation in 1871, the Moollah tore the seditious paper to pieces, and that he and other Moslems there pelted the rascals with rocks as far as Dabbol ;—would have killed them indeed, had not the Ratnagiri police there stationed saved their worthless lives. Know also, oh Bhutjee that that whitened sepulchre on that lofty hill has saved many a noble ship in stormy weather; that it is a beacon and landmark by which mariners working sailing vessels up against north-westerly gales, can and do always make their bearings by getting it in line with lofty cocoa-palms still erect on neighbouring hills. Know that the '*Pirsthán*' and the beacon palm trees are mentioned by Hackluyt in his valuable book on storms, by Walker, Moresby, and other eminent hartographers of the old Indian Navy !"

"Wáh ! Wáh !" cried the old man. "God is great ! as the Moslems say ! what abundant proof we have of His Omniscience and Power in the narrative thy '*gholám*' has just read ! He is verily '*a Jealous God !*' (as Missn'ry Padrès preach). He doth not permit the wicked always to flourish '*like a green bay tree.*' Sooner or later Shri Kâli (whom the

* Saint's place or tomb.

† Holy war of extermination of all Kâfirs (*i.e.*, unbelievers in Islam). (The above fact and a verbatim translation of the Proclamation was sent to *The Times* in 1872 by the author.)

Sahebs call '*Nimishis*' *) overtakes the sinner at the very acme of his prosperous career. And doth not Ishwar also mark the pious man and reward him—if not on earth, hereafter? Behold this holy '*Pir*' whose life is here told (patting the manuscript). His pious memory still flourisheth green among us. In death he lives again to benefit mankind! Truly the One God all worship is a '*Just God*'! Hán? Saheb!"

I assented with becoming gravity—ejaculating:—

"So mote it ever be! Amen!"

The good old Bhutt responded fervently "*Amen*" and we parted silently for that time.

* The old man meant "Nemesis."

(Author's note.—Every word in this Epilogue is literally true.)

CHAPTER XIV.

THE LEGEND OF RATNAGIRI.

(THE JEWEL-FORT.)

Prologue.

Ratnagiri is one of the many strongholds built by Siwaji, the Founder of the Maratha Empire, during the sixteenth century, ard has an interesting history. The author having resided there during most of his service in various appointments, felt a thrill of joy when his old friend the Chiploon Bhutt extracted the Sanscrit *sloks* relating to it from his wallet.

Ratnagiri is nearly 125 miles south of Bombay. The fortress projects into the Indian Ocean in the shape of a horse-shoe, thus forming two distinct fortresses connected by undulating ground like the frog of a horse's hoof. The southern heel of the shoe rises abruptly from the sea to a height of about 450 feet; the northern heel is about 100 feet lower. On the west side the cliff is exceedingly precipitous, in fact, unscaleable by any animals but goats. Nevertheless, the bastions and connecting screen walls (with which both forts are completely encircled) are built on scarped rock rising to an altitude of 20 to 50 feet, many feet thick. This formidable stronghold is connected with the mainland by a narrow neck of sandy soil. There is only one approach to each fort, up zig-zag steps cut in the rock; noble gateways flanked by bastions command the ascent, and are again protected by inner fortifications.*

Immediately under the southern heel or prong) the sea washes round under a scarp almost to the foot of the '*pakádi*' † or ascent, and then sweeps round in a broad curve, forming a spacious bay for about 1½ miles round, till it meets the mouth of the small tidal river Harcheri, (there about a hundred yards wide), when a sandy shore again curves in for about a mile till it encounters a lofty promontory jutting far seaward in a north-westerly direction.

Ratnagiri is thus half land-locked, but is an open roadstead exposed to the full force of the south-west monsoon, but completely protected from the north-west monsoon. The anchorage, immediately under the fort, is in 3 to 3½ fathoms at low water neap tides; the tide rises from 12 feet (low water neaps) to 25 and 30 feet (high water springs); the soundings from fort to promontory range from 10 to 20 fathoms.

---

* Called the '*Arkilla*' or inner fort.

† '*Pákádis*' are rock-cut, or paved steps and causeways.

From the north-prong fort, another sandy cove, about 4 miles long, curves round to '*Miria Donghur*,'* a large promontory jutting far into the sea, south-west and north-west; from the north-west another prong projects 1½ miles, thus forming an admirable harbour of refuge during the south-west monsoon, with an anchorage shoaling from 8 to 4 fathoms. The bay between Miria Donghar and Ratnagiri north fort is full of dangerous reefs.

Immediately under the southern bastion of the larger (south) fort on the sea face, is a cavern (enlarged by Siwaji's men) which leads into the heart of the fort, to which there was formerly access by a tunnel (long ago fallen in); it was navigable for small boats at half tide only (the roof being very low): by this exit the garrison used to sally forth and capture vessels becalmed in the offing. To the east the main land stretches away from the lowlands in a succession of laterite plateaux intersected by canõns and precipitous ravines clothed with (wild toddy) palms, jack,† teak, and other forest trees. The lowlands are densely covered (except on the rice lands and swamps) with Cocoa and Areca palms, and other large umbrageous forest trees, among which are magnificent '*Pipal*'‡

---

* Donghur means hills or mountains.

† A species of Dorian, bearing huge fruit on the trunk only, of a rich orange colour.

‡ *Ficus Indicus lancefolia.*

and '*Banian*'.* with wide-spreading branches. There is a large tank of spring-fed water on the curve between the two forts, and many tanks and wells, built or excavated in the town. This lies completely hidden in palm trees; its paved streets are narrow but very clean. Numerous picturesque Hindu temples, well surrounded, dot town and streets.

The population formerly (1600 A.D. to 1800 A.D.) numbered from 20,000 to 30,000 souls, exclusive of the fort garrisons: it is now 12,000, and steadily increasing.

Altogether Ratnagiri is one of the most beautiful and salubrious spots on the Malabar Coast.†

Traditions have come down from father to son that the Jewel Fort of Ratnagiri was more or less rudely fortified from the earliest times by the aboriginal Mhârs, who garrisoned it with Bhundâris in their employ, who were paid in kind or had rice lands and

---

* *Ficus Indicus dependens.*

† Ratnagiri was selected by Sir Mountstuart Grant-Duff, because of its being so healthy, as the residence of ex-King Theebaw of Burmah and his family. The author was commissioned to intern them there in February, 1886. They are still there, and always enjoy good health, though they take little other food and feed heavily on pork, dorians, and other indigestible vivers.—(Author's note.)

palm plantations granted to them, more or less rent-free, for this service, and for providing fish for the Mhârs and Sudras*. These fishermen never went out of sight of land, their boats being frail, out-rigged canoes with mat sails, bamboo masts and yards, and ill-twisted coir ropes for the rigging. Then came the Bâhmani Râj from Dekkan and Karnatic with Brâhmins, '*Raös*'† and more Sudràs ‡, rudely armed: they conquered the Mhârs. These Bâhmani Kings, struck with despair at the sparse population, gave grants of large tracts to Brâhmins and Raõs to hold in perpetuity on the condition that they should import labour and extend cultivation by reclaiming '*Khâjans*' § and laying out hillsides then covered with dense forest or tangled undergrowth. They were to pay rent in kind but it was almost nominal and very irregularly collected. The farmers or middle-men were called '*Khotes*.' ‖ There were only two or three paper factories in Western India, and the paper there made being produced from straw pulp was fragile, brittle

---

* Peasants and artizans.

† Raõs are the true Marâthas Kshatryas by caste) from the Syadri mountains and Ghâut plateaux.

‡ Sudras are also Marâthas, but of the labouring and artizan castes.

§ Salt swamps.

‖ Khotes are middle-men contracting with the Sirkar annually for the farm of the land tax.

and soon decayed in that damp climate. The deeds given to the Khotes were therefore either rudely carved on unplaned boards, or on sheets of copper, strung on copper rings.

The Khotes faithfully performed their contracts, terracing hill sides, and reclaiming large tracts with great labor. Thus, a considerable population was collected in hamlets and villages where water lay handy. At this time bands of wandering labourers from above the Syadri Mountains were attracted by the prospect of employment at fair wages paid in kind. To induce these '*Oopris*'* to remain, the Khotes gave them enough land rent-free for their houses and gardens, and granted to them lands already in cultivation at much reduced rentals on hereditary tenure. All other 'ryots' were mere tenants at will, bound each to give five days '*Vet bigar*'† gratis to the Khote in every year, and to pay half the produce of their little farms to the Khotes.

It is impossible to over-extol the admirable work of these Khotes in the Konkans: they and they only have brought waste lands under cultivation, built

---

* *Id est*, Wanderers—foreigners—interlopers.

† '*Vet*' and '*Vet Bigar*' is the gratuitous labour required by the Khotes, either in the fields, or as porters (*i.e.*, Bigaris) whenever the Khote travels.

'pákádis' down the precipitous ravines, reclaimed noisome pestiferous marshes. In a word—they have reduced chaos to order, introduced the village '*panchyhotra*'* system, and brought about a civilization even superior to that of the rest of Máhárâshtra above the Syadri range. (Tradé was by them attracted to the thousand ports and estuaries, and the '*Waishya*'† castes and sects flocked to Chiploon, Sangumeshwar, Jaighur, Ratnagiri, Râjapur, Khârepatam, Mâlwan, and Vèngorlè.

None of the civil wars in the interior, none of the incessant pirate raids by sea and land, none of the conquests by the Moguls and the Marâthas have more than temporarily retarded that civilization.

---

* *Panchyhotra* or village community consisting of (1) The priestly caste, the Brâhmins; (2) The Raos of the Kshatryas (or warrior) caste; (3) The Sudra castes: (Ryots) or cultivators, farm (hired) labourers, Lohârs (blacksmiths), Sutârs (carpenters), Dhungurs (herdsmen), Gowlies (milkmen), Sonârs (goldsmiths), Shimpis (tailors), Gâbeets (fishers), Bângris (bangle-makers and sellers), Hajams (barbers); (4) The Waishyas, and Wânis (shopkeeper and trading) castes and sects; (5) The Pâriahs or outcastes (of whom the Mhârs are the chief), Châmbârs (shoemakers, curriers and leather-workers, Halâlkaris (mutton butchers), Mhângs and Halâlkores (public scavengers), Beldars (stone masons and quarry-men), Kaikâris (basket-makers), Kathkaris (charcoal burners). No. 1 includes the Astrologer and the village Accountant. No. 2 the Patel, or headman of the village; also the Magistrate.

† Trading castes.

But, it followed (as a matter of course) that the aboriginal Mhâr owners of the soil went to the wall; not as slaves, for they are much too independent and warlike for that degradation: on the contrary, Mhârs became public servants, and occupied a very important position in the village community. He is '*ex-officio*' police constable, day-and-night watchman, guide, messenger, thief and stray-cattle tracker, pound keeper, and a human Encyclopœdia of village history; especially is he the final authority in all boundary disputes; his presence is absolutely necessary at the "beating of the village bounds" annually, at the erection of new boundary marks, at every inquest. He is the custodian of the temple, the '*Dhárm sâla*,* and the '*Chowki*,' † and responsible for the safe custody of criminals. The Mhâr must make himself acquainted with all strangers who may come to the village, fetch and carry for them, report about them to the Patel, guard their baggage, provide provender for their beasts, and see them (at least) to the boundaries of the village, not leaving them till he sees them in charge of Mhârs of the next village,—to whom he is expected to give full details about them. He must accompany the Patel to the '*Kacheri*,' ‡ when that official repairs there on any duty, and should there be a bag of rupees for payment of

* Rest-house.

† Lock-up.

‡ Office and treasury of the sub-district.

the last instalment of land tax, he must carry it. No appraisement of standing crops, no reaping of a field, no threshing out of the grain, no measurement of it, ever takes place in the absence of the Mhâr. He must see that the Mhângs scavenge regularly, that they remove the carcases of dead animals to the appointed '*Hudola*.'* If there be no Mhângs (which is the case in many Konkan villages) he must perform these low offices himself or make his family do so, and in the absence of Mhângs he officiates as the executioner. For these multifarious and arduous duties, he (that is to say the Mhâr community of the village) hold, a few '*bighas*'† of the worst lands rent-free, hereditarily, and receives a few seers of grain at the threshing floor : he also shares with the Mhângs whatever the hides of the dead animals may realize from the '*Chamburs*.'‡ The Mhârs' grain '*Huks*'§ vary in different villages and (in quantity) of the kind of grain, and the social

* A piece of waste ground outside the village used as the 'Golgotha,' where such carcases are dragged and flayed, and then left for dogs, jackals, and vultures to devour.

† A '*bigha*' is about ⅝ of an acre, English.

‡ Curriers.

§ '*Huks*' mean perquisites: the poor Mhârs often find it difficult to recover them, but there have been many decrees in the Civil Courts—awarding such claims made by Mhars suing as paupers. Mhârs are just as much Watandars as Patels or Koolkarnis (Headmen and village Accountants), and their lands cannot be attached or sold for debt.

position of the person paying it. Also the Mhâr gets what he can from travellers; never more than 4 annas per night and perhaps a double handful of grain. All these items do not aggregate much the year round; but their community (or such of them as are not on duty) eke out their slender incomes by quarrying slabs of laterite for any walls round fields, or houses that may be building, and by fetching firewood from the jungle, while their women make '*shen*' * cakes, which the '*Lohârs*' † use in their furnaces. The men take military service all over Màhàràshtra, and are renowned for their valour as common sepoys. They are (as a rule) very honest, and remarkably truthful. Their evidence in any boundary dispute may be thoroughly relied on. They will eat anything, except the flesh of wild swine, which they regard as sacred.

Mhârs being unclean (as outcastes) must live outside the villages, and on no account must they defile any one of the superior castes by permitting their shadows to fall across him or her, or by touching anything whatsoever that such superior is to touch, except animals. For the same reason they cannot travel by sea; all their journeys in the Konkan are on

* '*Shen*' cakes are made of cowdung sun-dried, and are largely used for fuel, especially by blacksmiths, as they emit intense heat and burn long.

† *Vide* ante.

foot. They are polygamists, and though permitted to worship at the '*Grâm dewul*,'* may not enter even the verandah, or allow their shadows to fall on any part of the structure. They must, of course, attend all weddings, funeral pyres, and ceremonies † and are called on to physic sick cattle. In a word, a village might get on pretty well without Patel, Koolkarni, or even the Khote, but it could not possibly dispense with its Mhârs. This dissertation on these outcastes is here given in detail because, not only are they the original proprietors of the soil, but they are the most numerous and prolific of all castes.

Towards the end of the 15th century the Moguls appeared on the scene, bringing with them a host of the lower orders of Moslems, and many Moollahs; many thousands of Hindus were circumcised by force, and made to conform outwardly to the religion of Islâm: their progeny became devout Moslems: thus the Konkans obtained immense numbers of fishermen and sailors. Great advances and improvements in ship-building, of course, followed, but these Moslems were not themselves expert in ship-building. The '*Sutârs*' ‡ of the Konkans, on the contrary, are adepts in the craft: nearly all the '*Sutârs*' acordingly took to ship-

* Village temple or god-shop.

† Burning.

‡ *Vide ante*

building. A remarkable thing is that on doing so, they substituted '*oza*' for the general terminal of '*jee*' to their names: thus, *Bâbajee* became *Bâboza*; *Mhâdojee*, *Mhâdoza*; *Nârrojee*, *Nârroza*, and so on. These Wâdias*, as they are also termed, now form a very numerous and important class of the community. Sutârs who worked up timber for other than ship-building purposes, retained the terminal '*jee*.' In like manner 'lohârs' working on the ships took the terminal '*oza*.' For very many years there has been a separation between the '*Jees*' and the '*Ozas*'; feuds sprang up betwixt them because the '*wâdias*' exacted heavy fees from the '*oza*' terminating '*Sutârs*' who desired to work as ship-wrights. They for some years ceased to eat together, and to intermarry.

The next important inhabitants in and near the Jewel Fort were the Chitpâwân Brahmins, of whom the principal families have been for generations the Prubhu Desais of Hurcheri, the Burvès, and the Phudkès. Another powerful Chitpâwan family had a branch at Ratnagiri—named the Atlays. All these were Khotes of many villages in many parts of the Southern Konkan, and the Phudkès and Burvès were also Saõkars and merchants on a large scale, whose *Hoondis*†

* Wâdias are hereditary ship-wrights. The Wâdia family at Ratnagiri were hereditary ship-builders for Siwaji and his successors, and for all the Peishwahs.

† Bills of exchanger.

were cashed without demur in any part of India. After the Mogul conquest came a branch of the famous Purkár's of Bânkote. This noble Moslem family had members who were commanders of the garrison, and settled there in a beautiful garden-house erected by themselves.

It has behoved me to recite all these details because all these families were more or less concerned in the series of terrible events narrated in the '*slokes*' that follow.

CHAPTER XV.

THE LEGEND OF RATNAGIRI.

(Continued).

"The first severe trial that the Jewel Fort had to encounter, my beloved children, was political and from external enemies. They had on scores of occasions attacked the stronghold both by sea and land. The pirate Ângria had landed his sailors and dread infantry once at Purangaum ten miles southward, and marched them round over the country I have described, to besiege the place by land, hoping at least to starve out the garrison and sack the town, while he himself pounded away from his fleet at sea with heavy cannon; but the Bhundâris and fishermen ambushed them at the mouth of the little Hurcheri estuary, only five men of them escaped wounded to Poorungaum. His cannon could not make any impression from the sea, being unable to fire at so great an elevation, but the garrison rained down red-hot shot on his decks, setting three ships on fire, then '*Shri Sâmudra*' blew a heavy south-west wind and drove them northward to Alibagh. Then did the garrison steal out by the tunnelled cavern, and capture the still burning three shibâds—left behind. Great was the 'loot,' * most valuable of all twenty huge

* Prize captured.

cannons which were forthwith dragged up and mounted on the bastions, and an immense quantity of ammunition.'

"Two years later, Ângria and the Habshi combined (though generally at war with each other), with the common object of reducing the Jewel Fort at all costs. Both these pirates had made repeated overtures to the chief of the Wâdia family to take service under them as ship-wrights, but the Wâdias rejected the offers with scorn. Therefore, did the pirates especially desire to capture some of them alive. On Sankrant day, no less than fourteen large war-shibâds sailed out from Jaighur; seven anchored in Miria Bay and landed a strong force, three engaged the fort from the sea, four put in at Purangaum and landed men as before. The force landed at Miria Bay was directed to march along the narrow neck of land to the foot of the northern fort, when they heard a signal gun-fired from the Shibâds attacking by sea. Both parties were to advance and attempt to carry both forts by assault. But the pirates had not reckoned on the Mogul General, Muhommed Ibrahim Purkâr, who met the Miria party at the narrowest part of the neck of land, outflanked and got into their rear. Not a single soul escaped to tell the tale to the infuriated Ângria at Miria. The Purangaum party were again foiled at the Hurcheri river ferry, losing many warriors as they were pursued to Purangaum itself.'

"Again Shri '*Sâmudra*'* displayed his power! The combined fleets were driven by a cyclone to the mouth of Jaighur river and might have succeeded in crossing the bar, but that they were left half manned, with crews so deplenished that they could not even man the enormous yard-arms: so they anchored just outside the bar, hoping to get in on the flood tide; but *Sâmudra* sent in a bore wave mountains high which swamped all but the two flag-ships and three others as they lay at anchor. Nine large heavily armed shibâds did the pirates lose out of fourteen on that occasion. *Great is Sâmudra! Sâmudra key Jay!*

"But these pirates are obstinate '*budmashes*'†; they *would* have the Wâdias somehow! So next year after the '*Dussora*' they sent a number of picked men overland disguised as '*Gosævens and Byrâgis*'‡ on a pilgrimage to a famous shrine half way to Ratnagiri, where the Wâdias would (as their spies reported) certainly be present for the great festival. Three of the elder Wâdias were captured after a desperate resistence; Ângria sailed off to Kolâba with one, leaving another with his *Killadar*'§ at Jaighur: the Hubshi carried the third off to Janijra, and imprisoned the

* The Indian Neptune.

† Rogues.

‡ Religious mendicants and pilgrims.

§ Fort Commandant.

"*gharib*"*—wounded though he was—in his state-prison on the islet Jezeerat; where, though tortured, starved, and loaded with heavy irons, the gallant fellow died, refusing to work for the Habshi: so did his brethren, imprisoned at Kolâba and Jayghur; wherefore the barbarous Ângria put out their eyes and cut off their right hands, in which miserable state they found their weary way back to their homes after many days. The Jewel Fort was never again attacked, and remains a virgin fortress." *

"What lesson do we learn, Khâwand, from this stirring tales? We learn to be loyal to our country, even at the hazard of our lives: we learn to pray to, and trust in, the gods; in firm reliance on their aid, to despise despair, and to wait with hope for brighter days to dawn."

"My next is a true tale of human lust, such as has too often disgraced this fair land. Verily, man is desperately wicked when he forgets the gods, said my old friend."

Thou knowest, Saheb, Soonder Wâdi; that spot of beauty in the South. Thou hast heard doubtless of the Sâwants who rule there. These Sirdârs are surnamed Bhonslay; are descended from the great Siwaji, and should be as noble in heart as all who bear his honoured

* Poor.

† The garrison surrendered to Col. Protheroe, 22nd September 1822, most of the men at once enlisted in the British Army.

named should be. But, alas ! this family has constantly disgraced the hero's name by their rapacity, cruelty, and licentious lives. It so happened that a few years after the events I have just related, the ruling Sâwant and his younger brother were on their way to Bombay, where the elder was to be wedded to a daughter of the Jungle Râjah of Jâwal*. It was a suitable match, in the matter of worldly wealth and position. It was suitable also—an' ye may say—because none of the other Sirdârs of the Deccan would demean their daughters by betrothing them to a young man who, despite his Bhonslay blood, bore the evil reputation that did Khèm Sâwant: only a '*paji*' † potentate like Chimnaji Raõ of Jawal would so condescend. May such evil-doers so mate always! and may the gods ever mete out them their deserts."

Sailing up from Vengorlè with a large retinue of debauchees like themselves, the brothers Sâwant put in one evening at Purangaum, where great rejoicings were afoot. A son of Phadkè of Ratnagiri was to be betrothed that day to a daughter of Burvè of that ilk. Bride and bridegroom were, of course, almost infants, but there were there two other ladies of great beauty; one, a Phadkè married a few years before to the young Prubhu

* This was a very small state lying between Trimbak, (Nasick District) and Tánnah. It was annexed for failure of heirs many years ago.

† Contemptible.

Dèsai of Hurcheri; the other, a Burvè, married to a young Atlay of Deorookh. The Sâwants were, of course, admitted to Phadkè's '*Wârra*,' * and partook of his hospitality so far as a Marâtha may receive it from a Brâhmin. Seated among the front rank of spectators at the accustomed nautch, the Sâwant; brothers saw the two beauteous young matrons and lusted for them.

After a brief consultation apart they adopted the following treacherous plan. They invited their host and the principal guests aboard their '*Pâtiamâr*' † under pretence of showing them the costly presents they were taking for the Jungle Raja's daughter. Next morning the Phadkè and Burvè party came down to the bunder with the ladies. It was Khèm Sâwant's intention directly he had them safe on board, to up-anchor and sail back to Vengorlè with his captives, landing all but the two young matrons at a port further down, or casting them adrift in the dinghy somewhere on the coast. The Sâwants, however, had reckoned without the faithful Bhundâris, who for centuries, have guarded the Phadkè family and their treasure Bábaji Bhundâri had observed the brothers lascivious looks during the nautch; he noticed further at the bunder that the main yards were already hoisted to the peaks, the crew at their quarters, and the ship merely attached to a buoy: he besought his master not

* Palace.

† Pattiamar here means '*Yacht*'.

to set foot in the '*hodis*' ‡ Khèm Sâwant had sent for them. Now Phadkè was an obstinate and resolute old man. Said he "Art turned a coward, Jee? that thou fearest for a Phadkè's honour! Ye Bhundâris have your '*koitis*',* we men-folk have our staves. What need of more '*bát*'†; we go, and may Shri Dewi protect us! So Babáji—abashed—embarked with his master's party, but secretly ordered his brother Bhundâris to jump into another '*hodi*' and accompany. They did so. When the two boats came alongside the *pattiamâr* the Sâwant brothers handed the two ladies (Phadkè and Burvè) up the companion ladder with deep respect. The Bhundâris—headed by Bábaji, of course, prepared to follow, but Khèm Sâwant tried to push their boat away exclaiming "*we want no rascally Bhundâris here!*" Bábaji and half-a-dozen of his men clambered aboard without more ado: a free fight followed; the ladies fainted of course. Phadkè and Burvè were unarmed but defended their women with their staffs: Bábaji lopped off the *tindal's* ‡ arms as he attacked from aft, his followers cleared the decks, driving the crew below, when they battened down the hatches. But the younger Sâwant—like a dastard—stabbed poor Bábaji in the back. Terrible was the revenge of his followers, who cast both the Sâwants overboard, and strung up two of the crew to the yard arms. Phadkè's party instantly

* Out-rigged canoe.
† Large bill-hooks.
‡ Talk.
§ Captain.

put off in their dinghy but the Bhundâris stayed to set the *pattiamâr* afire, afterwards cutting the hawser at the buoy. The last seen of the Sâwants and their ship, was the brothers wringing the water from their clothes, as the burning ship took the ground on the 'Gowkari' shore. Needless to say the Gowkari villagers lost no time in looting the vessel! Thus ended gloriously for Phadkê's party a most treacherous attempt on the honour of their family. My lord knows that Khêm Sâwant's maladministration * so disgusted many Sâwant families at Soondawári that they migrated to Miria Donghur. What lesson do we learn? Khâwand, from this true tale? We learn that lust brings its own punishment; we learn fidelity from the Bhundâris; we observe again the watchfulness of the gods over good men.

---

* A successor of this same Khêm Sâwant led the Sâwant rebellion of 1844-45 and the family dispersed a good deal after their abortive rising, a most disreputable branch settling, or being compelled by the Sirkâr to reside at Mhâr on the river Sâvitri, where the head of it (Hanmant Sâwant) disgraced himself as a writer of anonymous letters. Another branch (the best) settled at Rohê.

CHAPTER XVI.

THE MAHANT SWAMI OF NIPANI AT CHIPLUN.

Part I.

"Hearken, Khâwand! to the '*sloks*' that follow prefaced by solemn oration addressed by the most holy Máhant Swámi of Nipání to a vast multitude assembled to do him honor at Chiplun" (began my old friend the Bhutt, reading from his Manuscript). "Listen, oh ye People! My cherished disciples! Open your ears! and ye who now live in peace and plenty under the great Peishwah's beneficent Raj in this our beautiful Konkan, beloved by the Gods, watched over by the great Purèsh-râm (blessed be his name!). Ye Chitpâwans! favoured beyond all castes by all the Gods! Learn humility! Ape it, if ye have it not! Ye Kshatryas! Learn humanity! Then will Shri Krishna and his Rishis fight on your side, and smite your enemies in the hinder parts. Listen! ye Sudras all! so that ye who are now patient and frugal, may be more and more contented, labouring even yet more industriously. Then will the Gods, especially Shri Bhowâni, reward your toil abundantly, and give you of the fruits of the earth in due season. Listen! Oh ye Waishyas! Traders, Saõkars, all! Learn to be just and honest in all your dealings with your fellow-men giving good measure, pressed down and running over.

Ye, who are by nature charitable, be lavish to the poor, whom ye have always with ye! Then will ye not worship the holy 'Lingum'* in vain. Ye Mhârs and outcastes, down trodden, long suffering men! Listen! and hope! The Gods note your centuries of suffering and degradation. 'Tis a long river that has no gushing spring bubbling musically up at its source, as hath our sacred Wâshisti at Wâsi. Follow the the course the Gods in their wisdom have ordained for ye all. 'Twill lead to enlightenment and education, to honor and glory, if not to wealth. Despair not therefore, ye humble ones!

Oh! all ye my peoples of my heart! Hearken!"

"What a stirring appeal was this! Khodâwand" here interjected my old friend. "It was made (so saith the superscription) in Sankrânt of the year 1801 of the Christian era, before an immense concourse of all castes and creeds at the usual spot where the Elders of the Chitpâwan caste assemble. Many Moslems were among the audience, listening reverently. A thousand Mh rs and other outcastes stood humbly in the background, bare headed, leaning on their staves. Many thousands of Ryots and artizan Sudras squatted in front

* Emblem of the sexual act, sacred to Mahâdeo; a silver model thereof is worn by all lingayets next to the skin, attached to their sacred cords. It is, in fact, the emblem of increase and procreation.

of the Pâriahs, eagerly hearkening. A few hundreds of Waishyas, Bhâttias from Kutch and Mândavi; Goozurs from Sūrat and Ahmedabâd; Mârwârris from distant Rajputâna; a dozen '*jamma*' clad Parsis with their comely dames and lovely children, sat on chairs they had brought to sit upon. Our own Wânis, and many from the Dèsh had gathered in crowds. (Verily the worshippers of the bloated gods of greed and gain were well represented! Khâwand!) Around our great branching Banian tree sat in the place of honour, hundreds of richly attired Brâhmins of all sects; Chitpâwans, of course, predominating; and around and in rear, their backs to the sinking sun, in serried lines stretching far north and south a little '*Fouj*' * of armed Kshatryas, with grounded spears and arms crossed; (standing '*at ease*' as white sojer log say). Thy servant seems to hear as we sit, the blare of horns, the clash of timbrels, the sonorous beatings of huge war and kettle drums, and the monotonous tappings of many 'tum-tums', as the grand procession emerges from the town. First come troops of dancing girls, bedecked with garlands and flower chaplets; their male attendants posturing and prancing round the bevy of fair but frail women, and piping on their reed flageolets the while. Next marches a close phalanx of as noble warriors as the world can show; Kshatryas of the Syadris, clad in richly inlaid armour, bearing keen

* Army.

'*tulwârs*' * and embossed shields. Goodly are they to behold! taller than most men; their mustachios curled upwards as if in fierce pride; their keen eyes flashing fire-like; treading the earth heavily as one man, preceded by two warrior giants; the one to the right, the standard bearer, bearing the '*sön putki*' † saffron hued, of the great Marâtha nation; the one to the left ever and anon trumpeting on a long golden horn. This gallant band, Khâwand, is the great Swâmi's Body guard; 101 rank and file--(what Sâhèbs call the '*Guard of Honour*,' which with Sâhèb only numbers 100 men; but we Asiatics love odd numbers, believing that they bring good luck). Then follows a crimson and gilt palanquin, wherein on saffron-coloured gold-brocade is seated the Poet-Priest. Negro slaves on either side fan the holy man with Yák's tails and huge bunches of peacock feathers, and four others bear a tent like '*Chattri*' ‡ covering the entire conveyance. For this, Khodâwund, is a very great and holy man in good sooth! Hearken to the awe-stricken bystanders as the almost regal procession passeth by! 'Arè Baprè! baprè! Ha Deo âhè §?' asks that fat Wâni at the grain shop, to the Mârwârri who is dunning him. "Chè! Govindâssjee, Bhot burra Swámi

* Short curved swords.

† The pole is very high, and gilt or golden ('*son*').

‡ Umbrella, here a canopy.

§ Is this a God?

chè,'* replies Itcharâm. That gaping Gooroo nudging his friend murmurs, 'Arè Bhai! He was the most learned Oopâdya † at the Dukshina Poona College when but a '*Chokra*'‡: Bâji Raò, may dogs devour him! (see! Khâwand he spits on the ground!) Bâji Rao gave him the titles of *Máhá Oopâdya* § and *Sūnt Swâmi* ‖ and permission to keep and ride on elephants like a Rájah (!) whene'er he leaves his palace near Nipâni to visit Poona."

"'Yea! brother!' chimes in that lanky *lotah* ¶ vendor from his shop filled with brassware, 'that is true talk. But the Swámi did not fear to tell the Peishwah in private '*Durbâr*'** that his downfall approacheth very near from the hands of Elphinshtan Sâhèb, §§ because of his crimes and bestial life'! Wâh! Wâh! choruses the crowd, 'What a *Roostum* ¶¶ be this holy Swami! Did not Bâji Rao order him to be slippered for his temerity'? 'Slippered! quotha!' rejoins the lotah wallah.' Náheen! Náheen! Bâji Rao

* Guzerathi. 'Yes Govindâssjee; he is a great Swâmi (holy man).'

† & ‡ Literally, student.

§ Here, scientist. 'Maha' equals great.

‖ Chief, sacred priest.

¶ Brass water pots for drinking.

** Private audience.

§§ The Honourable Mountstuart Elphinstone.

¶¶ Hero.

feared the Máhá-Oopâdhya; sent him a rich '*Killut*'* and a royal '*Nuzzur*'† of 101 gold mohurs'!"

"Jey! Sũnt Swâmi, Mâha Oopâdya ki Jey! shout the crowds all down the street."

"(Yea, verily! Khodâwand! Gharib Purwa! commented the old Bhutt. This was indeed a great man, almost a *Râjudnya*‡! He is the bosom friend of our God-beloved Nâna Furnâvis: he is an honoured guest at every Court in Hindostân. Renowned not only for his purity and piety, his wisdom and powers of prophecy, but for his sublime charity—he is very wealthy—and humility, many of us believed that it was Buddha himself re-visiting the earth sent by Brâhma! What doth thy servant know!)"

"At last the palanquin has reached the ancient Banian tree: the chief of the Chitpâwan '*Panchayut*'§ takes his right hand; the principal Raõ (the Shirkè of Bahirughur) takes the left; they lead the holy man to the Guard of Honour: the Kshatrya *Subadâr Major*,¶ a grizzled veteran of lofty stature, scarred with many wounds, advances and salutes, tendering the diamond encrusted hilt of his *tulwar***

* Dress of honour.

† Offer of honour and respect.

‡ Son of a king.

§ Committee.

¶ The highest regimental officer of infantry.

** Curved sword.

to the Swâmi, who touches it, with a gracious smile at the noble figure before him. 'The Gods bless thee ever! Mahadow Raõ Shirkè, in bed, in board, in body, and thy children, and children's children within thee in thy virgin fortress!' Shirkè, bows reverently to the very earth. Then clash the timbrels; then beat the war drums; then bray the trumpets, as the holy man is assisted in climbing the '*Chobothara*'* round the tree: he seats himself for a few moments, while the whole canopy of heaven resounds with cheers, *Jey Sũnt Swâmi Máhárâj, Mahaupâdyá ki jey!*' The stenforian cheers, again and yet again reverberate in glen and ravine, on rocky mountains. (Men heard them, so they say, Khâwand even at lofty Wâsota and distant Helwak!)"

("Come, Bhuttjee! *draw it mild*," quoth I, "*why! thats from* 40 *to* 50 *miles!*")

The old man heeded not the interruption, but continued with uplifted palms, bare headed, his good old features lit up with pious enthusiasm: methought he was distraught!

"Was ever so grand a sight seen in this our Chip loon since Parèshrâm peopled it with us the twice-born—no, nor ever again will be, Khodâwund. What a picture for my lord to portray on canvas. Thy

* Raised terrace or platform of rough masonry round the tem of a large tree.

slave seeth it even now before his eyes, dimmed and bleared by sixty weary years of prayer and fasting! Can Khodâwund paint the scene ?"

"I don't know, old friend, but, by Bhowâni! I will try my level best depend on it!!" I replied. And then when I had liquored up in my way, and he in his, the old Bard resumed his recital :—

CHAPTER XVII.

THE MAHANT SWAMI AT CHIPLUN.—PART II.

"My tale concerns you, my poor and humble brethren, Mhârs and outcastes," continues the holy Mahant. "My heart warmeth toward ye; so great is the praise I hear bestowed upon ye by all the great men of Mâhârâshtra: my bosom friend the sage Nâna Furnâvis extols the uniformly peaceable behaviour of ye Mhârs, the confidence with which he can rely upon your loyalty, your fidelity in positions of great temptation. Our Generals never tire of vaunting your valour in battle and your endurance of hardships and fatigue that has broken down their best Pathân warriors. That wise administrator, whom I am proud to call my friend, Honourable Elphinstone Sâhèb, and his experienced Secretary Grant-Duff Sâhèb, tell me that some of their best sepoys are Mhârs; yea! Mhârs of the Konkan! This is high praise, my brethren all! My old heart was gladdened as I approached, by seeing the noble Shirkè Raõ of Buhiroo-ghur return the military salute of and remain in friendly converse as an equal and honoured comrade with Subedâr Major Râmnâk Bhiknâk, who stands humbly yonder as if he was a mere village 'Bhoomia,'* whereas he has won medals many from the '*Angreez*' for conspicuous courage on many a hard fought battlefield, and now receives the most liberal pension the British Sirkâr

---

* Village guide.

ever gives to a sepoy, and the title of Sirdâr Báhádur. Ye only want education to become great Generals! Even His Highness Bâji Râõ admits this, and vows that he is grateful to ye!!

I was grieved, oh! ye Brâhmins and ryots all, to observe the contumely with which ye permitted that hero to pass humbly to the rear of this vast assembly. I shall have serious matter to say to ye that toward, before we part. But to my tale.

As ye all know the stronghold, if I may so term defenceless huts on the outskirts of walled and defended villages which, mark ye! they shed their blood to defend at your bidding, leaving their own poor homes and families outside at the mercy of your enemies; the original stronghold (I say) of the aboriginal Mhârs lay between the foot of Buhirooghur and the foot of the Anuskura and Râm Ghauts, where they still outnumber all other castes together. Being expert masons and quarrymen, they have been only just able to live by letting themselves out to ye Khôtes all over the Konkan, for wages in kind of '*hárik*' * and '*natchni*' † from the sweepings of your threshing floors, washed down with polluted water from abandoned tanks, because ye refuse them access to pure wells, lest even their shadows may pollute them! Shame! Shame on ye!

* & † Millet—'*harik*' is little better than coarse grass. The grain must be boiled, or it is almost poisonous. The stalks used for covering floors, kill all insects.

But as in small communities, the world over, there were idle and drunkards among them, black sheep who would not work, but lived upon the labour of their fellows. These never-do-weels now and again wandered up over the Ghauts, making the acquaintance of Râmoshis and Mhângs all banded together for dacoity. Naturally our bad Konkan Mhârs fell into evil courses, joining in dacoity and highway robbery in the Deccan and Kârnâtic. Worst of all, they became the tools and decoys of the Thugs who infest all that region (whom may Shri Kâḷi curse!); misleading and misinforming unwary travellers; sharing in the spoil when the victims had been robbed and strangled: Aye! even acting as their grave-diggers! The acknowledged leaders of these bands of marauders were two; Ranjit Singh, an inhabitant originally of far Mooltân (in the Land of Five Rivers*) who had accompanied some Mogul troops southward and deserted with his horse and arms, and Wâghojee Naik of the Râmoshis of the Miraj '*Pergunnahs*'†. These '*harâm-khors*'‡ after a great and successful dacoity at Kolhapur, told the Mhârs, as they gave them their small share of the '*loot*,'§ that they would no longer be permitted to join in future expeditions, unless they guided the robber band to some wealthy town in the Konkan. "*If ye will do*

* The Punjab.

† Sub-districts.

‡ Doers of shameful acts.

§ Spoil.

this, ye shall be sworn into our band over a sacred dagger and shall share equally with us. If ye refuse," said Ranjit with flashing eyes, "*then*" (he drew his hand across his throat) *ye can guess your fate! Ye'll not leave this spot alive! And being unclean outcastes, none of us except the Mhângs, will sully their hands by touching ye when dead: vultures, dogs, dholes,* * *wolves and jackals shall devour your impure flesh—ye swine! Say then, how do you decide? Lo! ye are even now encircled by armed men; your own weapons were taken from ye when ye were drunken with our last victim's arrack last night!"*

The Mhârs perceived that this was so, and read in the threatening looks of their captors that their lives were not worth a *cowrie's* † purchase and they refused. They consented, and were at once sworn on the sacred dagger usually used, and the equally sacred or rather accurst '*roomal*' ‡ so deftly and fatally used by Ranjit Singh.

"*Go ye now, ye swine,*" threatened Wâghoji Râmoshi and Ranjit together. "*Go ye meet us in the caverns ye wot of above the busy town of Râjapur*

---

* Wild dogs.

† Small mottled shells, still used by the very poor as currency; about the value of a Portuguese 'rei'.

‡ Cloth or kerchief used by the stranglers, who usually folded a rupee in it. (*Vide* Meadows-Taylor's 'Confessions of a Thug') Dacoits like *Naikins*, are always sworn on a dagger dedicated to Bhowâni.

next Dussora! As ye wish to live, have goodly fat quarry marked down for us. We shall come in great force; will work on the same night (a moonless night mark ye) in at least two places; then, our work done, we will disperse by different Ghaut tracks, and meet again at Miraj to divide the spoil. Have all prepared therefore, ye sons of burnt fathers, this toward. Begone! may Shri Bhowâni aid ye in your quest! May Shri Kâli strike ye dead if ye fail to keep the tryst!"

The unhappy Mhârs departed hastily with sinking hearts; the task before them was a grievous one; the wealthy men they wot of were the benefactors of the Mhâr caste, and unfailing employers of their relatives! But yet they must be betrayed and robbed—aye! would almost of a surety be murdered and, perhaps their women ravished; for that Ranjit was a lustful beast! that Wâghoji liked nothing better than cutting off his victims' noses and putting the bleeding flesh into their mouths! Had they not seen him do it, many a time and oft! *

Sâhèb log—my chèlis! have a pithy saying '*Shaitân hâku lâgila, chalne zurur!*' † Those unhappy Mhârs had the shaitâns driving them, and a hundred

* During the Bheel rebellion (1858-59) I have seen a row of Mârwârris squatted in the Civil Hospital at Nâssik after Bhâgoji Naik's raids, with their noses cut off!

† 'Needs must when the devil drives.'

minor shaitâns to prick them on! But they did not, they could not draw back. 'Twas too late! They selected first a very wealthy Mogul merchant whose residence was above his '*Wakâr**' on the outskirt of Râjapur (which is not walled in) on the river side. Abdul Kâdir monopolized the Zânzibar and Muscât trade in those early days; he had a fleet of fifty large craft at sea, of which six or ten were always loading or unloading in the river: besides costly wares (such as ivory, silks and brocades and gums) in his '*Wakâr*.' He always had many lakhs' worth of pearls, diamonds, rubies and emeralds in his 'Khajina' and sacks of Spanish dollars, sequins, and rupees stowed in his *godowns*.† He maintained, of course, a strong guard of well-armed negroes and Pardèsis from *Ayoodya*; ‡ but one or other of them might be bribed to open a postern gate, or the others on duty might be drugged. If it came to the worst, a bag of blasting powder, easily brought up by boat to the very steps in a '*hodi*'§ propelled by muffled paddles, would blow in the whole gateway. The chief dacoits must decide how their attack should be made: the garrison of the Wakâr was only a Hâvildar and 12 men. The

---

* Warehouse.

† Cellars—English grafted on to the vernacular, meaning that one has to 'godown' to them.

‡ Pardèsi (up-country) Brâhmins are generally employed as watchmen: they come from Oude, *i.e.*, Ayoodya.

§ Canoe or 'dug out;' usually out-rigged.

town being full of armed men of all nations, the Subedar of the *pergunnah* saw no need of quartering more men in a place seemingly so well able to defend itself.

The second house was at Khârèpâtan, 6 koss off on the Viziadroog river: it is almost a miniature of Râjapur, and thronged also with men armed to the teeth. This *Wárra* also standing on the water's edge, was a much stronger place than that of Abdul Kâdir. Built of solid trap rock forty feet from the ground, it had no windows whatever outside, but the walls were loop-holed. There was but one entrance to the inner court-yard through a massive gateway with iron-plated gates.

The Mhâr spies learned that there was to be a great betrothal ceremony after the "Dussora"* at which many wealthy merchants would be present as resident guests: these would doubtless bring rich gifts; and all the wedding party would certainly wear all their best jewelry! The demon 'Cupidity' raged in their evil hearts! their eyes glistened! "*why! their share, one-hundredth part, would be worth at least five hundred rupees! Wah, Wah! yes it must be done. Kismèt! Nasib! 'Twas Shri Bhowâni's order!*"

The dacoit leaders sent spies many weeks before-hand to reconnoitre, and themselves visited both towns disguised as merchants, provided (of course) with forged

---

* All great undertakings are arranged at and commenced after this festival, especially by the predatory tribes, who then sacrifice to Bhowani.

hoondis * to show if need be, which their Brâhmin receivers of stolen goods skilfully prepared. They thus gained access to the private offices of both merchants I have named; even became intimate with them, and found out the exact position of their *Khajinas*, † pretending that they had a hundred camel-loads of *Kápus* ‡ on the way to the coast which they wished to ship to Zánzibar, or to barter for ivory and dates.

The appointed dark night came at last. Fifty of the band under Ranjit Singh repaired to Râjapur; Abdul Kâdir being (as they deemed) the more formidable of the victims. Thirty, under Wâghoji, were deputed to Khârèpâtan, where little resistance was expected. Ranjit Singh became uneasy as he crept with his followers along the river bank toward Abdul Kâdir's Wâkars. "*What doth this silence portend, Bhai?*" he whispered to the man next to him; "*we should have met belated roysterers returning from the brothels to their ships. 'Tis a bad omen! Silence is danger! However, let's to work, Jees!*" Lo! they had scarcely gathered at the gates, when the huge doors swung open; a torrent of grape shot from a brass gun mowed them down like grass, as a hundred fierce Arabs and Negroes pouring out fell upon them: others attacked them from the rear. Ranjit Singh fell dead at the first volley; forty of his followers were killed on the spot; five desperately

* Bills of exchange.

† Treasure vaults.

‡ Cotton.

wounded: only five escaped down the dry river-bed, favoured by the intense darkness. There was not a single Mhâr among the slain or wounded!

Meantime, how had Wâgboji's party fared at Khârèpâtan? Hearken, my chèlis! As the dacoits were clustered under the walls and at the gate, streams of molten lead and boiling oil poured on them from the loop-holes: huge boulders hurled from the flat roof struck them down: a body of brawny Bhundâris poured out of the gate, striking off limbs with their heavy *koitis* *; only five of the dacoits escaped!

Here again, no Mhâr was found among the slain; Truth to tell, compunction and remorse had induced two of the Mhârs to give secret *khubber* † to both merchants on a promise of free pardon, gladly granted: hence the hot reception the dacoits received at both places.

But, list ye all to the dread sequel! Not one of these recreant Mhârs survived: they were thirteen (an evil omen, as ye know!). Four were waylaid and murdered by the dacoits' confederates who hunted them down like '*Dholes*' ‡ hunt down a '*Sâmbhur*;' §

* *Vide ante.* Curved heavy bill-hooks, sharp as a razor, with which Bhundâris use to make the necessary incision in the cocoa palm crown, so that the juice may run freely.

† News.

‡ Wild dogs (*vide ante*).

§ Indian elk.

two drank themselves to death; two destroyed themselves; two quarrelled over a woman and killed each other; two only remained to tell the tale!

Now, mark the discriminating mercy of even Shri Kâli in her wrath, my children! The two Mhârs saved were those who had pleaded to the last with their comrades for mercy to the proposed victims; the two who actually warned them of their approaching danger! These two poor follows lived to a great age, making pious pilgrimages to all sacred shrines around (especially to Punderpoor), as *Byrâgis*, * returning at every *Mrig-sâl* † to their villages to preach penitence in their *Mhâr wârras.* ‡

What do we learn from this true tale? Oh Chèlis mine! We learn sobriety, industry, and that 'tis never too late to mend.

And, now, ye Khotes and Patels—all ye ryots, and villagers of the superior castes, a final word ye toward.

The cry of these poor outcaste Mhârs has reached the ears of the all but omniscient Nâna Furnâvis! He learns that ye treat these poor outcastes like dogs; that ye revile them; that ye defraud them of their hard

* Pilgrim mendicants (*vide ante*).

† The Mrig-sâl is the Indian Spring, from about 15th May t 30th June.

‡ The Mhâr' hamlet outside a village.

earned *huks* *. Our just *Punt Pradhân* † hath obtained a *durkhast* ‡ from the Peishwah, authorizing him to sequestrate villages from which such complaints reach the Durbar, to resume the inam lands of the Patel and Kulkarni, and (in bad cases) to compel the Ryots and Wanis to perform the Mhâr's duties by rotation. Be ye just, therefore, to your Mhârs that *Mâhâ Dyâl* §—*Eshwar* may be just and merciful to you, and your children within your gates. Be hospitable to the stranger within your gates; so will '*Vâruna*' ‖ grant ye timely and copious rains, and abundant fruits of the earth in due season!

And now, my beloved, I have delivered me of the wise and just Nâna's message to ye; I return to my Nipâni home never to leave it again; for I am an old man who has lived far beyond the usual span of life allotted to mortal man (a deep groan resounded through the vast assembly). Ye will see me no more! Ponder, each of ye, in your inmost hearts when alone, on these my words. Let me, thy humble Swâmi, be cheered in his last moments by the knowledge that he has this day sown good seed; that it has borne a plenteous harvest.

May all the gods bless ye! Amen!

---

* Perquisites (*vide ante*).

† Prime Minister.

‡ Edict.

§ Great God of Mercy.

‖ The Rain God.

The multitude rose to their feet in solemn silence, and prostrating themselves bare-headed formed a dense avenue through which the Holy Orator returned to his camp, where he rested in solitary prayer and meditation till day dawned, when he was borne away on a noble elephant to Nipani. In obedience to his express desire, not a soul appeared that morn in the streets or by-ways. It seemed as if Nature herself was awe-stricken into solemn silence."

EPILOGUE.

My good old friend, rolling up the manuscript, sat silent for some time with bowed head, great tears rolling down his furrowed cheeks. I, too, readers mine, had been deeply impressed, and did not care to break the spell. Rising, the old man raised his arms to heaven and solemnly ejaculated, "*Thy God bless thee and thine, Khodâwand, now and hereafter? And may that God and all mine own bless me too, a miserable sinner!*" Without another word he left me.

The Máhá Upâdhya, Sūnt Swâmy, Mohant (or whatever my readers chose to style him) is no mythical personage. Such a holy man existed in the 18th century. A very debauched descendant lived on the hill near Nipani in my time. He was killed by an accident to the mail 'tonga' in which he was riding to Poona in 1886 or 1887, and on his person were found a roll of notes to a large amount, and certain correspondence—showing that he was on his way to bribe a certain Eurasian, who pretended that he had great influence with your humble servant, the author of this book!

CHAPTER XVIII.

THE LEGEND OF BHYROOGHUR.

Bhyrooghur (or Bâhirughur) is one of the largest of the three hundred and sixty-five forts with which the Southern Konkan or Ratnagiri District is studded, and has a somewhat exceptional history. I read it in manuscript Sanscrit '*sloks*' (verse) in 1860 with my old friend the venerable Bhutt of Chiplun; but failed until a few weeks ago, to obtain a rough translation thereof. This I have here amplified, it being somewhat disconnected and fragmentary in style.

Bhyrooghur (as I prefer to spell it) lies, or rather rears itself to an altitude of some 3,500' feet in an elbow of the Syadri Ghauts between the Wáshisti and Jyghur rivers. It is connected by a spur with the undulating Mulla Ghaut at a point where the Syadris drop to about 2,500 feet. The fort is said to have been built by, or under the orders of, the great Siwaji, who nominated as its '*Killadâr*' (fort commandant) one of the Shirkè family—who had been one of his favourite '*Mânkars*' (great men) in his wars with the Moguls. The Shirkès, of course, were '*Kshatryas*' (or warriors) by caste. Since the British Sirkâr overthrew the last Peishwa (Bâji Rão), the family fell into decay. Several members of it, however, have served (probably do still serve) in the armies of Scindia, Holkâr, or the Guicowâr of Bâroda. I am not aware if any serve in the Bombay Army, but am sure that if they do, they have made their mark.

A branch of the family settled early in the last century in the city of Bombay as fruit merchants in a large way. Their principal shop was at the corner of the central row of fruit stalls in the Arthur Crawford Market: the chief partner was a member of the '*Panchayet*' or Committee of that Market; a man of considerable energy and intelligence, and of conspicious probity and enterprise. Of the latter quality I may mention as an instance, that it was he who first imported Almira grapes packed in barrels, filled with cork sawdust, also pears (which he called '*Vilayeti Pèroo*')* and apples from Kâbul. I trust he is still alive, for he was my good friend, and did right good service in the fruit and vegetable dealers strike in 1867. This by the way!

The first Shirkè Killadâr of Bhyrooghur's post was one of no small danger: he was quite isolated; forty-five miles from Jyghur, thirty from Gowalkote (near Chiplun), forty miles or more from Inchalghur (to the south), 60 miles (about) from Satâra. It is true that, at a pinch, he might obtain succour from Kolhapur, or even retire on that city by way of the dense Mândbeit jungles; but the Râjâh of Kolhapur had enough to do

* English quavas.

to take care of his own territory. The Kolhapur Chief of Inchal-Karanji, like himself, was boxed up in Inchalghur; the Killadâr of Gowalkote (a very small work, with a small garrison) could only just hold his own and shield Chiplun. Moreover, Shirkè's cannon were of small calibre, owing to the great difficulty of transport from the coast. But the bastions were in good repair; the defences well nigh impregnable, and the water-supply within the fort abundant: the twenty villages and thirty-five hamlets belonging to the fort's environment, though at long distances from each other were fairly populous and well-to-do, supplying the Killadâr with plenty of rice and millet; large herds of bison then roamed the Mulla Ghaut: wild boar were only too numerous: salted or half-cured Soormal (the Málábár coast Sturgeon) were bartered with the fisher-folk for grain; oil-nuts trees and coca-palms grew in every dell, goats did well on the slopes, and coarse sea-salt was easily procurable from the Ratnagiri salt-pans. Therefore, the garrison were abundantly supplied and had absolutely no need for cash.

This garrison, it is true, had very few opportunities of securing '*loot*': they rarely had occasion to raid around. Only once were they besieged by Ángria from Jyghur, but the valiant Killadâr sent that pirate back to his lair '*with his tail between his legs!*' In fact, Bhyrooghur was a virgin fortress; it never was taken by assault, so says Marâtha history. In a word the Killadâr Shirkès held their own, and more than their own ; being able on several occasions to send aid to the Chiefs of Miraj and Inchal-Karanji, and to the often terribly beset garrison of Gowalkote. When Ángria submitted to Siwaji, of course the troubles of Bhyrooghur were practically over, for they had no foes above the Syadri range. Very little '*loot*' was ever buried in that fort; what little was taken from Ángria, was faithfully remitted to Raighur. A vast store of grain of sorts, and of coarse salt, was found stored in pits as late as 1876-77, when the famine compelled the people to empty the '*peows*' (grain-pits); the salt being nearly black and quite worthless, is probably there now, for the fortress is utterly abandoned since 1817.

The '*pothi*' I have just received, relates to a romance in real life, common enough in those troublous times when every man's hand was raised against his neighbour ; when Brinjâris (Indian gipsies), Râmosis, Bheels, Arabs, Rohillas, and even Moguls banded together and roamed Mâhârâshtra as Pindâris, from Gwâlior to the banks of the Tungbuddra river, from Hyderabâd to Dhârwâr. Such romances are not uncommon in our own Emerald Isle at this day ; but the circumstances attending this particular tragedy were unusual, even in India.

Towards the end of the seventeenth century several families of the Sâwant Marâthas from Soonder wari* (generally called Sâwantwâri), disgusted with the atrocities and rapacity of the Chief of that petty State, migrated to Ratnagiri. The Sâwants are a particularly handsome, intelligent, and courageous sect of the Kshatrya Marâthas; much taller than even the Syadri Marâthas. Their women are renowned for their beauty and chastity, so find no difficulty in obtaining husbands from the highest Marâtha families of Kshatrya Marâthas of the Konkan: indeed, most Marâthas do not marry till both boy and girl have arrived at puberty; even then the bride remains at her father's house till she has matured—say, till 16 years of age. Her fiancè is then probably 19 or 20. Their women are not '*purdu nasheen*' (*i.e*, secluded behind curtains from male society, and obliged to wear veils in public); only the women of the nobility are so treated, or are wedded in infancy, for State reasons, and are '*purda nasheen*' as a matter of policy. The young people of both sexes meet frequently at each others' houses, at festivals, at the temples, and, both sexes being well educated, it follows that their marriages are often the result of true affection on both sides; not mere *mariages de convenance*', as with the Brahminical and Waishya (or trading) castes.

I have been present, an honoured guest, at many of their weddings. The ceremony is very impressive, and strongly resembles that of Christians, especially in

---

Soonder,' beautiful: '*Wari*, place or residence.

the actual action before the altar. The following description will not (I hope) be found tedious.

Bride and bridegroom arrive at the '*Gāūmti Dèwal,*' (the temple of the village tutelary deity) attired gorgeously: each comes from his or her parents' house accompanied by their near relatives. The two fathers mounting the steps into the outer temple, take off their shoes or sandals (as do all subsequently); they then ring the brass bell—pendant from the main crossbeam: this is to call the God's attention. The officiating Bhutt or '*Poojâri*' * awaits the party in the Holy of Holies (' the *Mâj Dèwal*'†): the whole assembly then squat on their hams around, while the fathers tender fruit, flowers in garlands, and bouquets to the *Poojâri* as offerings to the God. He receives the trays, deposits them at the foot of the altar, and proceeds to circumambulate the idol (usually a huge boulder, painted vermilion, with or without eyes). Meantime, the bride and bridegroom have been led by their parents in front of the idol, and seat themselves on their hams, facing each other,—knees touching knees: the priest—as he performs his circuit—muttering '*Mantris*' (sacred Sanscrit '*sloks* which no white man or Moslem knows). Anon, he drops Asoka, Champa, and Jasmine blooms on the idol. Anon, he anoints it with sandalwood and other fragrant

* Priest officiating.

† All this strongly resembles the Christian ceremony, and the procedure preliminary to it; a bevy of damsels follow and precede the bride -strewing flowers in her path,—like our bridesmaids.

oils. Anon, he lays fruit at the foot of the senseless stone, and a few packets of betel pân and unslaked lime (called '*Pân soopâri*') folded in gilt leaf. The last ceremony is that called '*Abishèk*' (the dropping of water, '*âb*', drop by drop on the idol). If the blooms immediately drop off the idol, or wither; if the water-drops seem to evaporate in steam, the omens are pronounced adverse, and the ceremony does not proceed that day. But, as the village '*Joshi*' (astrologer) has already cast favourable horoscopes for the bride and groom, and the officiating priest has been well fed beforehand with a goat, grain, ghee, or perhaps even with a cow, and has been promised a further liberal honorarium in cash after the ceremony, the omens are sure to be propitious, and the marriage proceeds. This is the most curious feature of all. The bridegroom's father hands him a plantain (*Banána*) which he peels; then shaking the pendant tinsel tassels that obscure his sight (as a horse tosses his forelock to disperse the flies), he pops the fruit into his mouth—to the middle thereof, and leans forward: the bride does the same, and takes the protruding half of the '*banána*' into her mouth: each bites off and eats the half he or she holds. This quaint ceremony is repeated with a '*pân soopâri*,' by the bridegroom. The bride repeats both ceremonies with a '*banána*' and '*pán*'—supplied by her mother. This concludes the ceremony.

The first time I witnessed such a wedding I asked the old '*Pâtel*' (Village Headman) what this curious ceremony meant. His reply was "Does not the Saheb guess? its meaning is '*Májha tuja! Tujha májha*' *what is mine is thine, what is thine is mine.*" Very terse and expressive are these four pronouns—are they not? readers mine! Do they not express exactly—but not at such length, "*with all my worldly goods I thee endow*" of our marriage service? The newly married pair then rise and repair hand-in-hand to the husband's father's house; preceded by the bridesmaids and children—strewing flowers: the onlookers plentifully assault the couple with showers of rice and millet. Then music and dancing follow the wedding breakfast (fresh toddy and curds in place of champagne). There is rarely any speechifying; the bride's wedding presents of clothes, etc., are shown by her mother in the 'Mâjghur' (inner chamber) to a select few. The women-folk embrace the bride—weeping in true orthodox British fashion; but the bridegroom does not kiss the bride; that would be indecent. Then the bride retires—to be arrayed in her work-a-day clothes. The wedding is over; but there is no honeymoon; the bride remains in her father's house till her mother-in-law decides that she is strong enough to bear children.

But, to return to our Legend.

About the end of 1700 A.D. (as I have said) the Shirkè then commanding at Bhyrooghur had an only son, a fine young fellow of 19, a splendid swordsman and athlete, a veritable Apollo withal, Mânkoji Rãõ by name. He had travelled a good deal in Upper and Central India, being well received at the Courts of Scindia and Holkar. He had resided during one cold season at Poona, where the last of the Peishwas had been pleased to treat him with marked distinction; for the name of Shirkè was a passport to any Court in Hindostân. Bâji Rão was then at the zenith of his power; unrivalled in rapacity, depravity, and cruelty. Trimbukji Dainghlia was his pimp, the fiendish Ghâtgè his Chief Constable; nameless crimes were daily and nightly committed in his palaces, at which the people of Poona shuddered, but dared not resent. No woman's honour was safe; no man's good name sacred to these demons; now Mânkoji Rão had been brought up in an austere and simple home, where obscenity was not tolerated. He had a beautiful sister, aged 15, residing with their father at Byrooghur. (Their mother was dead, and their education had been entrusted to their paternal aunt, a stern, resolute old dame). Mânkoji Rão was naturally disgusted at the licentiousness prevailing at Bâji Rão's new palace on Pârbutti hill, and his old '*wârra*' in the city, and would have returned home, but that his father (who desired his son to see the world) peremptorily ordered him to remain.

The Shirkè family was intimate with the Chief of the Sâwants—settled at Ratnagiri (Mhâd Sâwant *bin* Bhim Sâwant). This noble Kshatrya was closely related to the Chief of Sâwantwarri, who belonged to a distant branch of the Bhonslay; he was consequently descended from the great Shiwaij, and cousin german to the puppet Râjâh of Satâra. *He* also had a beautiful daughter of the same age as Mânkoji Rão Shirkè, and a son (Gun Sâwant), a year younger, whom he had despatched to Poona—to carry through some small negotiations with Bâji Rão for the Khoteship of Miria. It was the cherished desire of the two grand old Marâthas, that their sons should marry their daughters.

The young people were nothing loth, in fact were deeply attached to each other, and the double wedding was to be celebrated at Sangamèshwar on their return at the next 'mrig-sal' (spring season).

Bâji Rão's principal pander was a Gosâeen, who roamed far and wide seeking for attractive girls to gratify the Peishwa's lust. This devil, during a visit to Ratnagiri had seen both maidens at Mhâd Sâwant's house, and marked them down for his master. He suggested to the Peishwa to invite both families to Poona under the pretence that he (Bâji Rão) desired that the double wedding should take place under his own eye at Pârbutti.

But the Shirkè and Sâwant were cautious old birds not to be caught by chaff: moreover, they both detested and despised the Peishwa. They returned a curt refusal to Bâji Rāõ. "*They*—wrote they—"*were loyalists to the Marâtha Râj, to the great Siwaji's descendant, whom the Peishwa kept practically a State prisoner at Satára. They did not owe fealty to the Brahmin Prime Minister who had made the Bhonslay Râjâh a puppet, and, in common with most other loyal Marâthas of cleanly lives, they were disgusted at the license of the Peishwa's Court: no daughter of theirs should breathe the poisonous atmosphere of Poona. 'jyâda kay lihinè'? (what more needs to be written?)*"

Even the Gosāēen pimp was terrified at the outburst of fury with which Bâji Rāõ read this plain spoken * *khareeta*'. But neither master or man stuck at trifles, and both were adepts at villainous intrigue. Laying their heads together they hit upon the following plan. The Gosāēen should proceed to Ghèria (Viziadroog), and interview Dhoolup the hereditary High Admiral of the Marâthas, a noble of the highest family, but notoriously dissolute and impoverished. He was a sot and a debauchee, recklessly improvident. Most of his ancestral villages and Inâms were heavily mortgaged to a band of usurers of Râjâpur and Khârèpâtan. He was then an elderly man of vast stature, an admirable sailor, as bold as he was unscrupulous. Proceeding to Vizia-

---

* Letters of ceremony are written on glazed paper, sprinkled with gold-leaf: the cover is a rich kincob bag, fastened with silk and wax: it then becomes a *Khareeta*.

droog, the Gosāēen should bear Bâji Rāō's sign-manual on a mandate to Dhoolup's usurer creditors to look to the Peishwa for a settlement of their claims; the date of the document to be left blank. The Gosāēen was to show it to Dhoolup, but it was not to be dated or used until the latter had secured possession of the two Shirkè and Sâwant maidens aforesaid, and delivered them to the Gossāēen.

Dhoolup, of course, promised to do his best: he too had heard talk of the beauty of the maidens, and the idea came into his head that perhaps he might safely '*skim the milk*', or, in other words, have his wicked will of them before sending them on to Poona.

The Gosāēen suggested that the two families should be invited to visit Dhoolup; but the latter replied that they would no more accept his hospitality than the Peishwa's: the better way would be to meet them casually at Sungumèshwar, where they would surely do '*pooja*' at the Dussora: in the meantime the Gosāēen must '*lie low*' near the sacred town: he (Dhoolup) would gradually collect followers around the temple, and have a 'pattiamar' (ship) ready: the girls could be easily carried off to Panwèl where the Peishwa's Agents could meet them. The Gosāēen approving the scheme, Dhoolup began his preparations, despite the entreaties of his neglected wife, to whom he had revealed it in a drunken debauch. The Gosāēen secreted himself: the plot would certainly have succeeded but for the intervention (strange to say!) of Bâji Rāō's most trusty tools, Trimbakji Gainglia and Ghâtgè. It goes without saying that the Peishwa betrayed himself neither by demeanour nor action. With devilish cunning he overwhelmed the young Shirkè and Sâwant lads with favours; openly expressed his regret that their fathers were so inimical to their ruler, but said he could well understand such noble-hearted men being loyal to their sovereign at Sátara, whose position (of course) they did not understand. The simple youths were completely deceived, and wrote to their parents that the Peishwa was by no means so black as his enemies painted him. Shirkè's reply was prompt. "*Return at once, my son, from that wasp's nest, lest evil befall you both.*"

But Dainglia and Ghâtgè, who were bitterly jealous of the Gosāēen, spread about a rumour that the last named's mysterious absence, and his still more mysterious visits to Ratnagiri and Viziadroog concerned the Shirkè and Sâwant families, and was a bad omen for them. The infamous Foujdar of Poona City Ghâtgè paid a secret visit to the lads (who resided in the same Wârra). "*Májhe Jèwán ke batcha,*" he said, "*burra tuphán áhè ápalè Konkan madya. Apan doghè zarur paratilè páhijè! (My young heroes, there's to be a great tempest in your Konkan; you should return speedily!)*" Not a word more would the villain reveal.

The lads, however, took the hint, travelled with great speed *viâ* Sâtara to Chiploon, where a messenger met them from their fathers enjoining them to bring a strong contingent of armed men to the suburbs of Sangamèshwar without a moment's delay. They were only just in time! But their wily old fathers had already surrounded Dhoolup's gang. A fierce fight ensued within the very temples. The Dhoolupites were routed in ten minutes with great loss, and took to their boats. The Gosāēen escaped by the skin of his teeth. To cut a long story short, the double wedding took place at once, and the newly married couples '*lived happily ever afterwards*'.

Epilogue.

A history of the Dhoolup Admirals will be found in the Legend of Viziadroog.

This tale is doubtless true in the main particulars. It is, I believe, to be found among the Sânscrit manuscripts in the possession of priests at Sangamèshwar.

I may note in conclusion that the fiend Nâna Sâhèb of Bithūr was the adopted son of a respectable Chitpâwan Brâhmin, resident of Sangamèshwar; so also (I believe) was Tântia Topi. The latter certainly made a pilgrimage to the sacred temples there during his tour round Western India in the hopes of corrupting the Sirdars of the Deccan in 1856. Nâna Sâhèb, to my own certain knowledge and that of several other officials, also made two pilgrimages to Sangamèshwar subsequent to his overthrow in 1858.

CHAPTER XIX.

THE LEGEND OF DHOPESHWUR.

PROLOGUE.

My hoary old friend the Bhutt was always trying to inveigle me into a discussion as to the relative merits of Christianity and Hinduism. I had to dodge him like a hunted hare! for such discussions are of no avail whatever with old bigotted Brahmins, still less with atheistical young fellows who openly deride their own creed and superstitions, yet carefully attend to their religious ceremonies. Moreover, the pig-headed obstinacy of the former, and the "*swelled-headedness*" of the latter are mightily irritating in a warm climate.

At one of our seances, however, the old fellow touched upon a topic dear to the heart of all Christians, *viz.*, the purification from sins, and how to attain to that beatific condition. First, he descanted eloquently on the virtues of seclusion, silent religious meditation; and charity as practised by Buddha, as being the most efficacious means of washing oneself from sins. I assented cordially, of course; insisting, however, that silence was neither needful nor desirable, but a very palpable abuse of God's gifts to man. He certainly intended man to use his powers of speech freely; firstly, in praise and prayer to Himself; secondly, in consolation to our afflicted brethren, and in their education and exhortation. The good old fellow sat silent for some time, pondering on my arguments; then, looking up with a charming smile he startled me by "Do you know, Khâwund, that I myself have believed in your Messiah for many years, ever since I heard one of your best Missenry Padrès preach in Bombay. I don't mean that I believe in Christianity, of course, though thy servant doth admire it greatly; but I believe that there was such a God, a Son of God, who came down from heaven to benefit man; just as I believe that Máhá-Indra up there, Krishna and others of our demi-gods, were Sons of God. I don't see how you prove or come to believe that God has only one Son! why should not he have a thousand. Hân Khodâwand? Sâhèb can't answer that question." I retorted somewhat sharply: "Well, old gentleman! Though I'm pleasantly surprised at your half confession, I would prefer your reading another Legend, if it is all the same to you." He salaamed meekly and said: "What I have said, I have said, Khâwand! I said what I did as a kind of preface to the Legend I will now read, which describes the origin of our belief in possible purification from sin."

"Ah!" quoth I, "if that's so, fire away, old friend! I shall listen with the greatest pleasure; I'm sorry I spoke so sharply just now." Again salaaming the pious old gentleman pulled out from his wallet a well-thumbed Sanscirit '*pothi*' saying,—"This, may it please my lord, is the legend of Dhopèshwur which, as my lord knows, is the short for *Dhūt-Pâp-Eshwar* or '*The God who washes away sin.*' My lord has (as he has told me) often visited the temple at the village of Dhopèshwur, and the sacred hot springs that every few years bubble up at the top of Oonouri hill near the town of Rájápur; Hân Sâhèb." I nodded, and told him to read away. He took a deep drink from his lotah, and recited to the following effect:—

Part I.

THE TEMPTATION AND THE CRIME.

Ages before Brâhm sent Buddha into the world to wean man from overweening pride and luxury, but subsequent to the settlement of Chitpâwans at Chiploon and their condemnation by Puréshrâm to die like other mortals, there was a learned physician named Pándoba Waidya practising his profession in and around Chiploon. He knew the virtues of all the simples of the Konkan, the strength of mineral and vegetable poisons, how to combine the two together for the benefit of his patients, how to administer his drugs in minute doses for evil purposes. His besetting sin was avarice; this made him unscrupulous; he became renowned as far as Benâres and Lâknāō. Great potentates sent emissaries to him for virulent poisons wherewith to destroy their enemies, loose-lived nobles and lewd women of rank came from afar to consult him, or sent servants for love-philtres. He became passing rich, but ever craved more. He was forty years of age before any woman inflamed his passions: his child-wife died when he was but a boy, and he had never cared to re-marry; declaring that women were impediments to study. However, woman-hater though he was, he was bound by his creed to beget or adopt a son. But there were very few fathers in the Konkan wealthy enough to dower their daughters with coin or kind sufficient to make them worth Pándoba Waidya's mating with them. Pándoba employed the most astute go-betweens to find a suitable match for him, but for a long time in vain. It came to pass that when attending the old Deshmookh of Chiploon in his last fatal illness Pándoba Waidya saw the Deshmookh's grand-daughter, a beautiful girl of 15, but a child-widow. She was very learned; a good musician, and soothed her old grandfather with gentle hands.

Pándoba became ardently enamoured of Soondribai. He could not marry her of course, yet he could not and would not give her up. He employed sundry old crones and a '*bángriwallah*' (bangle-seller) to try and corrupt her mind. But Soondribai was both proud and innocent: her child-husband had died when she was six years old: she vividly remembered being taken to his funeral pyre before the corpse was stretched on it and that her mother told her that the elders were even then sitting in full conclave on her (Soondri's case) to decide whether she should be made to commit '*Sutti*' on that same pyre or not. "But," said her mother soothingly, "it does not really hurt much, and is soon over! Thou shalt have opium given thee in thy food and sweetmeats; gánja too, that will make thine eyes see double and stupefy thy brain. The dense resinous smoke will do the rest. And, think Soondri, my darling! how beautifully thou wilt be dressed for the great ceremony; only, of course, with no ornaments! Think what a glorious death to die! Think what a miserable life to live, if the caste Panchayut decide that thou shalt not burn, provided thou art dedicated to the service of Shri Parèshrâm up there when thou art become a woman. Thou wilt have to live as an outcaste in thy father's house! I, even I, thy loving mother, shall only dare to embrace thee furtively. Thou wilt be clad in the oldest, most threadbare, '*loogadis*' and '*saris*' (petticoats and shawl dresses) we can find; such as even a '*Sudrya*' (labourer) woman would not wear. Thy beautiful tresses will be shorn off; thou shalt feed on the refuse from the family platter and drink from an earthen lotah, and be the household drudge, despised—aye! even beaten by the very servants who are now thy slaves."

Soondri remembered that on their way home they encountered men—naked to the waist '*uagudu bdka* — (bare headed), who regarded her with sinister significant looks, and women who stared at her with pity, for she was a favourite among them. They (she and her mother) passed a hundred yards from the great '*pipal*' tree under which the Chitpâwan Elders were assembled in animated converse about her fate; then they entered Shri Devi Kâli's temple and laid flowers on the altar: then her father was seen approaching with down-cast mien, as if he had been shamed and disgraced, while their family Joshi by his side was evidently trying to console him; good old Govind Punt (of Shri Purèshrâm's shrine) who taught her, followed, his kind ascetic face beaming with joy. She had been reprieved by the Panchayut, and was henceforth to be his '*chéli*.' Then all was a blank; the poor girl fainted.

Then both her parents, who had treated her kindly on the whole, died of cholera, and Soondri was left alone to tend her paralytic grandfather doomed to succumb to his next stroke. Being practically a maid servant of Shri Purèshrâm her beautiful silky tresses had not been cut off: she was the most lovely virgin in the country-side; but alas! a widow, doomed to celibacy.

Such a girl was not likely to respond to Pândoba Waidya's advances. In vain the *tángriwallah*, as he fitted on rows of glass bangles on her shapely arms, descanted on the Waidya's wealth and position. It would be an honour—certainly no disgrace—to be his concubine! Let her recall how many young widows had escaped their cruel fate in like manner. The old hags, her aunts, and the wrinkled old bawd employed by Pándoba Waidya enlarged continually on the same theme. "What splendid ornaments and richly embroidered '*sâris*' she would wear in the Waidya's spacious '*Wârra*' (palace); an Arab palfrey to ride upon; a gilded palanqueen wherein to be carried up Máhá-Indra hill; slaves to fan and shampoo her; the best of food, the choicest sweetmeats, would be hers! Let her not be a fool! Let her say but one word and the Waidya would be at her feet; and then, he with his wealth would of course enrich the whole family! *Thoba Thoba!*' was ever a girl so '*bèwakuf*'.*

The old bawd waylaid poor Soondri whene'er she went abroad to the Temples and the bazaar, dinning all these specious arguments into her reluctant ears: they had no effect on the noble girl. Then the beldame, incensed at her obduracy, sneered, "Dost think oh! mule-like girl! to remain a virgin at the temple up there? (pointing to Mâhá-Indra). Why, there's not such a thing known among the temple servants! There are a dozen lusty young Dèwâlyas† who will ravish thee forcibly! aye! thou proud pea-hen; and old Bhutt's too, to whose lascivious embraces thou'lt have to submit. *Thoba*! fie on thy mock modesty!"

The innocent girl did not half understand the old hag's vile suggestions: she shuddered, drew her '*sári*'

* *Bèwakuf*—Persian for stupid or silly.

† Male devotees.

over her oval face and quickened her pace so that the foul tormentor was left behind. "Are all impure then?" she murmured to herself, "are there no modest women up there? Are all the men debauched? I'll ask good old Govind Punt; he won't deceive his poor chèli."

Little did Soondri guess that the very Chitpâwan Elders who had saved her from '*sutti*' only did so that they might thereafter gratify their senile lust on her person! men older than her own father too! Govind Punt, of course, said all he could to comfort her, but though pure himself, well he knew how all temples in those days reeked with impurity, and that Shri Purèshrâm's shrine was little better than others.

When the old bawd reported her ill-success to Pándoba Waidya, he assailed her with a torrent of foul abuse, refusing to pay her fees. "Go, you spawn of hell, and try again and yet again, or I will bewitch thee! Tell the girl that I am a wizard; that I can cast spells over her that will bring her voluntarily to mine arms!" The lewd old pimp knew this to be more or less true, for it was notorious that the Waidya had cured many of his patients by throwing them into a trance, when they obeyed every one of his commands. (*"This is what you Sáhèbs call 'meshmirizing', is not, Khâwand?"* said the old Bhutt, peering over his horn spectacles. I nodded, and he resumed reading) :—

The old beast lost no time in waylaying Soondri again. This time she began at once shrilly (it was a garden round a local shrine to Shri Bhowâni) "*Oh! Oh! Miss Prude! thine hour is come! Thou'st heard that the Waidya has studied the Black Art at Benâres? Hân? He is determined now to bewitch thee next time he comes to see thine old drivelling grandfather, and then thou'lt rue the day. May mine old eyes see thy downfall!*"

Poor Soondri was, of course, terribly frightened, having heard of the Waidya's witchery. Indeed, at an early stage of her grandfather's illness he had frequently been put to sleep by the Waidya's making a few passes over him. On her way home, she met one of her aunts hurrying to summon her to her grandfather's bed-side: the poor man had just had another (his third) stroke. The old lady told her that the Waidya had been sent for, and added, "*Now, dear Soondri, thou'lt be free! unless thou art an idiot thou'lt go to the Waidya, èk dam!*"

Soondri found the Waidya by her grandfather's side sure enough, but it was obviously useless to apply any of the usual remedies; the old man was moribund. Her sinister admirer left the room for a few moments to hypnotize the two servants and the old aunt (who was nothing loth): returning, with a few passes he put poor Soondri to sleep also, and then, while the death rattle sounded in the dying man's throat, he accomplished his fell purpose. After the hideous crime roused the three sleepers below, told them that Soondri had fainted when the old man died. The old aunt winked maliciously, having noticed poor Soondri's position on the mattress on the floor, and her disordered '*cholkhun*' (bodice). The Waidya had much difficulty in restoring the poor girl to consciousness. No sooner did she perceive her ravisher and her aunt together and felt her girdle unloosened, than she realized the awful truth. With the yell of a maniac she rushed out of the house and cast herself into a well at the back, striking her head against a projecting rock which was bespattered with her blood. A friendly '*punchayut*' brought in the verdict '*suicide while of unsound mind, owing to her grief at her grandfather's death*'; but all guessed what had really happened. Govind Punt openly denounced Pandoba Waidya as a ravisher and murderer, and cursed him solemnly at Shri Purèshrâm's altar!

PART II.

REMORSE AND RETRIBUTION.

From that moment the Waidya began to wither as it were, sleep was impossible to him; no drugs gave him rest; his food nauseated him. He wandered purposeless about the town by night and day, seeking the old bawd, with the avowed purpose of strangling her with his own hands. So terrible was the wicked man's remorse! Govind Punt offered up sacrifices of fowls and kids to Shri Purèshrâm for the speedy punishment of the villain, but soon the good man's heart was moved with compassion by what he heard of the Waidya's grievous condition. He pleaded to the mighty deity to bring the sinner to repentance. His prayers were wonderfully granted. The very next day, slaves brought in a litter and laid before the idol a miserable, emaciated wretch bearing still some semblance to the lately prosperous Waidya : so enfeebled was he that his voice was barely audible ! His slaves told the '*guru*' on duty that the master wanted to see Govinda Bâba. The latter came and squatted beside the sufferer, who feverishly whispered. "Govinda Punt, behold thy curse's work! thy just curse! Verily the '*lota*'* of my misery is full to the brim and running over! my sin hath found me out!" Quoth Govind Punt reprovingly "Say rather, my son 'âpalè pâp bhurile gèlè âhèt,' 'tis the *lota* (cup) of thine iniquity that is brimful ! Hast thou repented—oh, fearful man ?" "Yea! Govinda Baba, verily I have !" gasped the Waidya. "Tell me, holy father! tell me, what I must do to make amends"!

"Oh, my poor brother! nothing will now avail to bring my pet lamb Soondri to life again ! Let the dead past bury its dead. But thou ! poor mortal, perverted by devilish lust and pride! thou must do exactly as I tell thee, lest worse punishment overtake thee,

* Cup.

for the wrath of Shri Purèshrâm is still unappeased; lest after thy death thy soul pass into the writhing body of a serpent, or the skin of a mangy jackal!"

The sick man partially raising himself cried, "Tell me, oh tell me quickly, holy Father! thy servant will surely obey thee!" "Burè! Burè! mâjhè bhai! aikungya (Well, well, my brother, listen). Thou must sell all that thou hast of perishable and movable goods forthwith, and appoint a '*Punchayut*' to distribute the proceeds to the poor of Chiploon. Thy lands and houses thou must make over temporarily to the '*Panchayut*' of this Holy Shrine, who will manage thine estate prudently and render an account in due season for a purpose thou shalt presently learn." ("All this will thy sinful servant do!" solemnly swore the Waidya.) "Thou shalt at once repair to Oonowri hill whither the pilgrims are now hastening, for lo! news has come that the sacred well-spring of Gunga Mâtha is bubbling up in such volume as has never before been known. The sacred cows ('tis said) wander about the holy hill in herds with distended udders, yet will let no human hand milk them! These be strange portents, my son! Methinks thou art concerned in them! Do thou go and see without a day's delay. Bathe daily in the warm purifying stream and cleanse thy sinful body. There shalt thou be told miraculously how thou mayest cleanse thy blood-stained soul. Depart in peace! I forgive thee!"

Pandoba Waidya revived visibly at these gracious words. Not a moment was lost. The Temple's Secretary drew up a deed in favour of the '*Punchayut*' as regards the immovable property (real estate); a slave went down to Chiploon with another (duly signed) to a '*Punchayut*' of Sãõkars to realize his personal effects. Swift messengers were sent off to order relays of '*bigâris*' (porters) along the road. The Waidya stayed a few hours only in Chiploon to obtain a packet of goldleaf and some small change for the journey, and a '*Kamblie*' to cover his '*muncheel*' (litter), and a change of raiment. He took only a bag of parched grain and lentils for his sustenance, knowing that he would get milk, curds, cocoanuts, eggs and fruit in every village. Night and day he travelled, tarrying only for his daily ablution or to prostrate himself at any '*grâm dèwat*' (village temple) near the road side. It is 50 '*koss*'* from Chiploon to Rájápur by the nearest route (Ainowli and Deorookh). The fifth evening, at sundown, he slept at Hoonimân's temple at Rájápur, having been twice stopped by dacoits; who, not finding his secreted gold-leaf, or cash (which the Mukadam of each relay carried in his waistbelt) let him pass, on his giving them a '*hoondi*' payable at sight on his Chiploon Sãõkar. It was in the height of the monsoon; all the rivers and torrents were banks-full: many a

---

* A *koss* is somewhat less than a French league in the Konkan. In the Deccan it is two miles, till one gets east, then it runs to 4 or 5 miles.

time he had to wait till they subsided: often he was carried over slung to the '*muncheel*' pole, or had to be ferried across a swift stream in a sugar-boiler's pan, or to float over on inflated skins. But he was a new man, full of courage, honestly resolved to redeem his promises to Govinda Punt to the letter.

PART III.

MIRACULOUS INTERVENTION.

EXPIATION AND PURIFICATION.

He was amply rewarded. The officiating '*guru*' at Shri Hunimân's shrine told him that the omens were marvellously propitious and foretold that he (the Waidya) was in favour with the gods. "Khodâwand knows all these places!" quoth the old bard at this point. "'Twas to protect Shri Hunimân's '*palki*' from being wrecked by the thrice accursed Moslems at '*Sankrâut*'* in 1861, that my lord, like a '*Rishi*' † of old, did interfere with a few armed police, did shoot one of the '*pâji*' ‡ rioters and got forty-and-two more convicted by '*Ass-broan*' § Sâhèb the Fust Ashistant. Khâwand has also shewn me, thy slave, pictures painted by Louis Frank Sâhèb: a 'Sudra' he, but a

* Sankrâut is 13th January.

† Rishi means a demi-god.

‡ Pâji, shameful or shameless.

§ Mr. Lionel Ashburner.

clever artist; Hân ? Sâhèb!" I nodded saying "Right, but hurry up, you old duffer!"

The old fellow cried, "*What* did Khâwand call his Gholam? What abuse is this? Better smite thy slave over the mouth with thy shoe than revile him!" and he began to beat his breast, crying '*Thoba*! *Thoba*' (Fie! for shame!). "Why, old friend," said I, "*duffer* is a term of honor!" "Bhot barè! Khâwand, very well my lord, then I am very glad," said he, salaaming profoundly. After a long drink he resumed: "Now comes the most wonderful part of this true tale, Khâwand!" "Well, let's hear it then without more '*talk*'" said I, testily. He continued, meekly obedient:—

When Pándoba Waidya neared the Oonowri* spring, the multitude of pilgrims made way for him, as if they had been forewarned who he was and on what errand bent. Lo and behold! the warm water gushed up several cubits high (fountain-like), laving him all over; a herd of sacred cows crowded round him, licking his hands and feet; trotting off a little way, then trotting back, lowing in chorus. The pilgrims cried to him, "Follow them, Waidya jee! a miracle is to be vouchsafed to thee!" The Waidya obeyed: the whole herd ambled down hill as fast as their enormously distended udders would let them. Crossing the nearly dry river bed, they led him up a gorge; there, on a huge flat rock overhanging a waterfall they all stopped.

* From "Oon," hot or warm.

Immediately the surface of the boulder was covered with their hoarded milk, exuding spontaneously from their teats. A deep pool below the cataract became white as snow with the curdling, frothy liquid; the air was laden with the fragrant breath of the beasts, who jostled around, playfully butting him, licking his hands and feet. Then they began to scrape up the red soil (with which the plateau was in some parts thinly covered) with their feet—to prise up stones with their horns in rivalry, lowing the while melodiously. Some Bhutts who had accompanied the party ejaculated eagerly, "Lo! Pándoba Jee! the sacred beasts evidently mean that thou, who art so rich should build a temple here to Krishna on the very spot where they have voïded their milk!"

The Waidya at once collected a few large stones and, with the aid of the Bhutts erected an altar; a goat was dragged up and sacrificed to Krishna thereon; flowers and fruits were laid on the rude structure; the senseless stones being sprinkled with turmeric and saffron; sandalwood oil was smeared over them; bowls of '*ghi*', boiled rice, and plantains galore were laid before the altar, and all present circumambulated it, singing a hymn of praise of the deity. By this time most of the Hindu inhabitants of Rájápur, and thousands of pilgrims had assembled in the gorge, to see the miracle of the milk. A deputation of the Elders besought the Waidya to stay with them till he had built a temple there in obedience to Shri Krishna's behest. Pàndoba Waidya joyfully consented. Cried he, in trumpet tones which echoed and re-echoed around.

"Victory (or hurrah for) Shri Krishna! Permit this poor man's efforts to be completed. Here, at this very spot, my sins are washed away, by thy mercy. The temple thy slave will here erect I will thus name 'Dhut-pâp-eshwar.' Be kind to me a poor sinner.

The immense multitude joined in the prayer; the sacred cows being soon joined by the town bulls, camped on and never left the holy spot till Pàndoba Waidya had brought his pious old friend Govinda Punt from Máhá-Indra to consecrate the edifice. Liberally fed by the people, who ran up sheds for them, they multiplied exceedingly: but directly the sacred structure was opened for public worship the whole herd disappeared. Except a few long residents of Rájápur, all the others were incarnations of Shri Krishna's '*Gopis*' (milkmaid attendants).

Pàndoba Waidya expended two lakhs of rupees sicca * on that Temple, and endowed it with all his remaining wealth; filling its treasury with gold and silver ornaments and jewels for the idol's decoration on gàla days. He himself lived (or rather, slept) in a small hermitage outside the walls and became a holy

* £25,000.

'*Sunyassi* *'; his days and nights were passed in prayer and meditation. He died in the full odour of sanctity; his body was embalmed and carried in a sitting posture to Chiploon where he was buried in the same attitude.†

Thus were Pándoba Waidya's sins washed out, though they were black and many.

* Ascetic who has renounced the world. Such persons are buried in a sitting posture and are never burnt.

† His tomb was a handsome structure, 'tis said. It was blown up by the Moguls three hundred years later.

EPILOGUE.

My good old friend rolled up the manuscript reverently; then taking off his turban he prostrated himself three times to the ground. Replacing his head-covering, he addressed me with a pleasant smile:—

"Khodâwand! that is the legend of Dhopèshwur: every sinner of our Konkan castes and many from the Dekkan also repair there, to confess and worship whenever the hot spring bubbles up. Your honour has seen that the springs, of which there are seven, are now contained in cut-stone tanklets that are always full of tepid water. They bubble up hot and steaming, sometimes once annually for years together, sometimes after an interval of two or three years. What miracle is this, Khâwand? Why is the sacred water hot? Why does it rise and subside at uncertain intervals? How can it force its way to the top of a very high hill?"

I could only repeat the theory propounded by Geologists that the fountain-springs act by a syphon from hidden reservoirs in the bowels of some adjacent spur of the Syadri mountains at a higher altitude, wherein volcanic fires still smoulder; and that atmospheric attraction also affect their rise and fall. I reminded him that at the end of the hot season, before a drop of rain has fallen, after a long drought, water begins steadily to rise in wells and tanks hewn out of the laterite stratum of which the South Konkan is mainly composed. With this explanation my old friend departed, by no means satisfied.

o

CHAPTER XX.

THE LEGEND OF VIZIÂDROOG (GHERIÂ), AND THE PHONDA GHAUT

PROLOGUE.

Viziâdroog is one of the first strongholds that Sivaji caused to be built on the coast: it is often called *Ghêriâh* erroneously; the fortress being confounded with the *Ghêriâh* or girdling fortifications. It stands on a low rocky promontory jutting into the ocean in a north-westerly direction, and is separated from the mainland by a narrow neck of sand about 100 yards wide or less. Obviously, this promontory was originally an island. The estuary at the mouth, is about half to three-quarters of a mile wide, formerly navigable by native craft of 70 to 100 tons burthen, as far as the town Khâripâtam (about 22 miles), but now only so navigable as far as Waghotna (7 miles), and that only at high tide. The bar lies well out from headland to headland, and has from 2½ to 4 fathoms at low water neaps and about 5 to 6 fathoms at high-water springs: the soundings right under the fort walls (as one enters) are 3 to 3½ fathoms: the little harbour is practically land-locked, and is thus a fairly safe harbour of refuge from the south-westerly monsoon. About a mile up the south bank there was (and still is) a large dry (or graving) dock with sluice gates complete, in which the largest native craft known in the seventeenth century were careened for repair, and built. A village called 'Göödi' (*i. e.*, the Dock) buried in cocoa palms, lies adjacent under the scarp of an extensive plateau of sheet laterite rock: lagoons and smaller estuaries lie on either side of the creek, which is studded with several "eyots" * of small area. Viziädroog is about 36 miles from the foot of the Phönda Ghaut as the crow flies (about 50 miles by an excellent cart-road), with gradients 1ft. in 25ft. at most, bridged throughout, and passable for field artillery. Three rest-houses lie at the road-side. A small but commodious bungalow was erected in 1876, on the roof of the old powder magazine in the fortress itself, and an immense granary was roofed in: there are also two other habitable rooms on the ramparts. Thus, the fortress (which for many years after British accession held a considerable garrison) could still accommodate 2,000 men with ease, and the little town and Dhoolup's† Palace would hold as many

* The vernacular word for islets in a river is the same as in English. On both sides of the estuary and its branches and lagoons, many "Khâjans" (salt swamps) have been reclaimed by the enterprise of the Khotes. The "surmal" (Indian sturgeon) fishery is important. Large rock oysters, prawns, and crayfish, abound. There is very fair plover, duck and snipe shooting, and the estuaries abound with shoals of large sea-otters which afford capital sport.

† Dhoolup is the hereditary High Admiral of the Marâthas, who is a First-class Sirdar in these days.

more: the old ramparts, which still bear the shot marks of cannon, would take a deal of battering. In a word Viziàdroog would be invaluable as a fort whence troops of all arms could be transported to the Karnatic, should disturbances there unhappily recur; this was actually done during the Great Mutiny in 1857-58. Or, should it please the Almighty to afflict the Southern Maráthа again with famine, as a depôt to which food-stuffs could be easily transported by sea and rapidly conveyed to the *arid zone*, as was successfully accomplished during the great famine of 1876-77. There is already a network of narrow-gauge railway from Kolhapur to all parts of the South Marátha country and Karnatic. It remains only to construct (*i.e.*, prolong) the line to the fortress itself, (about 91 miles, including the Phönda Ghaut, only 15 miles of very easy gradients). The State—Local Fund—Municipal telegraph line crosses the road at Phönda or thereabouts. Thus, the entire new cotton crop of the Bijapur and Belgaum districts and of the Kolhapur and other of its dependent States, might (and would) be railed down, full or half-pressed and ginned, so as to be at the Fort by the beginning of May, reaching the Bombay Cotton Green before the monsoon breaks; or (if too late) being stored in the spacious granary and other store buildings till '*a break*' occurred in the weather—when a steamer could run down in 16 hours, and pick up what was left. Let the *South Marátha and South and West Deccan Railway Company* look to it. Every branch they may make to the coast will pay. There ought to be a branch from Kolhapur to Ratnagiri and its harbour of refuge Miria Bay (*viâ* the Amba Ghaut) besides the Kolhapur-Viziàdroog branch (*viâ* the Phönda Ghaut) above described. In no part of India (or at any rate Western India, with which the author is so well acquainted) is it more clearly proved that "Traffic begets Traffic." Both these Ghauts are short, with easy gradients; there is not one large river to bridge; the metals would be laid for half the distance or more, on sheet laterite rock, and would cost little to maintain; water is plentiful all along the route; excellent stone obtainable at the road-side. The Râjah of Kolhapur, the Chiefs of Miraj, Jutt, Waigaum, Senior and Junior Putwurdhans, the Punt Pratinidi, and the Chief of Inchālkaranji could be easily induced to contribute and would give the necessary lands gratis. Indeed, the existing excellent roads and bridges from end to end on both branches would need very little re-alignment for the railways, and cart-roads running alongside. What more can promoters want? Let the great Company above cited look to it for their share-holders' benefit.

Viziàdroog Fort, it will be remembered, was the Western India station selected by the Royal Astronomical Society for observing the eclipse of 1900. The first illustration (painted for the author by the late Louis Frank in 1877) was published in the St. James' Budget. The second was sketched by the author from the deck of H.M.S. "Clive", when he accompanied Lord Dufferin on a private cruise down the coast in 1887. *

All students of Indian History among our readers will, of course, remember that Viziàdroog was the scene of Clive's first so-called exploit when he was a subaltern in a Madras Infantry Regiment. "So-called," because the fortress, as a matter of fact, was not captured by Lieutenant Clive and Admiral Watson (of the Indian Navy), but capitulated to the Marâthas (who pounded away from a battery on the north head land) while Admiral Watson sent fire-ships up the river which burnt the enemies' fleet, and while Clive landed a force under a head-land to the south, which never came into action. It is a matter of history that Clive and Watson divided between themselves, treasure to the amount of one and a quarter lakhs † left in the Fort. Historians have hinted that this treasure, being prize-money, should have been treated as such. The objection is a little hypercritical. The treasure, obviously, belonged to the Marâthas to whom the Fort garrison capitulated. As they waived their claim in favour of the British Commandants personally, it can scarcely be termed prize-money. The point, however, is of

* *Vide* "Our Viceregal Life in India", by the Marchioness of Dufferin and Ava.

† About £15,000, if sicca rupees; or £12,500, if Company's rupees. (*Vide* Grant-Duff's "History of the Marathas".)

small importance, except to people who love to pick holes in Clive's character, while a memorial is being raised to the hero.

Thus much seems necessary in the way of Prologue.

The old Bhutt produced this legend with a self-satisfied smirk; wrapped in a *roomal* of red, white and blue striped calico; whereat I observed, "*Hullo? Bhutt-ji! why art thou sporting British colours?*" Quoth he quizzically, "*Khodâwund can surely guess why! seeing that these 'slokes' concern a Fort captured by the great Lard Clive when he was a callow youth. This grand feat (as it is now said to have been) was what led to the young Jawan's* subsequent fame. Naturally, the manuscript should be swathed in the colours under which he fought and won India; though he did cheat poor Nuncomar † with a treaty, and hanged him afterwards! Hân Saheb?*" *said he, slyly.*

"*Now, old friend, read away; I'm not going to discuss Lord Clive's action with thee—or anyone else!*

---

* Hero.

† We observe that Mr. Stanley Rice and '*The Times*' spell the name 'Nanda Kumar.' The Hunterianizing of Indian names is as harassing as the 'Bowlderizing' of the Bible and the Classics was 30 years ago. '*The Times*' and other journals who pride themselves on accuracy, yet print 'St Petersburg' for 'Petersburg'; 'Azores' for 'Acores,' might be content with Macaulay's version! it is good enough for us.

so hurry up!" said I, sharply. In great dudgeon the old man complied as follows :—

THE LEGEND.

When this our fair world was in its teens—so to speak—and so soon as our beloved Konkans became habitable after Pureshrâm (Indra) conquered and recovered it from Sri Samudra *; the only inhabitants were Mhârs who had migrated from the Dekkan. Being polygamists they multiplied exceedingly: Aye! tradition even sayeth, and evil-minded men still allege, that they took unto them concubines from the *lāngurs* † who descended the Syadris with them. "*How else is the lowly stature and apish features of some of them to be accounted for?*" contend these malicious men. But these aborigines are, for the most part, well grown, and of brawny build; well featured and high browed, most frugal and industrious. The few Sudras who migrated with them were, if not their slaves, certainly their servants—were employed to raise crops, to fish, and otherwise to work for them. Mhârs thus were the original owners of the red soil of the Konkans.

Ages rolled by before the Bâhmani Râj included the Konkans. The Bâhmani Kings found that two important industries existed in this otherwise unprofitable land, covered (as it then was) with primeval forest

* Neptune.

† Large black-faced ape.

and dense undergrowth, in which all the fierce beasts known to man, bred; yea! even the lordly Siw *, the giant Hatti †, the horned, armour-clad Rhinoceros, and other pachyderms, survivors of Noe's ‡ deluge; where immense pythons fascinated and crushed the hapless deer, and the cunning cobra lurked and hissed at every footstep.

The Kings found many tribes of dwarf black men smelting the purest malleable iron from the laterite iron stone along the '*Payeen Ghaut*' § and mountain spurs and strewn over the '*Ghaut Mhâta*,'‖ for which purpose they cut down fuel wherever they listed, to make '*Kâth*' where with to fuse the metal from its cells in the honeycombed laterite boulders. ¶

To their delight they also found the Mhârs with their S udra servants collecting gold! Gold of the purest—in the sandy bed of rivers as they dried up; gold in nuggets from the cells of quartz and granite seams that run from Mâlwan diagonally to the foot of

* Marátha for lion.

† Elephant.

‡ Noah.

§ Foot-hills.

‖ Mountain plateau.

¶ This industry was prohibited by Sir Richard Temple in 1876, because it wantonly denuded the hill-sides.

the Phonda Ghaut. Clever as the Mhârs are at quarrying laterite rock, their Sudra * servants were even greater experts in working quarries of granite. They drilled holes along the face of a cliff, into which they drove wedges of hard wood previously well steeped in water: then they lit '*shen*' † cakes and charcoal on the surface of sheet rock, or along the cliff face: the heat caused the wedges to swell, thus splitting off great flagstones and slabs as evenly as if they had been dressed by a stone mason. In quartz cells thus exposed, the miners found the precious metal in nuggets—great and small and in minute nodules, which they stored in hollow bamboos, and in crows' quills to be bartered with merchants in the Deccan.

"*The accursed lust for gold*" ‡ urged them on to compel the Mhârs to work night and day in chain gangs under the '*châbuks* § of cruel '*Mukuddums*,' ‖ who scourged them cruelly if they produced less than a certain ordained quantity whether they found it or found it not in the rock. This naturally led to the more fortunate miners being robbed and murdered by less lucky comrades unable to make up their day's tally, and to fierce onslaughts on the *Mukad-dums*, wherein much blood was shed on both sides.

* Labouring castes.

† Cowdung cakes—sun-dried.

‡ "Auri sacra fames"—Virgil.

§ Whips.

‖ Overseers.

The enraged Bâhmani Râjahs thereupon sent down a Subedar of sinister repute, cruel and tyrannical. He doubled the tasks, flogged, starved and maltreated the poor labourers continually; but without effect. They had many tame *langurs*: these they trained to come to the diggings over the trees, and to secret quills full of gold in their pouches. Thereupon the Subedar confined the miners in open spaces—fenced in with 'neorang,' (prickly pear) refusing to let their women visit them. But the Mhârs had already trained their *langurs* to dress up and mimic the *Mukuddums*. Their women now dressed up a huge patriarch of the herd to resemble the Subedar himself. The clever ape, staff in hand, turban on head, actually ambled up to the cruel potentate, spat at him, aiming a heavy blow at his head; whereat the guard set upon and slew that *langur*, casting his carcase to the dogs. This maddened both men and women, but, separated as they were, they could do nought but curse. A few nights after, the men confined in the impenetrable enclosure, heard womens' shrieks in the village: the sentries told them that Subedar was carrying off a young Mhâr maiden to his tent. This was more than could be borne: it was 'the last straw on the camel's back'!

Dissimulating their wrath, they went to work next morn as usual; but at a given signal they overpowered and killed their guards, and then tumultuously surrounded the Subedar's camp, dragged the villain from his tent to the open, to their yelling women, who literally tore him limb from limb; some even drinking of his yet hot blood from their *lotahs.* The remnant of the guard fled. The miners were at last free and left unmolested for many years, the Bâhmani Râjahs fearing to provoke a general rising of the Mhâr nation: they therefore sent some of their Durbar Officers with proffers of pardon and protection, provided the miners would pay an annual tribute of one maund of gold, and send hostages. This the miners agreed to. Peace reigned again; the miners easily paid their tribute, it was not a tithe of what they produced. But they stipulated (1) that one of the leading Sudra Maráthas (who began to be styled Râos about this time) should be Subedar in each pergunnah; (2) that all their minor officials should be nominated in rotation from the same caste; (3) that a certain number of Mhârs should be enrolled as watchmen in each village, with hereditary free lands to remunerate them, and the right to free fuel and shikâr, and power to levy *hukks* (or fees) at the village threshing-floors. Thus was the village *punchyotra* system first partially inaugurated. The Bâhmani Râjahs gladly acquiesced in these demands; being much in need of the troops quartered in the Konkans for other wars in the Karnatic.

There reigned peace, plenty, and security for life and property for some centuries. Then came the Mogul invasion, and innumerable inroads by Pirates,

'Durrya Wâghs' or sea-tigers (as they were called). The Konkans were overrun far and near by men clad in impenetrable armour, carrying deadly thunder and lightning tubes, and long spears. The Mhârs, unarmed, were powerless: the Marâthas or Rãos were as yet too few; the Brâhmins had not as yet spread far from Chiploon. Therefore, was the work of rapine continued till the great Siwaji's revolt against Aurungzebe, Emperor of Delhi. But ere "the great-little-man" had firmly consolidated the Marâtha Empire of his founding, many years were to roll by.

The Moguls, however, had then been for at least two hundred years established paramount at Dâbhol on the sacred Wâshisti, and at Râjapur on the Jaitapur river. Their Viziers naturally strove to make all they could out of the Phönda mines, where diamonds and emeralds had been recently found. They were much kindlier and juster taskmasters than the Bâhmanis; but greatly feared because they forcibly circumcised their conquered subjects, to convert them outwardly to Islam. In this they were greatly aided by certain Mollahs, of whom the chief resided at Dâbhol.

The Moguls worked the mines by day and night (by torch-light), feeding and treating the miners justly; but monopolizing every *chittak* of precious metal extracted. On the whole the Marátha population of the Konkans were tolerably content under Mogul dominion. Occasionally, some brutal subordinate carried off their women to their harems, but unless such miscreants were very influential at Delhi, the Kâzis afforded prompt redress. Meantime, Brâhmins with 'Khoti Sanads,' Moslem nobles and Rāos of the Syadri range similarly endowed, were doing grand work in reclaiming Khâjans and terracing hill-sides. The Moguls would doubtless have constructed aqueducts and extensive irrigation works, as in other parts of Hindustân, but a country with such a heavy and regular rainfall did not, in their Vizier's eyes, need them. What time the Brâhmins completed the *Panchyotras* everywhere, so well commenced by the aboriginal Mhârs. Commerce extended from Bushire to Muscât, from distant Suez to 'Lankha', from Calcutta to China and Japan. The indomitable English gradually drove out the Feringhi Franks, and stolid Dutch; superseded the effeminate Portuguese everywhere, and suppressed piracy. Fate decreed that in all these struggles by sea and land with these European powers the British should encounter Moguls and Marâthas, Sikhs and all the smaller States of the Eastern Punjaub and Scind; whose territories dropped like stricken deer under the paw-strokes of the British Lion. Gradually, but very surely, the chart of Hindustân was painted red.)

But our Muse is anticipating, and must retrace her steps to the sixteenth and seventeenth centuries, wherein the Marâtha nation was born, flourished and decayed never to revive again.

The great Siwaji, having built innumerable strongholds on coast and inland, and possessing a powerful navy, wherewith he was master of the Indian ocean from the Gulf of Kutch to Câthây, appointed one Dhoolup, a Rão of noble birth, who had distinguished himself in many a hard fought naval battle, to be his hereditary High Admiral; granting him numerous villages between Viziâdroog (his newly erected stronghold) in perpetual 'Enâm.' The best of these was 'Phunnusgaum,' about 17 miles from the foot of the Phönda Ghaut. At Phunnusgaum itself, in ravines and dry *nullahs* were the richest veins of gold ore; they extended to the foot of the Phonda Ghaut, whence an auriferous quartz reef passed diagonally south-westward to Malwan. All this gold-bearing region was included in the grant to Dhoolup.

But the High Admiral had not the wealth to exploit his mines; nor had he the leisure in those stirring times when he was constantly at sea, nor when at Viziàdroog, when he was engaged in building his '*Shibáds*' (largest man of war) and 'Gödi.' Moreover, he was by nature excessively lavish and licentious. One by one he mortgaged his 'Enam' villages to Sãokars of Râjapur and Khârépatan. These worthy cormorants at last refused to lend another *Kaori* unless Dhoolup also mortgaged to them his mining rights, wheresoever situated. They already, as 'gâhândârs' (mortgagees) had possession of both Phunnusgaum and Phönda, but the inhabitants refused to mine for gold without

Dhoolup's written order. Dhoolup was compelled at last to submit to the Sāokars's terms on condition of his receiving ten per cent 'Nuzzur' on the annual output.

The 'dustaiwâz' being duly signed they formed a league of eighteen ("What the Saheb calls a 'Shindykut,' Hân Saheb?" asked the old Bhutt. "Well, something like it," I responded). Then the Sāokars imported labour from afar (for the villagers still refused to work for them, notwithstanding Dhoolup's orders). This resulted in daily fights, of course. The Sāokars found that they had made a very bad bargain. Moreover, the mines at Phunnusgaum and Phönda were obviously exhausted, and they could not induce their imported labourers to exploit the quartz reef aforesaid; nor had they any ore-crushing tools or machinery for the purpose, and the people along the line of reef were unmistakably hostile. So they dismissed their men and closed the works.

But the people of Phunnusgaum and Phönda were not the kind of men to let the foreigners depart in peace. These foreigners were Negroes and Arabs, who had not only outraged the Hindu women, emasculated boys, and foully and bestially assaulted them, but had slaughtered and devoured their sacred cattle, and defiled their temples by herding swine, asses, and mules therein, out of sheer wanton brutality.

Accordingly, the word went round that when the foreigners should be assembled at the Dhoolup Wârra (which the Saokars used as their pay office) they were to be surrounded and slaughtered.

On that day there was a horrible butchery. The Negroes, well armed, fought with their usual reckless courage: the Arabs ensconcing themselves behind rocks poured in death-dealing volleys from their *jezails* and matchlocks. No quarter was asked for or given on either side. The trembling Sāokars barricaded themselves in the Mâj-Ghur (inner room) but were dragged out one by one: two were cut down by their own Negroes, infuriated at their cowardice: two were shot by the Arabs to whom they had refused the shelter of the Wârra, which they could have held for weeks successfully: two were hanged on the village 'bāobâb' * tree, and the baggage of the foreigners having been heaped up in the court-yard of the Wârra and fired, two were cast shrieking into the flames. The remaining twelve Sāokars, after being subjected to gross insult and scourged, were spared on condition of their giving up all bonds for debts due by the Dhoolup's villagers (two of their number were sent to fetch these under an armed escort!); they were also compelled to pay down five thousand rupees in cash by way of compensation. The villagers sought in vain for Dhoolup's 'dustaiwaz' (or deed) to destroy it: the

* Adansonia grande.

surviving Sãokars swore, holding a cow's tail, that it was burnt on the bodies of those of their number who had been roasted. This was afterwards proved to be false.

The villagers lost eighty killed, and one hundred and ninety grievously wounded, including several women and boys (who had fought like fiends). Not one of the foreigners remained alive to tell the bloody tale!

Thus ended gold mining in that region.

The massacre is still, and for many a year will be, spoken of with exultation by the villagers. Dhoolup was at sea fighting Ângria at the time. With the 'loot' he then gained, he richly rewarded his faithful tenants, and rebuilt his Wãrra at Phunnusgaum. But he swore by Shri Bhowâni that gold should never be delved for again anywhere on his estate; an empty oath! seeing that there was no gold left that could be extracted, and that his 'Enam' villages were in the possession of his gâhândârs' descendants and survivors, who, ere a year elapsed, foreclosed and bought them in at auction for a twentieth of their value.

When the massacre was reported to Siwaji at Raighur, he exulted greatly, for he detested Sãokars, and invariably punished oppressors of all classes with an iron hand. To mark his approval of the villagers' revenge, he sent rich 'Khilluts' to the Patels of each village, and doubled the 'Dharmaday' cash allowances to the temples of Phunnusgaum and Phäädä. Jey! Siwaji Maharaj! Maharaj Siwaji ki jey!

EPILOGUE.

"*A stirring tale of cupidity, reckless extravagance, aud dire revenge, is it not, Khodáwand* queried my old friend. I nodded assent. He went on musingly :—

"*Khâwund knows that Amrit Rāo, the present Dhoolup, is so impoverished by reason of his ancestors' extravagance, that his family would starve but for money occasionally sent to him by Máhárájáh Scindia, who is a connection of the Dhoolupeen* his wife Thou knowest that the Inam Commissioner— Major Couper Saheb, has found a flaw in his 'Sanads.† (in what 'Sanad' is there not a flaw!): wherefore the Dhoolup 'Jaghirs'‡ and Enâms§ will lapse to the Sirkar after Raghonath Rāō's death, the present Dhoolup's brother who is childless, as is the former up to the present time, though wedded for some years. What 'zoolum'‖ is this? Khâwand? Hath not our gracious Queen proclaimed that she will not let estates lapse for want of an heir male of the body? Why should Major Cowper Saheb's iniquitous 'dirkhust'¶ made before the Proclamation, now hold good, when there is still an heir in the younger brother, Dhoolup?*

---

* Dhoolupeen is the feminine of Dhoolup.

† Title-deeds.

‡ Ditto.

§ Lands and cash held on service tenure.

‖ Oppression.

¶ Decree.

I could only shrug my shoulders in silence, as my old friend resumed :—" *Khodâwand will pardon an ignorant old Bhutt! Thy servant asks again, why does not the generous and wealthy Sirkar undertake the management of the encumbered estates of Marâtha Sirdârs, so as to compromise and settle with their creditors, as it has been done in the case of the 'Grâssias' and Taluqdârs of Guzerâth?*" Again I could only shrug and say, "*Why? Bhutt Ji! echo answers 'Why'? in mockery! God knoweth why?*"

And so we parted for that time.

NOTE BY THE AUTHOR.

The author is able, of his personal knowledge, to bring the history of the Dhoolup family nearly up-to-date: it contains food for serious reflection by the Government of India, and the Right Honorable Lord Morley at this present time of *Unrest in India.*

In the year 1877, when famine was raging in the Dekkan, the author was engaged on the several works described in page 191, and was also pressing and despatching bales of fodder eastward over the various Ghauts. As a young Assistant Collector, he had known Amritrāõ Dhoolup well, a noble Marátha Chief, standing over 6 feet 5 inches in his sandals. He was of blameless life, and apparently much attached to his wife the Dhoolupeen, a buxom, well educated young lady about 20 years of age; Dhoolup being nearly 60. She was, of course, his second or third wife; all of whom died childless. His heir presumptive, therefore, was his younger brother Rugonâth Rāõ, nearly as old as himself, and also childless. As mentioned by my old Bhutt friend, they were in great want; were to a great extent dependent on Scindia's somewhat irregular, and not very large, remittances, and on the generosity of a well-known Chitpâwan Khote a merchant of Khârépattân, and the Prubhu Desai of Nârrâyengaum*, a near neighbour, (both famed for their

* *Vide* chapter "The would-be parricide" in "Reminiscences of an Indian Police Official," by T. C. Arthur.

discriminate benevolence). Some of Dhoolup's old tenantry also used to send him assistance, in the shape of grain and *ghee**, and the villagers of Viziàdroog and Gödi not only supplied him with fish and fuel but kept his Wârra † in repair.

It was very pathetic to hear this old nobleman refer to the past exploits of his family by sea and land. He received my first visit in *durbar* ‡ in his 'Wârra.' It was nearly as painful to me as it must have been to the Hereditary High Admiral of the fallen Marâtha Empire, to receive me in such sorry state. The very carpet on the cow-dunged floor, the very chairs we (he his wife, and I) sat upon, were borrowed from my camp: the only remains of the grandeur of the family were the usual paraphernalia for *pân-supâri* § richly chased silver utensils; priceless to a connoisseur of curios. The garlands, chaplets and posies for my decoration, were provided by the Desai aforesaid; the *âtdâr* ‖ and sandal-wood oil by the Khârèpâttan merchant, both of whom were present; as also were the *Patels* ¶ and *Koolkarnis* * of Viziâdroog and many adjacent villages, and the village magnates of Phunnusgaum

* Clarified butter.

† Palace.

‡ Audience.

§ Betelnut (areca in plantain-leaf, given to guests).

‖ Otto of rose.

¶ Headman.

* * Village Accountant.

and Phönda; all arrayed in their best. The Dhoolupeen wore costly ornaments, lent by the Patels for the occasion, and their wives provided the sweetmeats (sugarcandy, pastry, cardamoms and what-not). The *Hâvildar* * of the police party in the fortress, and the officials from the Custom House, to say nothing of the *Mâmlutdar* † of the *Tâluka*, ‡ his and my own armed sepoys and *Puttiwallahs* § as a guard-of-honour.

The Chief, after the usual compliments, proudly apologized for not providing a nautch for my entertainment. because (as he said) no naikeens were obtainable nearer than Goa (!), whereas of course, we all knew the Chief had not the wherewithal to pay a celebrated troupe then so near as Râjapur (12 miles distant).

With becoming pride he alluded to the past exploits of his ancestors, and told me that with his own eyes—when a child—he had seen the hulk of '*Jân Kumpani Bahâdur's*' ‖ good ship *Ranger* ¶ a few years after his father's pirating her on the 12th of September 1812: (he mentioned, of course, the date of the Samwatsarê or Hindu Calendar). "He had seen the

---

* Corporal.

† Chief Revenue and Magisterial Officer.

‡ A sub-district.

§ Messenger, men with puttas, *i.e.*, belts.

‖ The old East India Company.

¶ *Vide* Grant-Duff's History of the Marâthas.

stout merchantman broken up; some of her *Wânks* * were used in certain *Shibads* belonging to his good friend Rão Bâhâdur Khote Râmbhow seated there. May Ishwar bless him! (Râmbhow rose and salaamed). 'Áre! Áre! Mèhèrbân Saheb, the Sirkar used the best *wânks* procurable on the Sâvitri *Nuddi!* 'Tis a great, a good Sirkar; the Burra Râni's Râj will endure for ever, now that she has done justice to her subjects in the matter of adoption. Thoba! Thoba! His family was unhappily shut out from her bounty by *Captain Cowper Saheb's* † *durkhast.* ‡ *Pun, Ishwar krupâ kare.* (But God will be kind) I politely concurred, expressing a hope that the sun might yet shed beneficent rays on his ancient house. "*Nâheen, Nâheen Mèhèrbân Saheb*" he replied, sighing deeply, "*Tasa kadi gudnár nâheen* §. My brother Rugonâth Rão is in bad health. He and I must soon be buried in the Dhoolup cemetery outside; two more plain tombs; two more wasted lives! And then the great Dhoolup family will be extinct. Thoba! Thoba!" Tears trickled down the cheeks of several of the audience, but the old man sat stern and seemingly unmoved; his fingers playing convulsively with the

* Crooks or bends for the ribs of ships.

† Captain Cowper was Inam Commissioner for enquiring into titles.

‡ Decree.

§ That can never be

hilt of his 'tulwar'*. His prediction was speedily fulfilled; he died some three years later: his brother, Rugonâth Rão, speedily followed him to the cemetery. But, by God's mercy, a son had been intermediately born to the Rani † Dhoolupeen. I had left the District before, and did not revisit Viziàdroog till 1878, when (as Commissioner of the Southern Division) I paid my respects to the widowed lady, of whose most destitute condition I heard sad accounts on all sides. An old Marâtha resident, one Bâboo Kolgay (who acted as a kind of Thos. Cook and Son at the little port to travelling Sahebs) had prepared me to some extent to see penury in Dhoolup's palace, but I was inexpressibly shocked by the reality. The noble young widow received me with much dignity; leading a fine little boy of 4 years of age, clad in a wadded red cotton jacket, and tightly-twisted turban set jauntily on one side, a mimic tin 'tulwar'* in his waistband. The lady herself was clad in a thread-bare blue cotton sari, such as peasants of the poorer classes wear. Her ornaments were glass bangles, a single row of glass beads by way of necklace, and palpably brazen anklets; the whole not being worth a rupee! There was not a stick of furniture in any of the rooms: I perceived two coarse brown '*kumblis*' ‡ in an inner chamber,

* Sword.

† She was dubbed Rani out of respect.

‡ Blankets.

evidently the beds of mother and son. She was much emaciated; haggard with anxiety, her cheeks sunken from want of the ordinary necessaries of life. Yet she maintained a brave demeanour outwardly, repressing the tears that shone in her eloquent eyes. Having introduced her little son, she said, "I grieve, Mèhèrbân Saheb * that I have no 'khoorsi' † to offer your honour unless he will be pleased to sit on the balcony rail (which I did). Your honour seeth to what the Dhoolup's, once so powerful, are reduced. We should long ago have died of starvation but for the bounty of the villagers, who are themselves poor, what with salt tax, rent, house-tax, income-tax, shop and license tax. Ishwar only knows how many more they may be! But Burra ‡ Sahebs must get their *puggâr* § punctually. How could the world get on if Bhôt ‖ burra Commissioners did not draw their '*râjwân*' ¶ salariet month-by-month (this with covert sarcasm), Thoba what matter for a poor widow's poverty?" I could answer never a word. The lady continued calmly. "But it is a good Sirkar, though but a blind Sirkar, so all people say. We live in peace because it is rich and powerful. We are grateful; we see the Sirkar pouring out rupees like water to save lives in this fell famine sent by Shri

* Kind sir!

† Chair.

‡ Grand Sirs.

§ Pay.

‖ Most, very great.

¶ Princely.

Kali, as no former Sirkar ever dreamed of doing. Again, I say, we are grateful. What matter that I, humble Dhoolupeen, am starving with my boy, the heir to nothing, aye! not one *cowrie*, only to a noble name!"

The poor lady's voice broke down at this point, and she covered her still comely countenance with her *Sâri* *; the little man cuddling to her side and looking indignantly at me as if he thought I had brought fresh trouble on his mother.

After a short pause, I asked the Rânî if nothing could be done with her late husband's creditors. Her *Sâri* was hurriedly snâtched from her face, as she replied with flashing, scornful eyes:—

"Creditors! Thoba! Thoba! can one extract blood from a stone? their hearts are as the '*kala karak*' † of the Dekkan!"

I queried "What about the papers and sunnuds of the family and the Sirkar's *durkhast*, Rânî Saheb? Have you them?" The lady replied that she had, and calling to a young Brâhmin who was doing some 'chore' in a further chamber for her (she had no servant), she bade him fetch them from the strong room and which he did. "Thanks, Punditjee," ‡ she

* Shawl or scarf.

† Black rock, *i.e.*, trap.

‡ Mr. Tutor.

said and turning to me, added: "This, Mèhèrbân Saheb, is a good young Chitpâwan, still a student at the Dukshina * College, who generously devotes his '*Sootichè diwase*' † to teaching my little man to read and write for nothing! The Mèhèrbân Saheb may return his humble salaam without injuring his dignity."

"I should think so indeed!" quoth I. "Shake hands, Punditjee! I shall keep mine eyes on thee when thou hast finished thy course at College." The delighted youth salaamed to the ground. The Rani continued, "Thou wilt only waste thy precious time, Mèhèrbân Commissioner Saheb, by reading that roll of papers. The kind Desai of Nârrâyengaum, and Râmbhãõ of Khârèpâttan, have already studied our case in those papers; they say there is nought to be done; that Captain Cowper Saheb's *tarãõs* ‡ are never wrong; that no Government or *Shikitri* § Saheb ever yet dared to alter them. Mèhèrbân Commissioner Saheb is kind and very wise, but, Thoba! even he cannot find a *chook* ‖ in Cowper Saheb's *durkhâst.*" ¶ I said that might be so; nevertheless I would study the case, and consult good lawyers if need be. The Râni thanked me warmly, and we parted for that time.

---

* Dukshina was an old Marâtha Educational Cess, from which the Deccan College was maintained.

† Holidays, vacation.

‡ Decisions.

§ Secretary.

‖ Flaw, error.

¶ Decree.

I went through the documents very carefully with my friend and Assistant the late Nâna Saheb Sâthè. Instantly on his reading them out we both exclaimed simultaneously "Cowper Saheb has made a cruel blunder. The rules sanctioned for the Inam Commission declare that in such cases as this Jâghirs are to continue for two lives; whereas he limited it to one; the life of Raghunâth Rão deceased! They cannot even have read the documents in the Secretariat!" Impressing on Nâna Sâthè to treat the matter confidentially, I drew up a careful prècis, which Sâthè copied. I proved that the little Dhoolup was clearly entitled, under the Government's own rules, to succeed to the Jâghir, and to receive the 'mesne' cash allowances in arrears, with compound interest from the date of Rugonâth Rão Dhoolup's demise.

The Government of Sir James Fergusson (the Hon'ble J.B. Peile being Chief Secretary, afterwards Sir J. B. P. and Member of the Council of India) could not deny—did not by any means desire to deny—the justice of the claim, as I put it before them.

To make a long story short, I had the great pleasure of re-visiting the Râni Dhoolupeen three weeks later, to announce the joyful news. Needless to say, she was overwhelmed. The accumulations (amounting to some Rs. 7,000) were invested in the Savings Bank in the young Chief's name; a good tutor (his friendly young

Pundit was reading in Bombay for his degree of B. A.) was engaged for him, till he should be old enough to attend the Ratnagiri High School. The Dhoolup income, from zero became more tham Rs. 3,000 per annum. At my last visit to Ratnagiri in 1886, I found the Râni happily installed in the house of a leading Marátha resident, and saw the young Chief who had grown a fine young fellow and doing well at the High School.

I advised his mother to save, so that he might complete his education at the Râj Kumâr College at Râjkot*, and to ask H. H. the Maharajah Scindia, afterwards, to provide for the lad in his 'Rissâla.'† I hope soon to hear that the still young man is a 'Rissaldar Major' at least at Gwalior.

Moral.

The Powers that be in India and at the India Office may learn many valuable lessons from this " Ower true tale ", which I defy the most hostile Secretary of the Bombay Government to pick a hole in. *Imprimis.* There may be many Cowpers always to be found in our Anglo-Indian Bureaucracy : conscientious, laborious, but narrow-minded men, possessing about as much sentiment as a turnip, obstinate as a mule : such a man is a valuable servant of the State if he be in a position

---

* College for Nobles, established by Colonel Keatinge, Political Agent for Kâthiawâr.

† Cavalry.

where he is subordinated to men of larger minds, untrammelled by red tape, who do not regard the gaining of a rupee for the Sirkar's treasury as the "be-all and end-all" of every question and case submitted to them. Men, in short, who do their own work with a scrupulous regard to justice for both the State and petitioner, who read their papers, draft the G. Rs.* thereon themselves, and not believing that Cowper Sahebs are infallible, will not adopt Cowper Saheb's views without minute scrutiny.

There are many most excellent Governors who stolidly refuse to reopen a case that has been decided by their predecessors. *Non possumus* is their motto, and they piously stick to it. You see, readers mine, it saves a vast deal of trouble: what can this new evidence be worth? obviously nothing! What can Mr. Commissioner A. C. or B. D. know about it better than Cowper Saheb, or His (late) Excellency Governor Pordage, † G.C.S.I., etc., etc.? who was such a painstaking "*prancing pro Consul,*" ‡ who never (hardly ever!) was a puppet in the hands of his Secretariat, presided over by Secretaries whose objects in life were first, to draw their pay regularly, (*cela vá sans dire*): second, to earn it by systematically snubbing in

* Government Resolutions.

† *Vide* "The Treasure Island" by Charles Reade.

‡ Sir W. Vernon Harcourt's term for Indian governors.

offensive G. Rs., officials much their senior, and of twice their experience and sagacity.

I need not mention names: let my readers take any old Civil Service Calendars, and pick these well-known prize Secretaries, as Tom Thumb picked the plums out of his private pudding: lo! they are all (dead or living) recorded as K.C.S.Is., or (or if less pushing than they might have been) as mere Companions of these Most Noble Orders, who are as plentiful as the proverbial blackberry, wherever ye roam.

For many years (52 to be accurate), I have strenuously advocated officially, in the press, in my books, that the Government should establish an Encumbered Estates Courts (on the Irish model) for the relief of the landed gentry of Máhârâshtra, whether Hindu or Moslem, who are "*accablès des dettes de ses ancestres*" * I have been privileged to rescue more than one Noble † from his ignoble position of subjugation to Sãõkars by the enlightened policy of my Rugby School friend, the late Sir James Fergusson and Sir Richard Temple (another old Rugbean): but beyond these isolated instances, I have unfortunately been able to effect nothing. "Why?"—I ask again and again,

* Overwhelmed by ancestors' debts.

† *Vide* the case of the Pir Zadeh of Shahpur (Bijapur) in "Our Troubles in Poona and the Deccan" (by Arthur Crawford C.M.G. 1897).

as did my old Bhutt friend, "why should not the same State assistance be given to these unfortunates as was accorded to the "*Grassias* * and *Taluqdârs* † of Guzrâth, and has been accorded for thirty years past to the Ryots of the Deccan ?"

Was ever time more suitable than this, when the native mind is disturbed ?

I defy pessimists to show that in the long run such relief would cost the State one rupee. The result in popularizing British Rule will be worth "A king's ransom!"

With deep humility and becoming respect I submit these views to the Right Hon'ble Lord Morley and his Council. With no respect at all I call upon Mr. "Dinna-Keir-Hardie," † M.P., to do some good in this direction, that he may mitigate the mischief which his "*criminal utterances*" (I quote the *Times*) have just produced in East Bengal.

---

* & † Superior hereditary landowners on feudal tenure.

† The nick-name given Mr. Keir Hardie when he first distinguished himself (?) in the House of Commons.

CHAPTER XXI.

THE LEGEND OF SINDI-DROOG.

PROLOGUE.

Sindi-droog was the last stronghold that Siwaji built between Bombay and Goa to defend the coast. It has special interest for the student of Marátha history because it was planned by the great-little-man himself: he is known to have visited it several times while building, and to have personally superintended the masons on several occasions.

Tradition has it that the fortress was to have been called Sivaji-droog; (probably that was the original name); but that Siwaji preferred to name it the 'Siw' (or 'Singh') droog which in time became corrupted to Sindi-droog.*

It occupies the whole of an isolated, more or less, flat rock island situated only a few cables-lengths from a sandy bay curving southward to Vengorlè, and is even nearer to a group of lofty needle rocks of granite that jut out about a mile, leaving a small basin of very deep water between their projecting horns; the channel's westerly entrance to this land-locked cup is barely 50 yards wide: the curve of the basin ends in a sandy sloping beach with 3 fathoms of water at low water neaps: behind it, between the coast and the rocky (laterite) ridge peculiar to the Konkans, lies the populous town Mâlwan, protected as to the north by a small

* 'Droog' is sanscrit for fortress or stronghold fortified, and "Siw" or "Singh" is lion.

fortress in its midst. The sea approach from the north is further protected by the Shirè fortress built on an isolated flat rock about 4 miles from the town and 3 miles from the sandy shore east of the islet. Add to this that the coast is from that point studded north and south with sharp rocks projecting from the water, or awash at low tide; we, moderners, have therefore just grounds for pronouncing the fortifying of the Sindi-droog rock as an absolute waste of time and labour, we don't say of money, because the workmen were not paid money; theirs was mostly forced labour; but they were well fed and well treated; Siwaji being a most humane potentate, even on the battle field.

The little port of Mâlwan was of great importance to Siwaji, as the outlet of trade from the Southern Marátha country by way of the Ram Ghaut; Kolhapur lying about 80 miles due east, and Belgaum about the same distance, 75 miles southward of Kolhapur.

Moreover, Siwaji was specially attached to Mâlwan because that district supplied him with some of his best infantry; the sturdy and indomitable *Málwańis*, who were as reliable in battle as his famous *Máwalis** and *Hèdkaris*†, so highly extolled by all historians.

---

* The Mâwalis (also called the Ghâttis) are the Maráthas of the Mâwals or Ghaut plateaux.

† Hèdkaris came from far away down the coast; 'Hed' meaning 'down south'. Some historians insist erroneously that they were the real aborigines of the Konkan; others confound them with Helkars or porters from 'Hel' a load, and 'kane' to do or carry

INTERLOCUTORY.

With beaming countenance my old friend at our next seance produced and flattened out a musty roll of documents observing, "*Thy servant rejoiceth to have done for the nonce with battle, murder, and sudden death; with lust, cupidity and crimes therewith connected. This is in truth a triumphal march of events as it were, wherein the real Siwaji figures, successively as Politician, Architect and Engineer, Poet, Priest and King, and lastly as a demi-God. Each page of these 'sloks'* teems with gallant processions, or tells of tournaments and festivals, wherein the poor shared with the rich golden ornaments, the clas of arms and armour and shields in mimic warfare, the flaunting of thousands of proud pennants, and night and day the blare of trumpets and the clamour of kettle drums. Treachery, of course, there is, where is it not, Khodâ, wand?*"

Quoth I, "*All this sounds very promising, Bhuttji let's hear it.*"

---

* Verses.

THE LEGEND.

The great Siwaji was at the zenith of his power. He had carved out kingdoms for all his relatives, however distant they might be; for his favourite Generals, aye! even for most of his most renowned '*Mânkurs*'*. Scindia was firmly seated on the throne of Gwalior; the warrior Dhungar of '*Hohl*'† reclined with ruder grace on the Indore '*musnud*'‡; the Guzerâthi Herd § graced the ivory chair at Baroda. These were his principal Generals. A cousin Bhonslay, was regally installed at Nâgpur, nothing loth to reign henceforth in ignoble sloth and luxury. Another and nearer cousin, the best of all the Bhonslays, ruled wisely and well at Kolhapur over all Máhárâshtra south of the sacred Kristna, to the great content of the country. He, Siwaji himself, the head of all the Bhonslays, was titular Râjah of Satâra, but rarely resided there, preferring the solitary state of his fastness Raighur, whence—a veritable '*Mountain Rat*'|| (as Emperor Aurungzebe contemptuously styled him!)—he had sallied forth to pull the Mogul Empire to pieces, as a scribe pulleth from the packet of paper beside him sheet after sheet as he requireth them; as doth a rat nibble his way into a sack of corn and scatter the golden

* Great or powerful followers.

† Holkar.

‡ Cushions of royalty (*id est*, throne).

§ The Guicowâr, from 'Gay' a cow.

|| Thus did the Emperor call Siwaji when the latter began his raids.

grain to his followers of all castes and creeds, except the proud Râjput Princes, who ever held aloof from him whom they regarded as a low born adventurer. Every King and Kingling south of the Tungbuddra river was his tributary vassal. But he had yet to crush that mushroom Âdilshâhi Dynasty* of Bijapur and the powerful Nizâm still further east by Golconda glittering with gems (hereafter to be called Hyderabad) and away in the far north-west those pestilent Pathâns must be cajoled, for they supplied him with splendid fighting material. As for those scurvy Bengâlis, they were scarce worthy food for powder: at any spare moment, when nothing nearer troubled him, he could over-run their fertile country, and sack Calcutta as he had twice sacked Sûrat of rich spoil, but (his little eyes glistened with greed) not so rich as that to be gathered in that great city at the mouths of '*Mâh Gunga*' † and the sacred Brâhmaputra!

Thus communed the great-little-man in secret conclave with his favourite Mânkurs at Raighur during the Dussora festival of 1822. Ghorepurè, Shirkè, Phultunkur, the Pratinidi, his hereditary Commander-in-Chief; all counselled present rest, wherein the Marâtha Empire should consolidate, and agriculture be

* The Âdilshâhi Viziers at the and of the 16th century began gradually to secede and rebel from the Delhi Empire. (*Vide* Bijapur chapter in "Our troubles in Poona and the Deccan" by A. Crawford, C.M.G.)

† Mother Ganges.

generally fostered : those '*gharib ryots*'* ! they had behaved right loyally, been very patient, and suffered grievously. "*After all,*" urged Ghorepurè and Shirkè together, "*they are the back-bone of your Majesty's Raj! What could even our Máhárájah Siwaji do, were the ryots to rebel? Thoba! Thoba!*"—"*Ye be right! Mánhurs mine! we will e'en draw back within the impenetrable shell wherewith we have covered ourselves as doth the mud turtle : we will feed on the fat of the land till Shri Bhowáni tells us a propitious hour has come to protrude our snake-like heads and lick up those Bijapur beetles as 'Ghorepurès'† lick up flies! Han? mèrè bhai!*" quoth Siwaji slapping Ghorepure‡ on the back till he coughed again!

"*And to think,*" resumed Siwaji, "*that but a few years agone I, the 'Mountain rat', was actually caged like a rat at Delhi and escaped by the aid of my Mánkurs, being let down over the wall like a rat in a cage! Arè! mèrè Bhai log! Shri Bhowáni ever watches faithful worshippers.*"

"*Jey! Shri Bhowáni Máhá Dèvi ki jey!*" chorussed the assemblage.

---

* Poor peasantry.

† & ‡ This chief gained the surname of Ghorepurè from his having scaled the walls of a fort by means of Ghorepurays (huge ichneumons or lizards, which possess marvellous tenacity and prehensile power in their claws). The sepoys held on to the reptiles' tails as the latter crawled up!

"*Tomorrow night*," resumed Siwaji, "there is to be our *Durbar*,* when the *Surat* '*loot*'† is to be apportioned among ye, Mânkurs mine! Next day the 'Dussora' sacrificial ceremonies and our farewell to my beloved Soyerbai and that little '*budmash*' boy of mine. Then we must set out in state, visit Satâra for a while, and see with our own eyes that our 'Naib Subhedar' be not slothful, but just in his government. And then, mèrè Bhai log, to reside at Kolhapur a week or two with my royal and well-beloved cousin Bhonslay, who beareth my name. And so to inaugurate our newest fortress at Mâlwan, see the humble homes of my faithful Mâlwanis and reward them. Thither will come Sâwânurkar, our excellent and latest Mogul vassal. There shall we ascertain on the spot what truth there be in the tales told of our distant cousin the Bhonslay Sawant of Soonder-Wârri. We fear there be much foundation for his peoples' discontent! Thither is to come, as ye know, the Vakils of the Feringhis of Gōā! Ha! mèrè bhai log! we have an old bone to pick with those dogs some day‡! I fear them not; an effete and worn out race. But those Feringhi Angreez! we like them not: there be evil

* *Vide* Legend of Raighur.

* Spoil.

† A rogue (this in a jest): the son was Sumbhâji, Siwaji's *reputed* son, who brought the Empire to grief.

‡ For forcible conversions of Hindus to Christianity torture by the Inquisition, outrage of women, and general cruelty.

prophesies anent them! We must watch them closely and cajole them. Hân? Mânkurs mine! be we of one mind? Hoe?* then to sleep!

With that the secret Durbar broke up; slaves lit torches without, and each Chief betook himself pondering to his pallet of skins in his own poor hut.

This programme was carried out exactly. At daybreak of the third day after the Dussora, Siwaji and his Mânkurs aforesaid, took farewell of Soyerbai and her prime minister Annaji Dutto. They bent their way under Torna passing over the Bhore Ghaut. Three easy marches brought them by way of the sacred town Wai to Satâra, where Siwaji convened the Punt Pradhan,† and explained to them his programme for the year as aforesaid.

The Punt Pratinidi, as Hereditary Commander-in-Chief, was left as President of the Council. The Punt Âmât, being Siwaji's High Almoner and Steward of the Household, alone of the Pradhâns accompanied Siwaji on his triumphal progress southward. During the month of the Court's stay at Satára great

* Yes.

† The Pradhân or Council of State consisted of five Sirdars or Chiefs of the highest rank.

preparations were made. Elephants, camels, and mules were collected by thousands. Three several Brinjari tribes brought their pack bullocks to the number of 15,000. Troups of nautch girls, musicians, mummers and acrobats were, of course, among the camp followers. The camp below the fort contained not less than 150,000 souls, of whom 10,000 were splendidly mounted cavalry. Meantime, several of the Chiefs around had joined the camp; each with his own retinue. Phultunkur, Duflèkar (of Juth), Sânglikar, the Bhôre Chief's eldest son, and the Waigowkar. This gorgeous cavalcade marched by easy ten-mile stages to Kolhapur; for the difficulty in procuring forage was alone serious; would have been insurmountable had not the crops been still standing. Siwaji imperatively ordered that each evening the damage done should be assessed by a local *Punchayat*;* and the cash was immediately paid into each claimant's hands by the Punt Âmât's treasurers, so that the ryots blessed the magic name of Siwaji Máhárâj.

Betwixt Satára and the sacred *Kristna nuddi*,† Siwaji summoned the heads of certain '*Oochlia*'‡ tribes who infest that region. They came, not in fear and trembling as the Courtiers expected, but full of

---

* Committee or jury.

† Krishna river.

‡ From 'oochalne' to lift: thieves and pickpockets.

impudent confidence. Siwaji severely rebuked them for their persistent dishonesty. Replied an old grey-beard in his hundredth year, "Máhárāj '*gharib pur-wur,** ' do we not also worship Shri Bhowâni? 'Tis our daily '*bhâkâr* †' to thieve: 'tis our '*waton,* ‡' inherited from our ancestors from time immemorial: would'st have thy slaves starve?" "Nay!" graciously replied Siwaji, "but ye should confine your exploits to rich travellers, not prey upon your neighbours, carry off their cattle, sheep, and goats, or break into their houses in company with those cursed 'Beldârs § '!' After consulting with the '*Desmukhs, Desais, and Patels*' || gathered around, the Máhárájah continued, "Behold our good Sword Bhowâni; we swear on it that if we again hear that ye have 'looted' a neighbour, be it but of a kid, we will burn your village to the ground and hang your headmen. Look ye to it! Hearken! we have arranged with the Deshmukhs, Desais, and Patels that certain lands shall be set apart adjoining your villages, which ye shall hold as rent-free Enâms hereditarily so long as good reports of ye reacheth our Council of Pradhâns. We have spoken! Depart in peace!" Needless to say that the '*Oochlias*' hastened away joyfully from the dread presence to

* Of the poor protector.
† Unleavened bread.
‡ Hareditary service lands or cash.
§ Stone masons.
|| District officers and Headmen of villages.

convey the joyful news to their villages. They have faithfully abided by Shiwaji's order from that time.

The Râja of Kolhapur met his royal cousin on the south bank of the Krishna *nuddi* in great state. The sacred *nuddi* was in flood from heavy late rains; four days and nights were passed before the enormous host had crossed. Siwaji himself was ferried over on a raft of bamboos resting on inverted '*chatties*.'* Then the princely cortege hastened on to Kolhapur, where ten days glided pleasantly in feasting, tournaments and sacrifices to the Gods. Meantime, all the Chiefs and Sirdars feudatory to Kolhapur, flocked in to present their *nuzzurs*† to the Mâhârâjah Siwaji; the Patwardhan the Mirajkar, Manglèkar, Inchalkarinjikar, and the Killadar of Pânalla. This added several hundreds more to the procession down the Râm Ghaut. The vanguard reached each camp before the rear guard had left the last camp. For 500 yards on either side of the track the crops were swept off by the feet of the beasts of burthen as clean as the hair on a man's chin is shaven by a barber. Sending on the main body of his followers to Mâlwan, Siwaji and his Mânkurs branched off at the foot of the pass and paid a brief visit to his distant relatives, the Bhonslay Sâwants of Soonder-Wârri; very stern was he with Khem Sâwant and his brother, who

* Large earthen or metal water-pots.

†Symbol of fealty—always touched and returned.

angered his Majesty not a little by their turbulent attitude and insolent speech. They were commanded to join the camp at Mâlwan forthwith, and to report themselves daily to Ghorepurây till further orders. A pleasant ride of 25 miles brought Siwaji to his camp within the Málwan fort. The great conqueror of Máhárâshtra, however, stopped once to receive the *nuzzur* of the Patel of a village where there be an eyes-enchanting natural lake, wherefrom the ryots irrigate many thousand '*bighas*' * of rice land, and to inspect the extensive teak forest planted around it by Mânaji Ângria. The Sâwant brothers followed sulkily in the rear, evidently guarded by Mânkurs: they muttered moodily to each other, wondering what the Máhárájah had really heard of their latest misdeeds at Purangur. They were soon to know: arrived at camp, Siwaji at once summoned them to his presence, refused their *nuzzurs*, and thus sternly accosted them: "Degenerate kinsmen! Because ye are Bhonslays, think ye that ye can outrage my people with impunity? We have heard of the crime that ye did attempt at the Phuakè's and Burvès double betrothal! Our sentence is that ye be suspended from your Jaghir and Enâms for twelve months from this day. My faithful '*Killadar*,' † will administer Soonder-Wârri. If ye be wise, travel, make pilgrimages

* About ⅝ of an acre.

† Fort Commandant.

to Punderpur, Nassik, and Benâres. Ask the Gods to pardon your crimes. Wash at 'Oonowri,' prostrate your sinful foreheads at Dhopèshwar, so shall be cleansed your foul stains of blood and lust! But! an' if ye repent not and we hear more of ye in outrages!" (His Majesty's eyes flashed with fire) "On your heads be it! By our good sword 'Bhowâni' we will hang ye at your own threshold! We have spoken!"

Arose the shout "Jey! Siwaji Máhârája! Máhârâj Siwaji ki jey"!

Having performed his ablutions piously, and partaken of a frugal meal with the Mânkurs, Ghorepurè and Shirkè, His Majesty discussed the programme for the weeks before him. First there was his royal cousin of Kolhpur to be received in special Durbar; next the Chief of Sâvânur and other petty Sirdars were to be introduced, and '*Killats*' * presented to them; then the omens must be consulted by the Joshis. Suddenly, during the discussion the booming of cannon came from the South. "Ha"! cried Ghorepurè, "methinks the Envoy from Gōā approacheth. Máhárâjah mine!" "Be it so! See that he be received with the honors due to a nephew of the great Albuquerque," said Siwaji; "such be the Envoy's name the Punt Pradhân write us." "On our eyes be it, Máhârâjah!" responded the Mânkurs and the Punt Âmât. "We have

* Dresses of honor with other presents.

staked out his camp beside that of Sâvânur, where he can foul his own nest as it seemeth good to him. But let him beware of offending Sâvânurkar's Arabs!" "Ye have well done," quoth Siwaji, "the swine can be wanton with their Naikeens far from our ken!"

Next morn the Mânkurs—headed by the Punt Âmât received the Portuguese deputation at the landing place, when they were saluted by 21 guns from Siwaji's silver battery, and courteously conducted to the presence; Siwaji advancing to the border of the golden carpet, received a profound salute from the Capitano. Then Siwaji led him to the seat of honor at his right hand, and the usual ceremony of '*Pân and Attâr*'* being performed in solemn silence, the Máhárájah accosted Capitano Albuquerque as follows:—"We are grateful to the King of Portugal and the Âlgârves for deputing to Us a Capitano so renowned for gallantry in naval warfare. What is't His Most Faithful Majesty has instructed thee, oh, noble Capitano! to communicate to Us?" queried the Máhárájah, fixing his keen eyes on the envoy. "May it please the great Siwaji, it is simply to ask thy gracious permission to cross the frontier with armed men, so that we may chastise the Sâwant Chief of Soonder-Wârri who hath insulted the Royal Flag of Brâgânza," was the dauntless reply of the Capitano.

* Offering of betel-leaf and oil of roses.

"Ha!" muttered Siwaji, scowling at the brothers Sawânt; "Here be more of thy villany, Khem Sâwant!" Then to the Envoy: "Tell thy Royal Master to send '*Vakils*'* with proofs of any misdeeds of our vassal and kinsmen. But let not a single sepoy set foot over the frontier; 'tis for Us to punish our vassals and kinsmen" At this, a certain half-caste Lieutenant standing behind the Envoy, interrupted insolently, and stepped forward, his hand grasping the hilt of a broad-sword. Instantly, the Máhárájah arose in wrath: "Away with the ill-mannered knave, who dareth to interrupt our Durbar, oh, Capitano! An 'twere not that he is protected by a flag of truce our own hands would smite him down!" the Máhárájah cried. The man was removed. Continued the great Siwaji, "Let not that miscreant again land, oh Capitano, an' he would keep his head on his shouldiers! And thou! we pray thee to betake thyself and suite to the camp prepared. Send thy *Vakils** with such proofs as ye have of our caitiff Sirdar's wrong-doings: we will consider the same; thou shalt have justice from Siwaji Maharaj; we shall not meet again oh! Capitano! We ourselves are called on affairs of State to the city of the *Adilshâhis* †, but my faithful Killadar of Belgaum will, in due course, avenge at the very gates of Gōā the many foul wrongs our subjects have endured at the hands of thy Sirkar. We

* Lawyers.

† The Adilshâhi dynasty of Moguls who set up a kingdom of their own in defiance of the Mogul Emperor at Bijapoor.

have spoken! Depart on the morrow in peace for this time." The Deputation departed in silence to their camp, whence at early dawn came messengers to report that a serious tumult had occurred 'twixt the Sâvânarkur's people and the Goanese. It seemed that so great was the din in the formers' camp that the Capitano went in person to request the Chief to command quiet. He was challenged by the guards, disarmed and dragged before the Chief—seated at that late hour of midnight in Durbar with his followers. Hast ever seen an Arab camp at night? Oh, reader mine! Verily it be a strange sight to see, and fearsome withal. A ring of watch fires surroundeth the rude encampment; at every fire two '*Jewans*' * with matchlocks and fuses burning: and on a sentry rising, yells, *Hooshyâr hay* †? "Yâkub Khân!" "Hooshyâr hon ‡!" yells the sentry at next watch-fire. "Apna Jezeel teeyâr hai §?" roars the first man. "Han! teeyar hai!"‖ then—bang! bang! go both their matchlocks in the air! and then the challenge passeth similarly round the camp. In the centre thereof is the Durbar tent of the Commandant; brass swivel guns ranged irregularly about: the weary chief must so sit on his kinkob cushions till it pleaseth his uncouth warriors to

* Warriors.

† Are ye alert?

‡ I am alert.

§ Is thy matchlock ready?

‖ It is ready.

retire. They crowd the tent to overflowing; Rohillas of mighty stature—armed with spear, sword and targe: swarthy Negroes—clad in leopard skins with a bundle of broad-bladed cut-and-thrust spears, '*Asseghais*'—the ruffians call them: wiry Arabs with short, razor-edged scimitars at their sides, leaning on silver-wire bound matchlocks of small bore, eight feet long: all smoking '*tumbako*' * of the strongest; all gesticulating, quarrelling or embracing, or singing obscene songs. Thou could'st cut the foul atmosphere with thy knife, reader mine, so thick is it. The clash of arms and shields, the bray of brazen trumpets, the beating of huge kettle-drums and piping of shrill shawms, ever and anon mingled with the wild challenges of the ring of sentries is maddening. And this the swine call taking a rest!

But to my tale. The Commandant had no power nor desire to quiet his 'Jewâns'; whereupon the Capitano and his guard strove to return to their own tents, were jostled, spat open, gave back blows and returned with many wounded within the line of their own sentries, when Siwaji's night patrol separated the combatants with difficulty. At daybreak the '*Cristaos*' † betook themselves to their ships: the Capitano refusing to give or return salute and vowing by his Sovereign and

* Native coarse tobacco.

† Christians.

Virgin Lady to be avenged for these gross insults to his King and to himself the Royal Envoy. Little recked the Máhárájah ! be sure !

That day the great cannon already loaded on platform boats, were hoisted into position on the ramparts, where the great Siwaji inspected them (101 in all) with greatest satisfaction, and resting his right hand heavily on some still soft mortar, left a deep imprint of his royal hand which can be seen to this day.*

On the morn following, the Máhárájah and all his suite were rowed from Mâlwan to the great spiked water gate of the fortress in gilded barges, and Siwaji landing —was decked with garlands. He then proclaimed in his clear tones that Sindi-droog was ready for all foes and dedicated to Shri Bhowâni. The usual shouts of applause rent the air; and then, oh readers mine ! one after the other the huge cannon belched forth their flames of welcome in a Royal salute. Many animals such as kids, rams and cocks were sacrificed to the Goddess; the Joshis, examining the entrails, pronounced the omens to be all most auspicious; and then the Máhárájah betook himself to his tent to fast and pray till dawn.

For why ? Hearken ! my '*Chelis*' ! †

---

* It is shewn to this day.

† Disciples.

The Conqueror of Máhárástra a simple, even a humble, votary of Shri Bhowâni, was next day to inaugurate his own effigy in a splendid temple erected within the fortress ! he was thenceforward to be worshipped as a God, as Shri Siwaji !

The Máhárájah was himself most unwilling, but all the Joshis, Bhutts, and Bâwas declared that the omens were unanimous, and that Shri Bhowâni herself had ordained this great honor to her most powerful protector. Siwaji sighed deeply, but must fain consent. Accordingly, on the morrow a great procession led by nautch girls and music escorted the Máhárájah to the confines of the temple (all bedizened with flags of saffron, red, white, and blue hues) : there, a huge bull buffalo was sacrificed after being beaten to a jelly by Bhundaris' clubs. The priests pounced upon the smoking quivering entrails directly the beast had been disembowelled. They rose, smearing their bodies with the hot blood and anointed the Máhárájah therewith also, shouting 'Jey ! Shri Siwaji Máháráj—Shri Deo Siwaji ki jey !' for the slimy coils they vowed by Shri Bhowâni, were plainer in omens than ever ! Siwaji, again sighing deeply, mounted the '*chowthara*'* and seated himself under a canopy of purple silk beside his effigy. And all the people with renewed shouts prostrated themselves bareheaded, and worshipped him as a demi-god incarnate !

* Plinth.

Siwaji again sighed ; he presaged evil, despite the favourable omens : he betook himself shuddering to his tent and denied all visitors, even his trusty Ghorepuray and Mânkurs. And he was right, as his history hath related.

EPILOGUE.

"This, Khodâwund, is the last of thy servant's collection of Konkani *Pothis*" quoth the old Bhutt with a satisfied smile. "And it is the last I shall hear from thee, Bhuttjee! for many a day, for I must betake me to Belgaum in a few days to take charge of the responsible post of Commissioner of the Southern Division conferred on me by His Excellency Sir Richard Temple," replied I; "but thou wilt write to me, old friend, and if peradventure I revisit Chiploon, thou must read me thy *Pothis* of the Deccan."

We parted affectionately, the good old man calling down blessing upon me from all his Gods. I never saw him again; so my readers will not again be bored by his senile prattle. The Legends of the Deccan (if ever finished) which will form a fitting sequel, were picked up here and there in my peregrinations about the Syadris during the next eleven years, from other Bhutts and Sirdars of the Deccan and Karnatic.

CONCLUDING NOTES.

The worship of Shri Siwaji Máháráj continues to this day at Sindi-droog. The Rájah Bhonslays of Kolhapur annually visit the fortress for the purpose. The shrine is richly endowed. On the anniversary of Siwaji's canonization a solid gold mask is fitted on his effigy; a silver one at other times. These were given by Rájárám Bhonslay who died at Florence (I think, early in the 'Nineties').

My readers unread in Hindu religious customs may deem it strange, even improbable, that Hindus who worship horned cattle, or (at least) hold them to be sacred, should sacrifice buffaloes; but it is so, and, until quite recently, the poor beasts were literally beaten to death (to a jelly in fact) with clubs before their throats were cut at certain festivals. Stranger it is that high caste Brâhmins should dabble in the bloody, smoking entrails of the yet quivering victim, eagerly turning them over to seek omens! But this also is so. My good friend the last '*Diwánji*' * of Ângria's Kolâba was much addicted to this sanguinary form of religious ceremonial. He spent large sums on such occasions in doles to priests, and on dinners to multitudes of Brâhmins. He it was who gave Rs. 22,000 to me for the head-works of the Royal Albert Water-works of Âlibâgh on the occasion of His Royal Highness the Prince of Wales' (now King Edward VII) visit to Bombay in 1876.

---

* Minister.

In other respects the Diwânji was most humane to man and beast; so grotesque and distorted do become the intellects of even high born and highly educated Hindus when clouded by superstition!

True Tales of the Konkan.

CHAPTER XXII.

"MY COUSIN THE CONVICT."

In the year of Our Lord 1862, I was Senior Assistant Judge for the detached Station of Ratnagiri on the Malabar Coast, (about 130 miles) south of Bombay. I was also *ex-officio* Superintendent of the gaol (it was before such officials were provided); I was also Sheriff, required to preside at executions! A queer *olla podrida* indeed!

The gaol had been over-crowded till the beginning of that year (it held 350 males and 40 females); but we were then, happily, to be spared future drafts of Chinese, Malay, and Papuan convicts from the British Straits Settlements, desperate ruffians (mostly pirates), under life sentences for piracy, or dacoity with murder.

During that year, however, the great "Share Mania" set in at Bombay, produced by the American Civil War, so enhancing the price of cotton (the then chief Bombay staple of export) that silver poured into Western India like water, at the rate of two and three millions worth of ingots every month, far faster than the Mint could coin it. Speculation ran stark mad. I question whether John Law's South Sea Island schemes were more rabid and insane. To Bombay city, therefore, flocked every rogue and ruffian from the interior, as to an "Eldorado"—some few of these gentry succeeded, became millionaires and, perforce, honest—men. The majority, of course, fell from bad to worse, and were "run in" by the Police again and again, so the City's Prisons (three in number) were so overcrowded that malignant fevers began to rage, and sporadic cholera killed the convicts off like flies, and still the cry was "They come!"

His Excellency, Sir Bartle Frere (God rest his noble soul!) was Governor, and prepared always for any emergency. He passed an Act, through all its stages, at one sitting of his Legislative Council empowering him to transfer convicts to the great central gaol at Tânnah, 20 miles distant, or to any other prison, should need arise.

It did arise; one fine morning an Indian Navy paddle wheel steamer brought me down 80 convicts, of sorts and sizes, mostly under short sentences. They were "overflows" from Tânnah.

The *ex-officio* Superintendent of the Tannah gaol was the Judge (to whom I was subordinate). He wrote me a sympathetic demi-official letter, specially commending to my care an Eurasian (whom I will call "Johnson"), who was serving out a seven years' sentence for forgery and embezzlement, inflicted by Her Majesty's Recorder at Penang.

"This poor creature," wrote the humane Judge, "has interested me greatly, and will so interest you also. He will not tell me his history; but he is a man of superior education and manners. He was sent from Penang to us with a mob of pirate convicts who would certainly have overpowered their guards in the sailing ship by which they came round, had not this poor fellow, Johnson, who knows all their dialects, discovered and revealed the plot, so that the Captain had time to put in at Trincomâli and strengthen the escort. For this great service, performed at the risk of his life (for the conspirators found out that he had '*betrayed*' them), the Governor of the Straits Settlements has reduced his seven years' sentence to six (methinks he might well have pardoned the poor devil!). He will not live out the rest of the 5 years remaining, the Doctor tells me. He was sent to Tânnah on the off-chance that the climate of the Konkan might prolong his life. The unhappy man is in a gallopping consumption; of course, he has been mostly in the Infirmary. When he has been better, I have employed him on clerical work in the jail office, where he has been safe from attack by the pirate ruffians who came over with him. Bishop Meurin the R. C. (Jesuit) Bishop of Bombay, is in correspondence with the Jesuit Fathers at Penang. You will hear all about Johnson's case from them, no doubt. Meantime, I have made a strong representation for mercy for him, to Sir Bartle, who has backed it up officially to the Governor of the Straits Settlements. The miserable man's case is the harder, from his being lame from a severe spear wound in the foot received in the storming of a stockade during the Burmese War."

It goes without saying that I was, also, much interested in poor Johnson, who rallied a good deal in the genial sea breezes of the Coast.

My jailer (Mr. John Xâvier, a stalwart Eurasian) reported that Johnson had given him valuable information, not only about the pirates who had been his fellow passengers from the Straits, but also about some desperate villains already in my gaol—Wâghiris (a wild tribe from Kâthiâwâr) who, to the number of seventy-five, had recently been sent to me. These desperate dacoits (Johnson told Mr. Xâvier) were known to be ripe for an outbreak at any moment. (Two years later these Wâghiris did actually overpower and disarm their out-door guard, and escaped with their arms, but the neighbouring villagers brought them back one by one. I had then left Ratnagiri.) He also informed Xâvier that some half dozen Bombay gamblers, lying under short sentences, ossessped no end of money in currency notes, also opium that they had concealed under their arm-pits, in the folds of their turbans, and in their *lángootis* (loin-cloths). So, at the next Sunday morning inspection parade, I had these men stripped and searched. Sure enough! Johnson was right! One man had two notes of Rs. 100 each; another had ten notes of Rs. 10, and so on. And *all* had opium and tobacco smuggled into my gaol, with the connivance of my own warders, whom, of course, they had bribed! How superficial must have been the official searches at the Bombay House of Correction, at Tânnah, and finally by my own warders, when the rascals first landed!

There were "wigs" (I mean turbans) "on the green" that Sabbath day—much "weeping, wailing and gnashing of teeth"—but the culprits (convicts and warders) never suspected Johnson of being the informer: they only cursed their patron goddess, Bhowâni, and spat vehemently behind the jailor saheb's broad back!

Time rolled on, the hot weather mightily revived Johnson. Dr. H—D—, the Civil Surgeon, began to give hopes that he might yet live to return to Penang.

In April, I received from Father Bonifâce, a Jesuit Priest at Penang, a full history of the poor man's antecedents. It was very pitiful. He was the illegitimate son of a Colonel in the Madras Cavalry by a Tâmil woman. His father had so far done his duty by his boy, that he had him very well educated, and obtained a clerkship for him in the Commissariat Department, in which position he (Johnson) went to the first Burmese War. At the storming of a formidable stockade, before which the Madras Infantry had been badly repulsed, Johnson (though a non-combatant) volunteered to serve in the last assault. The stockade was won, but Johnson in his eagerness to get to the front, miscalculated his distance in leaping an inner trench, and was speared through the foot so badly that he was invalided with a small gratuity. Getting a passage to Penang, he speedily obtained a good position as Manager to an Eurasian Merchant and land-owner, and fell in love with his daughter. After their marriage his father-in-law made him a salaried partner. All would have gone well, but, unfortunately, his young wife was vain, flighty, and most extravagant. She ran him heavily (for him) into debt and at last ran away with some ship's mate. Happily, they had no children. But before she went she borrowed, in her husband's name from usurers, who, of course, came down upon poor Johnson. His father-in-law had gone to China, leaving him in sole charge. The Sáŏkars served him with legal notices—ruin stared him in the face! His father-in-law was attached to him—would certainly clear him of debt when he returned. When that would be Johnson did not know. In his despair he forged his father-in-law's name to a cheque sufficient to pay his peccant wife's debts, hoping to be able by speculation to replace the amount, and conceal his forgery. But the usurers (Malay money-lenders are of the "Isaac Gordon" type) were well aware of the forgery--they bought the cheque up, and holding it *in terrorem* over poor Johnson, forced him to embezzle again and again to pay the black-mail they levied from him.

His father-in-law returned somewhat suddenly—he would have known nothing, but a secret enemy of Johnson's sent an anonymous letter denouncing him—Johnson, when confronted with his infuriated parent confessed—but the latter, refusing Johnson's offer to refund him the defalcation from the proceeds of a successful private speculation in rubber, prosecuted—with the result to Johnson I have mentioned, seven years' penal servitude beyond the seas.

The same mail brought letters to Sir Bartle Frere from the Straits Government intimating that Johnson's case was being considered, and one from the Coadjutor of the Roman Catholics at Penang, to the effect that Johnson's father-in-law had repented of his harshness on learning that Johnson had forged merely to pay his own daughter's debts, and that he was ready and eager to restore him to partnership, and held no less than Rs. 7,000 as Johnson's salary and share of profits to hand over to poor Johnson on his release.

A memorial also had been presented by influential residents to the Governor, recounting Johnson's services in the Burmese War, and on board the convict ship—praying that he might be pardoned.

Dear old Sir Bartle would have pardoned him in a moment, but the Governor of the Straits Settlements at that time was a Colonial Official of Mr. Commissioner Pordage's type *—a " man in buckram " when in his official uniform—in a word, he was swaddled in red tape and suffering from stupidity. He could not understand " why Frere and others should make such a fuss about a half-caste forger—Only a ' convict, begad'! So His Excellency continued to 'sit tight' and consider the case !"

Johnson was naturally much cheered by all this good news, he actually put on flesh! The tears rolled down his wan cheeks when I read what the good Jesuit Father wrote of his father-in-law's generous behaviour—" Oh, Sir," he cried, "he is a good man, indeed! I'll work for him like a slave—please God I live and it doesn't rain !'

This last phrase (jocularly, but profanely used by Anglo-Indians) poor Johnson really meant seriously—for he well knew that the monsoon would kill him.

Mr. Xavier, the jailor, in his glee ejaculated to me " We'll give him such a 'send off'—won't we, Sir? If that Straits Governor will but do the straight thing in time! But will he, Sir, think you ?"

* *Vide* " The Treasure Island,' by Charles Read.

June came—the monsoon burst on the 5th, as usual. Next day poor Johnson's hacking cough returned—he daily weakened. All the gentlemen of the little Station came to see and read to him in the Infirmary—Their wives (God bless them !) made jellies and broths for the poor man—and never failed to ask how "poor Mr. Johnson" was, as they passed for their evening drive.

On the 10th the poor fellow burst a blood vessel, and Dr. Horace D—y told me it was then only a question of a few hours. We all took it by turns to sit up with him. I was with him on the 6th day at 4 A.M., his voice had sunk to a whisper. Seeing that he was at the point of death, I raised him gently and asked if he had any last message—he gasped, "My poor wife! I forgive her—God bless—her good—father! God forgive my father, Colonel—" (he mentioned a name well known in Indian history) "God bless ye—all !—and forgive me, a mis—." The life blood gushed over my arm—he was dead and at peace, poor dear fellow! for he was !—he was my own illegitimate cousin !!

This revelation was, of course, startling enough—but in the middle of last century there were few Anglo-Indian families without Eurasian connections. Concubinage with native women was not then regarded as a very heinous social offence (except, of course, in the case of married men), because English marriageable ladies were few and far between, and it was difficult and expensive to take furlough to England.

I knew Johnson's father, the Colonel, (long dead) to have been a distinguished soldier—his treatment of his bastard son showed him to have been just, humane and generous—the poor fellow lying stark and bloody before me had been, despite his crime, a good servant to the State in many ways—he was at last at peace! *Requiescat in pace*—what more was to be said, or done, than to convey his last words to the living, and to bury him decently?

I kept my newly discovered secret to myself, of course, and "the Station" was somewhat surprised to see me Chief Mourner. We gave him, as that good fellow Xavier, the jailor, said "a good send off" to his grave in the pretty little English Cemetery. Every English gentleman in our small Station was present and followed the coffin—every lady sent a wreath; the District Collector and Magistrate, the Police Superintendent, the Civil Surgeon; Mr. Trott the Deputy Magistrate, and another Eurasian Subordinate Judge, were the pall-bearers. And then a plain laterite stone tomb, surmounted by a noble teak Cross carved in my School of Industry, was erected to poor Johnson, at the cost of "The Station." Much good feeling was shown by all—men who were on bad terms shook hands across poor Johnson's grave, when the good Pâdrè had pronounced the Benediction with tearful eyes. Ladies who were 'cuts' about their Ayah's tittle-tattle, kissed and made friends at 5 o'clock tea that evening, and marvellous to relate!—there was no row at the station croquet lawn, so sobering and morally beneficial was to us the death of our poor "brother"—though he was only a convict.

Postcriptum.—

I may, perhaps, mention that when the Jesuit Father at Penang acknowledged my letter with poor Johnson's messages, he wrote that Mrs. Johnson had returned to her father's house—a chastened Magdalen —The ship's mate deserted her (of course) at Hong Kong, whence her father's commercial agents paid her passage back to Penang, where "the fatted calf" was killed for the poor returned prodigal. She was warmly welcomed, moreover, by the Eurasian Community.

"Lord" bless you! Sir!" said Mr. Xavier, when I told him—"Why! of course she was! We don't mind such little matters—Our women (bless 'em!)—they all do it!" Exactly one month after Johnson's burial, his free pardon arrived at the Bombay Secretariat!

CHAPTER XXIII.

THE KIDNAPPING NAWÁB.

The author of this paper not only knew this enterprising Prince well, but was instrumental in bringing about his downfall in 1860. Yâkub Khân was his family name, he was an Abyssinian (or as otherwise called, a Habshi; Habesh being the Vernacular for Abyssinia) of very ancient race who, somewhere about 1200 A.D., sailed down the Red Sea in well-manned and armed "Dhows" and "Shibads" * and set up as pirates on the Malabar Coast (even in the Gulf of Cambay) from Kutch to Kumta.

There were many of these sea-rovers in these regions from time immemorial. Every petty king and princeling along the African Coast—every Arab Chief along the shores of Arabia Felix, of Zanzibar, and of Muscat pirated; not only did they intercept all merchantmen of whatsoever nationality, but they landed

---

* A "Dhow" is a huge lubberly craft with one or more upright masts and a main yard often 100 feet long, a lofty poop and fore cabin, and nearly upright bowsprit; it can only sail well before the wind. Natives call them Ocean "Tongas" (buffalos). A "Shibad" has two masts leaned forward with two lengthy yards also. It is very speedy on the wind and sails very closely to it. Both crafts are half-decked.

and often established themselves in fortified positions whence they raided the country round for slaves and ivory. At that early date, probably the only genuinely honest traders by Sea were the Moplahs of the Island of Socotra, and they were just as eager to capture slaves as the professional pirates, especially after they had settled under the Zamorin of Calicut, as farmers and foresters, for which, of course, they needed much foreign labor. Along the Malabar Coast, the Habshis found many rivals in piracy, of whom the most successful were the Ângrias of Kolâba (just opposite Bombay). All those sea rovers sailing under the black flag (or "Jolly Roger" as the white men called their ensign), not only preyed on the Moplahs who for centuries monopolized the trade of India and the Persian Gulf with Egypt and Europe (by way of the Red Sea), but they preyed upon each other, the Marâthas, and the Moguls. At last the fleet of Vâsco de Gáma rounded the Cape of Good Hope, and gradually the seaboard of Hindostân, and the Straits of Malacca became dotted with their Colonies—the Dutch followed : lastly came English and French.

Ere many years elapsed, white men appeared in much better equipped vessels armed with heavy guns, and of large tonnage ; their crews, desperados of al nations. These white pirates with their square-rigged ships could outsail all the lumbering lugger-rigged native craft and could tack against headwinds, wherea the latter are compelled to "wear" and thus lose much way.

History does not specially mention any French or Dutch pirates; but there were at least three Britons, one of whom, the redoubtable Captain Kidd, had already earned the reputation of being the most bloody villian of Western Waters. The phrase to "Kydnap" is said to have originated from this villain's evil deeds. It was originally spelt "Kydd-nab," meaning that Kydd had nabbed ships, crews, and passengers. Later, when children were frequently carried off by Gypsies in Enland, and young lads by the Press Gangs of the British Royal Navy, the phrase implied that the "kids" (or children) had been "nabbed", and "nabbed" easily became corrupted to "napped".

When the islands of Bombay and Salsette were granted by the King of Portugal and Spain to England as the dowry of his daughter Prince's Catherine, on her marriage with Charless II, the old British India Company leased them from the Crown for an annual rental of £10 in gold. So little was the gift valued in those benighted times! "John Company" had a small fleet to maintain and provision: there was great difficulty, however, in procuring beef, owing to Hindu prejudice against killing the sacred cow. In this difficulty the Government applied to the then Nawab of Habsan residing at his Island Fort Jinjira (which is Arabic for "Island Fortress"). That potentate agreed to supply that needful flesh meat alive. An Offensive and Defensive Treaty was signed between the Company and the Sidi Nawab* who was thus the first ally the British had in Western Hindostân. The treaty† (which still holds good) was couched in a few lines, and was faithfully observed in after years. This, however, did not at all deter the Habshis from pirating the merchant men of "Jan Kumpani Bahadur": nay, from carrying on guerilla war with their British Allies. On one occasion the Habshi even laid up his fleet at Sewri for the monsoon months, actually bombarding Fort George and reducing the Government and garrison to a starving condition till they bribed them heavily to withdraw at the end of the monsoon.‡ So far from ill-blood following this little interlude, the strange alliance was cemented. British envoys and traders were permitted to visit Habsan, were received hospitably in Fort Jinjira itself, but were never allowed to reside in the Habshi's territory.

* The Portuguese ignorantly termed the Habshis, Siddees, Seedees, Sidis, (the word is differently spelt in old documents) Negroes and the British (nearly as ignorant) continued the error, though the Habshis do not in the least resemble Negroes or Siddis in stature or features, being fairer than the Portuguese themselves, of generally lofty stature, and handsome featured.

† *Vide* "Aitchison's" Indian Treaties and Sir W. Lee-Warner's book on Indian States (I forget the title).

‡ *Vide* Grant Duff's History of the Marâthas. "The Bombay Monthly Magazine" (of which only a few years' copies were printed), "Campbell's Bombay Gazetteer", and Dr. DeCunha's istory of Portuguese India".

History relates that a certain dunderheaded Governor of Bombay in Council, dismayed, at the terrible mortality among their white soldiers, from malarious fevers on the then insalubrious Bombay Island, actually proposed to the Court of Directors in Leadenhall Street, that it should exchange Bombay for Rajpuri Bay (in which Jinjira is situated) and Mazgaum at the head of the tidal creek. Needless to say the Court of Directors severely snubbed the fools, ordered them to prohibit their seamen and soldiers from drinking so much arrack, to lead more sober and cleanly lives themselves, and, above all, to look more to the sanitary condition of Bombay. *

* The mortality among Europeans was never less than 30 per cent; that among the British Artillery cantoned on the Sewri Road was often 40 per cent or more. The Sea then divided Bombay into a group of small islands, the tide ran right across the City from the harbour to Khetwati, so people coming to market had to wade across at "Pydowni" ("Pai" feet and "Dhone" to wash). At low tide all the flats were noisome pestilential swamps right up to Worlee and Mahim, for the sea washed deep between Worlee and Malabar Hill and tidal rivers flowed from Bandara to Sion (or Lion) fort surrounding the large Island known as the "Neat's Tongue". The Fort was separated by another arm from Colaba (not to be confounded with Ângria's Kolaba opposite) which was called "Old Woman's Island." Governor Hornby, in 1744, built the Vellard (Portuguese for Causeway) from North Malabar Hill to Worlee, in anticipation of sanction by the Court of Directors, who promptly suspended him for his extravagance (it was estimated to cost a lakh of rupees). But his suspension took six months to come round the Cape in those days. Hornby "douceman" pocketed the document and

Between the "fifties" and "sixties" the Grand Old Kidnapping Nawab, of whom we are writing, had no special or personal grievance to allege against "Jan Kumpani Bahadur", but he was a truculent potentate leading a life of debauchery, cruelty, and extortion; the mere rumours whereof terrified his peaceful neighbours at Bombay, and horrified the Government of the day.

The old Treaty, though unabrogated, was practically a dead letter, the Bombay Commissariat Officers being by this time able to obtain plenty of beef from the interior. Nevertheless the Nawab closed Habsan absolutely to the British. The Governor of Bombay, of course reported to the Governor-General, Lord Dalhousie, the gross misbehaviour of their next door neighbour and were (also as a matter of course) asked why they did not annex Habsan,* that being His Lordship's well know "panacea" for all native trouble. But His Excellency the Governor of Bombay and his Council (such men as Rivett-Carnac, George, "Clerk

---

had completed the Vellard called after him, before his successor landed. Thenceforth the Court of Directors ordered that all despatches should be first opened by the Chief Secretary alone. In later years, Lady Jamsetjee built the Mahim, Bándra Vellard; Sion Causeway and Colaba Vellard were constructed between 1850 and 1865: thus all swamps except the Flats were reclaimed from the sea.

* When Lord Dalhousie, on a subsequent visit to Bombay, inspected the Charts and saw the proximity of Habsan, he is reported to have exclaimed "Good God, why on earth do you hesitate to annex the rascal's little State."

of Umballa," and Mountstuart Elphinstone) were far too wise and prudent to adopt a course that would have stirred up a hornet's nest in their vicinity, at a time when all India was alarmed at Lord Dalhousie's annexation policy on the slightest pretext, especially whenever he found no heir of the flesh to succeed to any Jaghir (estate held on service), Tenure or "Inam." Nothing in Hindu eyes was more sacrilegious—adoptions being essential (wherever no male heir of the flesh exists) to secure a son to perform, not merely the funeral but the annual rites and sacrifices of the deceased. The very salvation of Hindus depends, according to their creed, on such ceremonies. No native Potentate, no noble or landholder, felt himself secure. Native allowances and lands granted for the maintenance of Hindu temples by ancient deed or (in their absence owing to their mutilation or destruction by white ants or time) by long prescriptive right that had never been questioned by the most rapacious Delhi Emperors, were resumed or curtailed.

Overt rebellion first broke out in the Bombay Presidency in 1844-45, when the Sâwants of Sâwantwadi * were with some difficulty subdued at and about Belgaum and Dharwar in the Southern Marátha Country.

---

* A petty Marátha State at the foot of the Syadri Mountains near Vingorila, whose Chief is a Bhonsla, and so descended from Siwaji.

Disaffection simmered on below the surface, but did not (because of Bombay's proximity) burst into flame when Kolâba was annexed across the harbour, on the demise of the Marátha Chief Angria without heir of his body. Then followed the annexation of Satára on the same grounds, where a descendant of Sivaji, the Great Founder of the Marátha Empire, was reigning nominally (a puppet of the Poona Peishwa) up to 1817.

This unrighteous policy declared, almost in so many words by the Queen's Proclamation of 1858, to be unrighteous, resulted, as all the world knows, in the Great Sepoy Rebellion of 1857. Had the Nawáb of Habsan been an enlightened and well disposed potentate, he would have been morally justified in ceasing to hold intercourse with a Government so seemingly unscrupulous, which might at any moment pick a quarrel with him, and annex his petty territory. But this particular Nawáb (as has been mentioned above) was both truculent, debauched, and daring. For many years he and his "Sirdars" (nobles) had been in the habit of kidnapping women from British territory. Once within Habsán, no more was heard of them, let their husbands and families do what they would. Habshi agents employed and heavily bribed village "Patels" (Headmen) not only to hush up such crimes but to aid in kidnapping girls whose husbands were employed at a distance from their homes. Such a case occurred in 1859 * when the Patel of a village near Severndroog (or Hurnai, as it is now called) sold the girl wife of a Marátha gatekeeper employed on the Great Indian Peninsula Railway, to a Habsán slave-dealer for a large sum. Her husband, alarmed at receiving no intelligence of the child's arrival at puberty, returned suddenly and questioned the Patel, who assured him that his virgin wife was safe, but had removed with her relatives to a somewhat distant village to which he (the Patel) would accompany him. Meantime, Bábajirao (the husband) heard disquieting "gup" that a Habsán slave dealer had been seen in close "confab" with the Patel just before the girl disappeared, and that the latter seemed to be very flush of rupees. However, he accompanied the Patel very foolishly alone: their path lead through dense jungle. A few days later vultures were observed by a herdsman hovering at a certain spot, where the man found poor Bábajirao's body, already nearly consumed but easily identifiable by his belt and blue uniform. The Patel, pretending great grief, declared that he had left the poor fellow at the confines of the thick jungle aforesaid, on his volunteering to proceed alone on hearing that the Patel was due at the "Thana" (Revenue Officer's Station) with an instalment of tax overdue. The skull of the corpse being shattered and there being other claw-like wounds on it, the *Punchayet* (Coroner's jury) recorded that poor

*The author was then an Assistant Magistrate in the Ratnagiri District. This case is briefly mentioned in his "Reminiscences."

Babajirao had been killed by a man-eating tiger (not before heard of). The Patel reported accordingly, and in due time a reward of rupees one hundred was offered for the mysterious man-eater's skin by the District Magistrate at the Author's suggestion, though the latter discredited the tiger tale altogether, and instituted certain enquiries among the villagers, personally. At last one of the village Mhârs (guides and messengers) admitted before the assembled villagers to the Author, that he had accompanied the Patel and Bábajirao as guide, that the Patel cut Bábajirao down from behind with a "koiti" (bill-hook), inflicting other wounds and fracturing his skull with his iron-shod staff—that the Patel had bribed him (the Mhâr) to held his tongue and that he had done so.

The Author arrested the Patel then and there, making the Mhâr Queen's evidence: the case went to the Sessions, where, however, the Judge acquitted the accused for want of sufficient evidence. But the learned Judge (Charles Forbes) reported to the "Sudder" or (High) Court that he was morally convinced that the Patel had murdered poor Bábajirao. The "Sudder" Judges took the same view, and moved Government in the Political Department to institute inquiries in Habsán. The spies sent found that the girl was in a harem of a near relative of the Nawáb himself. Nothing could be done, however, as the Habsán "Durbar" (Ministry) reported that the girl stated that she had voluntarily left her home.

The next case occurred in 1861 when the Author was acting as District Magistrate of Ratnagri, and in Camp at Kelsi (a small village on the coast, 20 miles south of Jinjira). A merchant personally petitioned him, in great distress, to obtain the release of his brother, who (he alleged) had been forcibly abducted by the Nawáb's people three months before, and was (he had learned) lying in the State prison on the Island of Jezeerat (close to Jinjira) in a dungeon loaded with a heavy collar rivetted to fetters (which the Nawáb called "Habsán bangles") so that the poor wretch could neither stand, lie down or eat and drink unaided, being manacled over his doubled knees, with an iron bar passed under his knees, trussed like a fowl much in the posture of school boys "*cock fighting*" (as they call it).

The petitioner who was a "Máhájan" (great man or banker), produced a former petition presented to the Junior Assistant Magistrate and endorced by that foolish young official "there is no redress to be obtained from this Sirkar (Government). Petitioner should go to the Nawáb of Habsán." The Author at once sent the petition to the Chief Secretary (Sir Henry Anderson) by express runner with the petitioner's affidavit, which was to the following effect:—

"My brother, against my advice, began to trade with the Nawáb, some years ago, and lent money to certain of his relatives, who refused to repay the loans.

On this being brought to the Nawáb's knowledge, he gave my brother the revenue farm of a large village for three years in liquidation of the debt. My brother made a very good thing of the farm, but foolishly refused to bribe the Mootsadi Parbhus (hereditary Parbu Ministers of the Nawáb). Hearing that these worthies were intriguing to ruin him, and that they had already reported to the Nawáb that my brother's accounts were fraudulently kept, my poor brother managed to escape in an open boat to Kelsi. Three months ago, however, we were much surprised to see a 'Pattiamar' (Native lugger) flying the Nawáb's ensign, anchored in our little road-stead one fine morning. From this, a boat put off and landed one of the Habshi nobles and one of the 'Mootsadi' Parbhus. These high personages promptly presented themselves at our house, porters carrying presents accompanying. After the unsual complements the Parbhu Minister produced a 'Kharita' (or letter in a silken bag) addressed to my brother in most complimentary terms expressing H. H. the Nawáb's great regret at the false accusations with which my brother had been assailed, his accounts have been found quite honest: H. H. invited my brother to Jinjira to farm half a Tāluk' (sub-district) for 7 years.

"When the deputation had left, both my brother's wife and I tried in vain to dissuade the former from accepting the Nawáb's offer. He yielded reluctantly, but it was necessary (so he said) that he should pay the deputation a return visit of ceremony on board the pattiamar. We cast ourselves on the ground, embraced his feet, but he persisted, and was rowed off to the ship carrying cocoanuts and bananas. Directly our 'hodi' (canoe) reached the side, we saw my poor brother hauled up over the gun-wale, we could even hear his screams, but the ship was merely attached to a buoy and the yard was at mast head: so they sailed away swiftly. Arè aré, thoba,' 'bom marro'd' (*i.e.*, beat his mouth with his palms) 'Khâwand krupa karo' (My Lord be kind), get the great Sirkar to rescue my poor brother for Ishwar's sake," cried the Mâhâjan.

Having taken the petitioner's statement on solemn affirmation, I despatched an express runner to the Chief Secretary. Sir Henry Anderson replied demi-officially that Lord Elphinstone was very indignant, the more so that he had just received a secret envoy from the Begum Saheb (Fatima Bibi) widow of the late Nawâb, complaining that she and her son Sidi Ahmed Khân * were imprisoned in Jezeerat and expected every day to be poisoned, because he desired an illegitimate son called the "Buxshi" to succeed him at his own death. His Lordship had, therefore, determined to bring the Nawâb to book at once.

While His Excellency was deliberating the matter in Council, news was brought of another most serious

* The Present Nawâb.

outrage: An Indian Navy ship employed in making a deep sea survey of the Coast, landed a boat's crew under a Habsan headland to fill the ship's water casks, whereupon they were attacked and stoned by the Nawáb's ragamuffins. This brought matters to a head of course. Two companies of Native Infantry, some Sappers and a Company of the Marine Battalion, with a light Field Battery were embarked on the Indian Navy paddle wheel steamer *Victoria* (Captain Chitty) under the orders of Mr. E. P. Robertson, District Magistrate of Thanah (who was Political Agent of Angria's Kolâba). On arrival in Rajpuri Bay the *Victoria* steamed up under the walls of the fortress of Jinjira, and Mr. Robertson was landed under a strong escort. The "Killadar" (Commander) of the fortress at first refused to open the big sea gates and manned the battlements, but Mr. Robertson sent word to the Nawáb that unless he were at once admitted, Captain Chitty would shell the fortress and Sappers would blow in the sea gate: so the Nawáb ordered the British Envoy to be admitted to his presence and listened surlily to the British Sirkar's ultimatum.

This required the Nawáb instantly to deliver his Jezeerat prisoners to the Envoy with all British subjects in the fortress or elsewhere in Habsan detained as slaves or as concubines. The Nawáb was further informed that the British Government would thereafter place a Political Resident at Moorood (opposite the fortress) for whom he (the Nawâb) must at once build and furnish a suitable Residency: he had also to pay down a heavy fine in cash and to give an undertaking in writing to defray the cost of the expedition; finally he was to pay such compensation as Mr. Robertson should award to the Kelsi Mâhâjan and other persons aggrieved. The Begum Saheb (Fatima Bibi) would (the Envoy informed him) reside in Bombay with her two sons. To all these demands the old rascal reluctantly subscribed, at the unanimous advice of his ministers and nobles, whereupon the expedition returned to Bombay, having previously released and sent to their homes nearly 500 British subjects who had been, from time to time, abducted, mostly as concubines.

The Kelsi Mâhâjan, of course, was handsomely indemnified for his sufferings, and the Junior Assistant Magistrate who neglected his duty, received a tremendous "wigging".

The old Begum soon died, her son Sidi Ahmed Khân Yâkub Khân was sent to the "Râjkumar" (Nobles') College at Râjkot (Kâthiâwar) with a younger brother. Sidi Ahmed did well at College, and remained a ward of the Author till of age, when (September 1879) the latter installed him on the "Gadi" (Cushion of State) with full powers as a Judge and Magistrate. His career has been eminently honourable and he received the honour of K.C.S.I. at her late Majesty Victoria's Golden Jubilee.

Mr. Larcom (son of Sir Thomas Larcom, Chief Secretary of Ireland) was the first Resident and did excellent service during the interregnum. Habsán is now perhaps the best administered Mahommedan State in Western India. Thus ended what might have been a very nasty business.

CHAPTER XXIV.

A TRUE TALE OF A PERSECUTED MUSSULMAN OFFICIAL.

Somewhere about the year 1850, there was in the Revenue Department a very promising young Mahommedan gentleman who, for certain reasons, I will call Abdul Fareed. He belonged to the principal Moslem family in the Konkan; his grandfather had risen to the highest post in the British Service—*viz.*, a Deputy Collector and Magistrate—before he retired on full pension at sixty-five years of age, to his home at Bankot at the mouth of the River Sâvitri. When Major Protheroe, after the fall of the Peishwah Dynasty, was deputed in 1822 to storm the forts in that region one after another, this old man was more than 80 years old, but he persisted in accompanying the Major, acted as guide on several occasions, and actually led the assault on a hill fortress near Siwajee's old stronghold, Raighur. The old hero's son and, subsequently his grandson, Abdul also entering our service, followed in his footsteps. The grandson Abdul, was a Mahalkari (or sub District Officer) in what is now called the Kolâba District, when something approaching what is now termed a famine occurred in the Northern Konkan, and he earned the encomiums of Government by the efforts he made through his relatives in Bombay to import food grains for the starving people in his charge.

It was as common then, as it has ever been since at such calamitous times, for parents reduced to the last depths of despair, to expose their infants and desert them at some spot where it was probable they would be soon discovered, in the hope that some charitable person might find, take charge of, and rear them. In this way a little girl about eighteen months old was found at a roadside in Abdul Furreed's jurisdiction, and brought to him. He took the infant into his family and his womenfolk cherished and brought her up. Fearful that his conduct might some day be misrepresented, he reported to his official superior what he had done, and that it was his intention to bring the child up as a member of his own family. He received, in due course, the commendations of Government for his charity. Time passed and he was promoted to a "Mamlat" (sub-district) at a distance. There, he incurred the enmity of the Brâhmins, who lost no opportunity of trying to injure him in the eyes of the Collector and Magistrate. Anonymous letters, accusing him of every crime under the sun, poured in. Conspiracies innumerable were got up against him, but Khan Sahib Abdul Furreed, though he continued to triumph over his enemies, and retained the full confidence of his chief, became disheartened. His request to be transferred to some other district, where he hoped to encounter less hostility, was refused; Abdul Furreed, who had some private means, thereupon tendered his resignation on the ground that he could not hope to prevail always against the secret machination of his enemies. His chief refused to accept his resignation, and with much difficulty persuaded him to stay on and not to give his foes the satisfaction of having driven him away.

This chief not long afterwards left the District, and was succeeded by a gentleman who knew not Abdul Furreed. This was the opportunity his enemies desired. In a marvellously short time they concocted a diabolical conspiracy, with the aid of some of his own Marâtha peons. The body of a Brâhmin widow was found in a well, and Khan Saheb Abdul Furreed was anonymously accused of having had her brought to his house by certain peons, and finally, after having violated her, of having, with the aid of other peons, caused her to be thrown into the well. He was suspended from office, committed to the Sessions and after lying in jail for nearly six months, was arraigned for murder. He had not the means to engage an English barrister—in fact, there were very few in those days who would undertake a case out of Bombay. He would not trust any Brâhmin pleader, and there was no Mohammedan Vakil, so he defended himself. After a very long and patient trial, in which he ably exposed certain discrepancies in the evidence of the peons, he was acquitted

He would no doubt have been reinstated had he cared to petition, but he felt himself to be hopelessly disgraced, and preferred to retire to his native village, where he shut himself up and lived a life of complete seclusion with his family, rarely permitting even his brothers to visit him.

As a matter of fact Abdul Furreed had no acquaintance whatever with the family of the deceased widow, whom he had never even seen: and circumstances afterwards came to light, which proved beyond doubt that the unfortunate woman when drawing water from the well had accidently overbalanced herself, fallen in, and been drowned. This collapse of the case against Abdul Furreed, so far from discouraging his enemies, emboldened them to enter upon a fresh system of persecution. Abdul Furreed was pursued into his retirement a hundred and fifty miles distant, by continuous accusation of corruption and malversation of public monies, in all of which, however, he came out triumphant. Then, for about two years, with the exception of scurrilous anonymous letters to himself, and petitions to the magisterial authorities, none of which were ever traced to their source, Abdul Furreed was left in comparative peace. He built a wall round his property to secure privacy, and devoted himself to the observance of religion, and to horticulture, of which he was passionately fond. He also devoted much of his time to preparing a series of notes on the conquest of the

Konkan, which would have been of great value had they ever seen the light.

In the meantime the little waif, whom he had charitably taken into his family years before, arrived at a marriageable age. She had been named "Khatiza", had been cherished and educated in his Zenána, and taught to regard him as her father. It was known among the Mahommedan gentry throughout the country-side and in the neighbouring Mahommedan State of Habsán, that he was trying to obtain a suitable husband for her, and was prepared to give her a very handsome dowry, considering what his own means were. It would be difficult, one would have thought, to distort his admirable behaviour in regard to this poor child, into a ground for accusing him of any fresh crime. But his old enemies had, of course, made themselves fully acquainted with his early history, in the hope of finding some vulnerable point on which they might attack him, and they knew of the incident of the discovery of the infant girl Khatiza, and of her having been adopted into Abdul Furreed's family.

So long as she was a child there was nothing that he could be accused of in regard to her: but it was different when she had arrived at maturity. They could then, and in their diabolical hatred, they did, make all kinds of infernal suggestions. Anonymous letters were constantly received by the authorities warning them that a fresh and terrible tragedy was impending at Abdul Furreed's house: that he had given way to drink, that he had evil designs on Khatiza: that she was only saved from his violence by the ladies of his own Zenána, who shielded and protected her: that these ladies sought to place her with one of his elder brothers for safety, "lest there should be a repetition of his former crime", but they could not break through the restrictions with which he had surrounded his prison-like house.

The Magistrate was besought to surround and search the house, to summon the ladies, and take their evidence: and to release Khatiza at all hazard—the writers knowing no greater indignity could be offered a Mahommedan gentleman than the searching of his house, or the summoning of his womankind for any purpose. Needless to say that these anonymous communications were treated with contempt, though they were filed, and enquiries made in the hope of tracing the writers.

I myself received documents of this kind, month after month, and having struck up a warm friendship with Abdul Furreed's eldest brother, consulted with him as to the best mode of terminating, once and for ever, this diabolical persecution. Mahomed Furreed was advanced in life, a man renowned for his blameless life: he had always shown the greatest sympathy for his younger brother, who, however, had repulsed all his advances. After many consultations, it was agreed between us that there was but one way of checkmating Abdul Furreed's enemies, so far at least as the insinuation regarding Khatiza were concerned. Abdul must be persuaded to let her leave his house and be placed under Mahomed's protection till she was married, as it was hoped she soon would be. My friend Mahomed tried in vain to induce his younger brother to assent, telling him of the interest I took in the matter and my object; he showed Abdul also some of the vile letters I had received, but these only made him more obdurate. Finally, I resolved on making an attempt to see Abdul myself, and not long afterwards I visited the village of the Furreed's, told Mahomed what I was about to do, and myself went and asked to see Abdul at his own house. As may be imagined there was much commotion when I knocked at the gateway: an ordinary visitor would have been treated very unceremoniously, but I sent in my name with a note from Mahomed, and simply asked to see Abdul for a few moments at the gateway, adding that I should not go away till I did see him.

After a considerable interval, the gate was opened by as fine a specimen of the Mahommedan race as it has ever been my good fortune to see. Nearly six feet high, and broad in proportion, erect in carriage, with a long beard that fell nearly to his waist, clear-cut but massive features, with intelligent eyes, and an expression in them of deep despair, yet of resignation: it was impossible to associate such a man with violence or depravity. A few hurried words passed between us: I, apologising for my intrusion, and striving to excuse it—he, with tears streaming down his face, trying to maintain a calm appearance, while in broken words he said "I never thought to see a Saheb's face again." We seemed to take to each other at once. With all the grace and dignity which distinguish a Mahommedan, he asked me into his house, into a handsomely furnished room, fitted up as a library, where for nearly two hours we discussed his past history and most unfortunate position. I told him that his brother was the most intimate native friend I possessed—that I had made it my business to master all the details of the infamous conspiracy of which he had been a victim, in the hopes of being able by some means or other to reach the authors of it. I recounted to him the hideous case of Vinayek Deo, the "would-be parricide" (which I have published * separately) which I had just disposed of. I impressed upon him the great importance, for the sake of his family, of his coming out again into the world and showing his enemies that they had not utterly broken him down; but it was all of no avail, so far as his own personal feeling was concerned. He persisted that he was a broken-hearted man, hopelessly disgraced in the eyes of the world, and all he desired was to be permitted to die in peace. I then gradually brought

* "Reminiscences of an Indian Police Official."—Chapter I.

the conversation to the question of the girl Khatiza, told him what his enemies were insinuating about him and her, and suggested that the one way to stop these attacks, and above all, to protect her fair fame, was to place her in his brother Mahommed's family and let her be thence married. He was deeply moved, declaring that the child was to him in truth a daughter (he was, I may mention, childless). He went out and brought her in to see me—a bright-eyed, delicate-looking child of about thirteen years of age appeared, whose deep filial affection for him was apparent in every gesture. When she had gone he told me he would follow the advice given by his brother and myself, and would lose no time in placing Khatiza under the latter's protection. Mahommed, who lived close by, was sent for, and in my presence accepted the trust, and in the course of a few days the girl was installed in his house, from which in the course of a few months she was well married to a notable in the Habsán State. In the meantime, we decided that the Furreed family should offer a large reward (five hundred rupees I think was the sum) for any information that would lead to the discovery of the writers of the latest anonymous letters. The Chief Magistrate's consent was obtained to my officially publishing the notification. Of course we had little hope that any reward would have results, but at any rate the notification showed that the authorities were in earnest, and that it would no longer be of any use to send anonymous letters to or about Abdul Furreed, while Khatiza being no longer under his roof there could be no foundation for fresh accusations. I frequently visited Abdul Furreed afterwards, and for several years afterwards, when I had left the district we kept up a correspondence. When he was dying, some twelve years ago, he sent me a farewell message, telling me that, "thanks to me," he should die in peace. I may mention that when in great affliction about twenty years ago, I received a charmingly sympathetic letter from Khatiza, who is the happy mother of a large family.

CHAPTER XXV.

A TERRIBLE TALE OF THE SEA.

This is also a true tale that came under my official cognizance in the year of our Lord 1860, when I was an Assistant Magistrate in the Ratnagiri Zillah (as it was then termed). My favourite headquarters were at Hurnee, in the picturesque fort Severndroog, one of a group of five small fortresses built at various times, *viz.*, Futteh-Ghur (Victory Fort), Karak-Ghur (Rocky Fort), Severn or Sooverndroog (The Golden Citadel), and Jinjira (the Island Fort). The first two were built by Siwaji, the Founder of the Marátha Empire, the third by the first Angria, the fourth by the Sidi or Habshi (Abyssinian) Nawáb of Jinjira, as was also his impregnable stronghold of the same name 40 or 50 miles from Hurnee northward, and only about the same distance from Bombay. The Jinjira fortress at Hurnee was erected (as tradition says) by the Habshi from "trap" rock, blasted from a ledge that jutted out eastward from Severndroog, which is only about 300 yards distant. The Sidi Pirate with some 2,000 followers, working at night only by torch-light, built it to enable him to capture his brother Pirate's four other forts above named. He must have been a plucky old sea-dog that Sidi and persevering withal; for the stronghold, partly hewn out of hard rock, partly built of enormously roughly faced stone blocks cemented by shell lime*, rises more than 60 feet and covers (I think) about 3 acres. It must have taken several years to complete and arm with heavy guns in the teeth of Angria's heavier metal, firing night and day at point-blank range, while the latter's warships hovered around trying to cut off the Sidi's supplies. The Sidi, however, succeeded as he deserved to do. Toolaji Angria was killed in the Sidi's assault—(his tomb adjoins a small English Cemetery in the Bay).

But the Angrias soon recovered their four forts on the Mainland, and the Habshi withdrew his garrison from the Jinjira Island Fort, because of the water-supply failing: a malignant type of typhoid fever decimated his men, and (strange to say) Jinjira became so infested with Cobras and Foorsas (the "fer de lance" of the Isles de France, the "Kairait" of Northern India) as to be uninhabitable. Every hot season still the English Forest Department fire the long grass and reeds, killing thousands, but the reptiles nevertheless breed as freely as ever.

In a chapter on "Wrecking" in my work entitled "Reminiscences of an Indian Police Official," I mentioned incidentally certain circumstances which I may term

* No 'Portland Cement' equals this as it was then made by slave labour. It was worked up with various gums and horse hair. When destroying certain bastions, we might break the stones, but could not break the cement joints by blasting. All Konkan forts were thus built.

the prologue to this veracious historiette. For the development of the sequel I must relate them at greater detail at this point.

The Severndroog Fort was captured by the Indian Navy by assault without the loss of a man—a European garrison was then quartered therein for some years. But discipline being exceedingly slack and arrack cheap and abundant, the garrison was killed off every few months by *delirium tremens*, or by cholera during the mango season, till Hurnee (like the northern suburb of Bombay—Mâtunga) was called "The white man's grave." At last the white soldiers were replaced by Sepoys of the Native Veteran Battalion (the "Guttrums" as they called themselves) whose headquarters were at Dápoli 8 miles inland. Then Hurnee was selected to be the Head Revenue, Magisterial, and Police Station of the "Taluka" (sub-district) and the "Mamlatdar's" (Native Magistrate) "Kacheri" (office) was located in vacated barracks in the Fort with Treasury, Lock-up (or prison) and duly arranged "according to Cocker." A small bungalow of three rooms, with a spacious 12 foot verandah, adjoining a tank of excellent spring water, where the officers of the Detachment used to live, was allotted to the Assistant Collector and Magistrate, who had charge of the Hurnee and two other Talukas—his office being held in another small building over the water gate which was formerly the mess-room.

Seated in the verandah of this Baby Bungalow, I faced due North and commanded a lovely view of the coast for 12 miles to the mouth of the Savitri River, which divides the Ratnagiri District from Habsán Territory—the South Konkan from the North Konkan. It was in March, a fierce northwesterly gale had been blowing three weeks (as is usual at that season). Day after day I had sat in my long chair watching the turbid Indian Ocean breaking on the sandy cove below me. The Hurnee fishermen, bold seamen as they are, dared not venture outside the tiny harbour under Fattehghar and Karak Forts where, and under the lea of every headland, for many miles hundreds of native latteen-rigged vessels were sheltering at anchor. Anon a "school" of Spermaceti whales* spouted out at sea (sure sign of a continuance of the gale). Anon a huge Surat "Battiála" (two-masted, half decked of perhaps 150 tons) or a swift "Shibád" (timber ship): or a black-hulled one-masted Arab "Dhow" † larger than either, scudded south, the waves washing even over her lofty poop-cabin. I knew them to be from Zánzibar, bound to Rájápur 80 miles south, deeply laden with coffee, camphor, gums, wax, honey in quaintly carved gourds, shellac, fruit [such as

* The native sailors greatly dread these mammals, which sometimes smash their smaller craft in pure mischief. They are worshipped as 'Hussein Saheb.'

† Dhows with main yarde 120 feet long can only lumber along the wind and the natives call them Ocean buffaloes.

pomgranates 'Moosambis,' *i.e.*, Mozambique limes, and dates] which would be exchanged for Swedish Iron bars, Brass and Copper sheets, Teak logs, Cocoanuts, Copra (dried coçoanut kernels), Rice, Hemp, Turmeric and Toddy.

During the night of the 28th day of the gale, the wind rapidly went down. I was drinking my early cup of tea in the verandah, when I descried in the offing a huge black object rising and falling on the wave crests. I made her out with my Dolland telescope to be a large Surat Battiála, probably one of several I had seen the previous evening labouring off Bánkot.

Despatching a peon to the Custom House with a message that if they would man their biggest boat we would try to tow her in, I hastened down in my pyjamas and a couple of men carrying brandy and blankets in case there should be any half drowned poor devils aboard the wreck. I found the Deputy Collector of Customs eagerly awaiting me, with kedges and hawsers already stowed "forrard" in their long boat to which they had affixed an out-rigger. The tide being on the turn and the wind with us we soon ran alongside the hulk and made fast to the stump of the mast, which, broken 6 feet from the half deck, lay overboard to windward, and was thumping the hulk to pieces. The sea swept the vessel fore and aft as she wallowed in the trough of the billows. There was no human being aboard so far as we could see, and both her boats (such craft usually carry a long boat and a dingy on deck) were gone. The only living creature was a rat which scampered along the gunwale from stem to stem as the hull rose and dipped. We could not (dared not) approach very near, lest we too should be swamped; otherwise I should have tried to save the poor animal. His bright little eyes peered so piteously into my own face, as if to implore aid. At last he took courage and leaped out towards the beam of our out-rigger, fell short and was swept away. The Khalássis (sailors) took to the oars to tow, but their hawsers were only two inch coir ropes, which broke like pack thread, so we were forced reluctantly to abandon the hull, knowing that it would certainly be driven ashore at ebb-tide on a bluff some miles to the south.

Late that evening I rode round the sandy cove towards Anjirla and observed half a dozen fishermen hauling at a large chest that had been washed up and left high and dry by the receding tide. I knew the men of course: they were good honest fellows, headed by the Patel of a little hamlet at the end of the cove. They called out that they would by and by carry the chest up to the Kacheri and deliver it to the Mamlatdar. I went out into camp early the next morning for a fortnight; in due course the Mamlatdar reported that the chest had been brought in, and that he had taken the depositions of the Patel and other fishermen who found it, because it had been hacked through at the back and its contents abstracted. He had held a *Panchayet* (jury enquiry) on it also, because there were certain red stains inside, so it looked as if there had been foul play at sea. The finders deposed on oath that it was just as they found it. They were respectable men. What would his Honour the "Asheestant Saheb" wish to be done? His humble servant respectfully suggested that the chest, being of solid well-seasoned teak, and clamped with heavy copper handsomely carved clamps, would make a suitable Treasure Chest for the Sirkar. He had not attempted to force the lid open; it was secured by two massive patent padlocks, and a steel bar connecting them. The hole at the back was as big as a man's head; so one could see that the chest was quite empty etc., etc.

On my return to Hurnee I went straight to the chest as it lay in the Kacheri yard, and sent for a blacksmith who easily drew the staples. The moment the lid was raised, my eye delected that the chest had a false bottom. We prised up the planks. Lo and behold the compartment was crammed with rich silk petticoats, little tin boxes lined with cotton wool, containing strings of pearls, rings, gold, silver, and ivory armlets, necklets, anklets (such as wealthy Bhattia women wear), also a fat roll of bonds and two years obese account books in the Guzarathi language! A jury of "Sonars" (goldsmiths) valued the jewellery at Rs. 30,000. The clothing (which was sewn in oil silk) was also valuable, being embroidered with seed pearls. The ledgers and deeds told us the name of the merchant to whom this 'treasure trove' belonged. So I wrote at once to Mr. Charles Forjett, Commissioner of the Bombay City Police. He replied that the owner was one Khimji Dhanjibhoy, a Bhattia "dalál" (agent or broker) employed at Zánzibar as Manager of a branch of the great Merchant Banking Firm, Sewji Jiwji and Co., who deposed that their Manager Khimji aforesaid, having reported himself too ill to remain at Zánzibar, had asked to be relieved in the preceding November. They had accordingly sent out a substitute by steamer, and Khimji had written to say that he, his wife and two children and his wife's sister were sailing in an Arab "Dhow" for Rájápur or Bombay in February. Khimji was an old and much esteemed employè of their Firm, had been 10 years at Zánzibar, and Insurance certificates of cargoes had already arrived, that was all they knew, and so on. So I transmitted the "treasure trove" to Mr. Forjett to be held in deposit for Khimji's heir, for whom he would advertise; but I retained the heavy treasure chest for the use of our Government, offering to pay its assessed value (Rs. 50) which I suggested might be well bestowed on the honest finder of the "flotsam." This may be taken as terminating the first episode of the tragedy.

PART II.

Meantime, the coastguards were keeping a sharp look-out for the derelict "Battiálla," drifting about, a peril to all the fleets of fishing boats and native merchant craft. She drew much water when sound, but water-logged as she was, and in deep water, she travelled very slowly. The Ratnagiri Police too were active at Rájápur (at my instance) enquiring whether Khimji and his family had landed from an Arab "Dhow" at Jaitapur on the Rájápur River, beyond which only small craft can ascend at high tide.

Before any answer could reach me from Rájápur or from Mr. Forjett, who was seeking intelligence as to whether Khimji had sailed in any Arab "Dhow" direct to Bombay—several corpses of Arabs and Surti sailors had been washed up below Hurnee—but there had been several wrecks, during the gale, of craft beating up the Coast. On the fifteenth day after the derelict drifted past Hurnee, however, the bloated bodies of a huge negro and a "Surti" (inhabitant of Surat), from his dress evidently a "serang" (Native Captain) were found stranded on the Burrondi rocks at low tide, and in their waist-belts were gold mohurs, Spanish dollars, and Turkish sequins, while the negro's leather waist-band also contained a pair of large emerald earring pendants, a woman's necklece of gold beads, and a pair of diamond nose rings. I sent them to Forjett by a coasting steamer that happened to touch: they were identified by Khimji's father-in-law as ornaments usually worn by Khimji's wife and her sister. The mystery began to clear up, but the denouement was delayed till the middle of May, when the derelict took the rocks at the mouth of the Wâshishti River nearly fifty miles south of Hurnee. She was found to be a Surat "Battiala" of 600 sandies (159 tons). Her name painted on the stern in Guzeráthi was "Durya Báhádur" (Lord of Ocean)—her cargo had consisted of half-pressed bales of short staple cotton, which, wetted with the gale, had opened her seams but had afterwards kept her afloat. Her register number (Surat No. 255) was cut into her riband or string plank. Her State cabin at the poop was nailed up. Hatchets soon cut through the panels. Then the murder was out! Lying about the small chamber, in distorted attitudes, were four corpses in advanced stage of decay—that of a man, two women, and a child. The man's skull appeared to be cleft to the chin. One of the women's heads was barely attached to her trunk by muscles—the other woman had seemingly been strangled with a cord still round her neck—the child's head was battered in. It was found impossible to remove the putrifying remains—the inquest was therefore held aboard the wreck. Identification, of of course, was impossible. The only verdict could be "wilful murder by persons unknown." The vessel had still remaining of her cargo, a few bales of festering cotton and "copra" (cocoanut kernels), "Moodhas" (straw bound bundles) of rice, on a layer of the largest sized bamboos. The crew's cooking pots were gone and all clothing. The Police smeared the after part of the wreck with pitch and made a bonfire of it as the only mode of cremating the corpses.

Gradually, we gathered in the threads of the ghastly tragedy. The Custom house entries at Jaitapur showed that the "Durya Báhádur" sailed from that port for Bombay with a general cargo on the 10th of February—commanded by Serang Kanji Premji, inhabitant of Surat—Crew, a mixed lot of Arabs and Sulus, 22 in number—Passengers, Bháttia Dalál Khimji, his wife (Laksmibaie), daughter (Soonksibaie), and sister-in-law (Anandibaie). The manifest of a huge Zánzibari Dhow still anchored within the bar, showed that Khimji and his family had embarked at Zánzibar in January with a negro slave attendant, entered as Kwâja Singh. The serang and crew of the Dhow (who were engaged in caulking her seams) perfectly recollected all the five passengers' names, and their big Treasure Chest which, being too large to stow in the cabin, was lashed to the cross beams of the Dhow outside the door, so that Khimji could get at it. They remembered transferring it to the "Daraya Báhádur's" long boat.

The Custom house register at Kelshi (a small but busy port 9 miles north of Hurnee) supplied the last link in the chain of evidence. The Bhattiála "Durya Báhádur" was entered as having anchored under the Kelshi head on the 20th of March to shelter from the gale. The Inspector and Peons remembered that two elderly Bhâttia ladies and a female child of about ten years of age had landed during the afternoon to obtain fruit, vegetables and milk, accompanied by a richly-clad negro eunuch, whom they called "Kwâjajee." The sailers who rowed them ashore in the Battiâla's dingy, gossiping at the liquor shop, had spoken of a "Shett" (Merchant) on board who had a large treasure chest that he usually sat upon and would scarcely ever leave. The Surti serang of the Bhattiâla and the eunuch held a long animated discussion outside the grog shop, while the ladies were bargaining in the bazaar. All re-embarked and the "Durya Báhâdur" put to sea for Bombay with a land breeze at dawn.

Lastly—the Battiâla's long boat had drifted ashore a few days later at Anjirla, and as it had been reported the "Darya Báhâdur" had been seen labouring vainly to beat up against the North-Westerly gale, the Inspector concluded that she must have foundered with all hands.

What had actually happened was this—no doubt.

The Negro eunuch had made up his mind to rob, and, if need be, to murder Khimji and his family before they reached Bombay with the chest—the "Lalla" (eunuch) well knew its contents—he also knew the value of the women's jewels. He did not intend to go to Bombay. Not he! He detested the place, for he had knifed a man there ten years before, and was "wanted" by Akbár Ali, the Detective Inspector. What he wished was to land at Jinjira in Habsán, with the contents of that chest, with which he would bribe the "Mootsadi" * Parbhus in the Nawab's service (that Nawáb who hated the Angrezi)—the Parbhus would get him into the Nawab's favour—he, Kwâjah Singh, the eunuch, would sell Khimji's pretty little daughter to the Nawáb or to one of the Sidi nobles for a good round sum, would purchase rice fields, secure contracts and concessions, farm the Nawab's revenue, become a Máhájan † and have a lot of slaves himself,—as for the older women they would do to grind his corn, shampoo him, and so forth. But that "budmash" (rascal) Khimji, who had him flogged at Zánzibar—the humble "Lálla" would tear out his windpipe. Of course, he must bribe the crew and serang of whatever vessel they sailed in from Jaitapur to scuttle the ship off Habsán. When Khimji (Shaitan take him!) was dead, if the women would not come away quietly on the long boat—well, they must be strangled or some way done to death—then—Máshállâh—hey for Habán! Khwâja Lálla ki jey! Allah Akbár. Great is Mahomet his prophet!. This simple plot, no doubt, was carried out just as I have suggested, but the Lálla had not reckoned on the fierce gale, or dreamed *he* would be drowned.

---

* Mootsuddi, that is literally "Seal-holding"—hereditary minister.

† Literally "Great man."

Thus were five poor creatures murdered, a whole ship's crew of 22 men drowned, a valuable vessel lost with a still more valuable cargo, all to satisfy the insatiate cupidity, the *auri sacre fames* of a Negro eunuch.

Readers mine—these crimes were of almost daily occurrence on the Western Sea-board of "Jan Kumpani Báhádur" in the first 60 years of the last century. For seven months of the year—from October to June, hundreds of thousands of labourers, hundreds of traders, were compelled to make their way to Bombay by sea in native craft of sorts and sizes—for the land journey was tedious and costly, and lay through wild country infested by Thugs and Dacoits. What could be simpler than for the Serangs and Tindals to rob and murder, or (at least) to extort rupees from the sea-sick passengers by starving them for want of water. So the game went on right merrily and profitably for the crews. Who could know that they oft-times scuttled their ships after selling their passsengers as slaves in Habsán or at Junaghar, Cambay, or Kutch, and the cargoes to wreckers along the coast. All this I have described at length in the Chapter on "Wrecking" in my book aforesaid. They be true tales of the sea; as true as taxes and "nuthin's truer nor they be" as Mr. Barkis declared on his death-bed at Yarmouth *.

* *Vide* "David Copperfield"—(By Charles Dickens).

Printed at the Pioneer Press, by Geo. Sim, No. 650—28-8-'09.

BY THE SAME AUTHOR

REMINISCENCES.

OF AN

INDIAN POLICE OFFICIAL

Some Press Notices of 1st Edition.

"The Times," 7 *June*, 1894.

"Indian crime affords many striking illustrations of native character and many episodes of a more or less dramatic complexion, and the Author's long experience enables him to turn these elements to a very good account......"

"The Standard," 18 *July*, 1894.

"The Author does justice to the many good qualities which have survived the centuries of anarchy, superstition, and oppression through which the native races have passed......"

"Athenaeum," 4 *August*, 1894.

"There are (Indian) publications so good in the matter and so agreeable in manner as to justify their appearance; and amongst them we are glad to include the *Reminiscences of an Indian Police Official*......"

"The various stories are humorously told, even when the Author was victimised...... This interesting volume is well printed and the illustrations by Van Ruith deserve commendation......"

"Westminster Gazette," 1 *August*, 1894.

"We take it that not many (Indian Officials) have his facile pen. He contrives, while bringing out the dangers and difficulties which beset our Indian rule, to fascinate the reader by his inimitable powers of story telling."

"The Speaker," 14 *July*, 1894.

"The English reader is introduced to sundry scenes and characters possessing the two qualities, not often combined, of novelty and authenticity...... The book opens out to us a glimpse of Indian life and manners from a point of view well worth taking."

"St. James' Gazette," 7 *July*, 1894.

"The book is readable and interesting from beginning to end... (The Author's) reminiscences may be added to those which, like Forbes' "Oriental Memoirs," give us a true and vivid conception of Indian life and character, such as can only be imparted by those who have studied the people with sympathy and insight.

"St. James' Budget," 13 *July*, 1894.

"The compressed incidents above related can give one but an inadequate idea of the interest and attraction attaching to these stories...... The book is illustrated with many views of local scenery and native life."

"Pall Mall Gazette," 17 *July*, 1894.

"The stories are too long to quote or analyse, but they should be carefully studied by those who imagine that our country's veneer of civilisation has made any fundamental change in the leopard's spots...... They are all told in a clear, animated, and attractive fashion."

"The Saturday Review," 7 *July*, 1894.

"The Author was quite justified in giving us the seamy side of Asiatic life......and he is careful to note all the pleasing traits in native character......A conversation between an English loafer and the Patel, with the bad Hindostani of the one and the utter bewilderment of the other, is, in its way, nearly equal to Mr. Rudyard Kipling. Several of the illustrations are very good."

"The Daily Chronicle," 6 *June*, 1894.

"Altogether we have to thank the author for a very interesting and informing book, the illustrations to which are instinct with life and reality."

"The Daily Graphic," 7 *July*, 1894.

"The book, while it ostensibly deals only with the criminal aspects of Indian Society, throws side-lights upon certain out-of-the-beaten-tracks phases of native life that will be both novel and interesting to most English readers...... The chapters quoted are among the most interesting of a very interesting book......"

"North British Daily Mail," 16 *August*, 1894.

"This is a volume of some interest......by one who knows what he is talking about...... Very interesting chapters......"

"Scotsman," 11 *June*, 1894.

"*Reminiscences of an Indian Police Official* will be found even better than such books as 'Pandoorung Hurree' (by Sir Bartle Frere), or 'The Adventures of a Thug' (by Meadows Taylor). The tales are mostly brief and very well written...... full of incident and abounding in local colour. This book may be confidently recommended to general readers as well as to those specially interested in our Indian Empire......"

"Morning Post," 17 *July*, 1894.

"This is a remarkable work as a study of Indian character and crime, based on the personal experiences of a keen observer. A very readable volume...... Throughout admirably illustrated by Horace van Ruith."

"Black and White," 23 *June*, 1894.

"These grim studies of Asiatic wickedness are impressive from the very simplicity of the method in which they are told...... The Author relies aconic veracity for his effect, and wins complete success."

"The Globe," 30 *August*, 1894.

"The *Reminiscences of an Indian Police Official* have both interest and value and are to be welcomed, they are the cream of thirty-five years' experience......and furnish data of which politicians, and statesmen even, may be glad to make public and practical use...... They are adorned by many graphic drawings."

"Morning Leader," 21 *July*, 1894.

"Mr. Arthur Travers Crawford is a man with a distinct literary gift, and his *Reminiscences of an Indian Police Official* are marked by an energy and vivacity that makes them very excellent reading."

"The Field," 4 *August*, 1894.

"The incidents of which the author gives particulars in no way resemble the sensational tales with which the public have been made familiar by detective geniuses...... The book is nicely illustrated and contains much that will be interesting to the general reader."

"The Times of India," 18 *June*, 1894.

"Graphic and fascinating stories of Indian crime and Indian criminals......worked out with fine dramatic instinct...... It would be odd indeed if the volume were not one of the most interesting of the season...... The book in short is a delightful one from cover to cover, and the illustrations by Van Ruith are very charmingly and very effectively reproduced."

"The Friend of India," 10 *July*, 1894.

"There is much of real value in this book......written with considerable dramatic effect, and with some literary skill......should be most valuable to Members of Parliament."

"The Englishman," 3 *July*, 1894.

"A book of very deep, if painful interest...... We have to thank the Author for a very interesting and informing book, the illustrations to which are instinct with life and reality."